ATLA Monograph Series
edited by Dr. Kenneth E. Rowe

1. Ronald L. Grimes. *The Divine Imagination: William Blake's Major Prophetic Visions.* 1972.
2. George D. Kelsey. *Social Ethics Among Southern Baptists, 1917–1969.* 1973.
3. Hilda Adam Kring. *The Harmonists: A Folk-Cultural Approach.* 1973.
4. J. Steven O'Malley. *Pilgrimage of Faith: The Legacy of the Otterbeins.* 1973.
5. Charles Edwin Jones. *Perfectionist Persuasion: The Holiness Movement and American Methodism. 1867–1936.* 1974.
6. Donald E. Byrne, Jr. *No Foot of Land: Folklore of American Methodist Itinerants.* 1975.
7. Milton C. Sernett. *Black Religion and American Evangelicalism: White Protestants, Plantation Missions, and the Flowering of Negro Christianity, 1787–1865.* 1975.
8. Eva Fleischner. *Judaism in German Christian Theology since 1945: Christianity and Israel Considered in Terms of Mission.* 1975.
9. Walter James Lowe. *Mystery & the Unconscious: A Study in the Thought of Paul Ricoeur.* 1977.
10. Norris Magnuson. *Salvation in the Slums: Evangelical Social Work, 1865–1920.* 1977.
11. William Sherman Minor. *Creativity in Henry Nelson Wieman.* 1977.
12. Thomas Virgil Peterson. *Ham and Japheth: The Mythic World of Whites in the Antebellum South.* 1978.
13. Randall K. Burkett. *Garveyism as a Religious Movement: The Institutionalization of a Black Civil Religion.* 1978.
14. Roger G. Betsworth. *The Radical Movement of the 1960's.* 1980.
15. Alice Cowan Cochran. *Miners, Merchants, and Missionaries: The Roles of Missionaries and Pioneer Churches in the Colorado Gold Rush and Its Aftermath, 1858–1870.* 1980.
16. Irene Lawrence. *Linguistics and Theology: The Significance of Noam Chomsky for Theological Construction.* 1980.
17. Richard E. Williams. *Called and Chosen: The Story of Mother Rebecca Jackson and the Philadelphia Shakers.* 1981.
18. Arthur C. Repp, Sr. *Luther's Catechism Comes to America: Theological Effects on the Issues of the Small Catechism Prepared in or for America prior to 1850.* 1982.
19. Lewis V. Baldwin. *"Invisible" Strands in African Methodism.* 1983.
20. David W. Gill. *The Word of God in the Ethics of Jacques Ellul.* 1984.
21. Robert Booth Fowler. *Religion and Politics in America.* 1985.
22. Page Putnam Miller. *A Claim to New Roles.* 1985.

23. C. Howard Smith. *Scandinavian Hymnody from the Reformation to the Present.* 1987.
24. Bernard T. Adeney. *Just War, Political Realism, and Faith.* 1988.
25. Paul Wesley Chilcote. *John Wesley and the Women Preachers of Early Methodism.* 1991.
26. Samuel J. Rogal. *A General Introduction of Hymnody and Congregational Song.* 1991.
27. Howard A. Barnes. *Horace Bushnell and the Virtuous Republic.* 1991.
28. Sondra A. O'Neale. *Jupiter Hammon and the Biblical Beginnings of African-American Literature.* 1993.
29. Kathleen P. Deignan. *Christ Spirit: The Eschatology of Shaker Christianity.* 1992.
30. D. Elwood Dunn. *A History of the Episcopal Church in Liberia, 1821–1980.* 1992.
31. Terrance L. Tiessen. *Irenaeus on the Salvation of the Unevangelized.* 1993.
32. James E. McGoldrick. *Baptist Successionism: A Crucial Question in Baptist History.* 1994.
33. Murray A. Rubinstein. *The Origins of the Anglo-American Missionary Enterprise in China, 1807–1840.* 1995.
34. Thomas M. Tanner. *What Ministers Know: A Qualitative Study of Pastors as Information Professionals.* 1994.
35. Jack A. Johnson-Hill. *I-Sight: The World of Rastafari: An Interpretive Sociological Account of Rastafarian Ethics.* 1995.
36. Richard James Severson. *Time, Death, and Eternity: Reflecting on Augustine's "Confessions" in Light of Heidegger's "Being and Time."* 1995.
37. Robert F. Scholz. *Press toward the Mark: History of the United Lutheran Synod of New York and New England, 1830–1930.* 1995.
38. Sam Hamstra, Jr. and Arie J. Griffioen. *Reformed Confessionalism in Nineteenth-Century America: Essays on the Thought of John Williamson Nevin.* 1995.
39. Robert A. Hecht. *An Unordinary Man: A Life of Father John LaFarge, S.J.* 1996.
40. Moses N. Moore. *Orishatukeh Faduma: Liberal Theology and Evangelical Pan-Africanism, 1857–1946.* 1996.
41. William Lawrence. *Sundays in New York: Pulpit Theology at the Crest of the Protestant Mainstream.* 1996.
42. Bruce M. Stephens *The Prism of Time and Eternity: Images of Christ in American Protestant Thought from Jonathan Edwards to Horace Bushnell,* 1996.
43. Eleanor Bustin Mattes. *Myth for Moderns: Erwin Ramsdell Goodenough and Religious Studies in America, 1938–1955.* 1997.
44. Nathan D. Showalter. *The End of a Crusade: The Student Volunteer Movement for Foreign Missions and the Great War.* 1997.

Myth for Moderns

*Erwin Ramsdell Goodenough and
Religious Studies in America
1938–1955*

Eleanor Bustin Mattes

ATLA Monograph Series, No. 43

The Scarecrow Press, Inc.
Lanham, Md., & London
1997

BL
43
, G66
M38
1997

SCARECROW PRESS, INC.

Published in the United States of America
by Scarecrow Press, Inc.
4720 Boston Way
Lanham, Maryland 20706

4 Pleydell Gardens, Folkestone
Kent CT20 2DN, England

British Library Cataloguing in Publication Information Available

Library of Congress Cataloging-in-Publication Data

Mattes, Eleanor Bustin, 1913–
   Myth for moderns : Erwin Ramsdell Goodenough and religious studies in
America, 1938–1955 / Eleanor Bustin Mattes.
      p. cm.—(ATLA monograph series ; no. 43)
   Includes bibliographical references and index.
   ISBN 0-8108-3339-5 (alk. paper)
      1. Goodenough, Erwin Ramsdell, 1893–1965.   2. Religion historians—
United States—Biography.   3. Religion—Study and teaching—United
States—History—20th century.   I. Title.   II. Series.
BL43.G66M38 1997
200'.92—dc21
[B]   97-8875
                                                                      CIP

ISBN 0-8108-3339-5 (cloth : alk. paper)

To Evelyn Goodenough Pitcher

Erwin Ramsdell Goodenough
(Yale University Archives, Manuscript
and Archives, Yale University Library)

Contents

Figures

Series Editor's Foreword

Since 1972 the American Theological Library Association has undertaken responsibility for a modest monograph series in the field of religious studies. Titles are selected from studies in a wide range of religious and theological disciplines.

We are pleased to publish Eleanor Bustin Mattes's fresh study of Erwin Ramsdell Goodenough, a major figure in religious studies in North America in the first half of the twentieth century. The author studied at Smith College and has an M.A. from Girton College, Cambridge; a B.D. from the Yale Divinity School; and a Ph.D. from the Yale Graduate School. She has published *In Memoriam: The Way of a Soul: A Study of Some Influences That Shaped Tennyson's Poem;* articles in *American Notes & Queries Supplement, Women & Literature,* and *Anima;* and reviews in *The Review of Religion* and *Christianity and Society.* She is a member of Phi Beta Kappa and the Modern Language Association. Currently she is professor emerita of English, Wilson College.

Goodenough, once a Methodist minister, became a historian of religion at Yale and published innovative studies of Philo Judaeus and Jewish symbols, especially those of Hellenistic Judaism. He also authored two statements of his agnostic perspective, *Toward a Mature Faith* and *The Psychology of Religious Experience.* Mattes's training at Yale Divinity School enables her to shed fresh light on Goodenough's thought. Especially rich is the way she explores Goodenough's encounter with major figures in modern religious and social thought—Newman, Tillich, and Niebuhx as well as James, Freud, and Jung.

Kenneth E. Rowe
Editor, ATLA Monograph Series
Drew University Library
Madison, New Jersey

Acknowledgments

I am deeply grateful to Evelyn Goodenough Pitcher, a longtime friend, for urging me to write a biography of her former husband, Erwin Goodenough, and providing me with her memories of the years she spent with Goodenough, access to all her materials, and suggestions of people to interview. I also appreciate the willingness of Cynthia Goodenough, Erwin's widow, for me to engage in this biography and for her generous permission to use the materials to which she holds the copyright. To my husband, Alfred, I am grateful for his encouragement and support throughout.

Goodenough's children have my warm thanks. Ward provided me with the collection of letters his father wrote during his Oxford years and numerous photographs and invariably had answers to my questions. Ursula and Daniel, in our interviews, have given me information, impressions, and insights, as have James and Hester in our correspondence.

Many others have enriched this book through interviews and conversations: Mary Ludlum Davis, who attended high school with Erwin; Amos Wilder, who knew him at Oxford and Yale; Gladys and Paul Minear, who recalled their impressions of Goodenough when Paul was studying for a Yale doctorate; Dorothy Mierow, daughter of Charles Mierow, a professor at Colorado College, who remembered the Goodenoughs' visits to her home during the summer when Goodenough taught a course at Colorado College; Claude Lopez, Goodenough's research assistant during his work on *Jewish Symbols;* Harry Buck, who knew Goodenough through their association in the American Academy of Religion; Robert Pitcher, who became acquainted with Goodenough when Robert's wife, Lucile, was president of the board of the Eliot-Pearson School at the time Evelyn Goodenough became the director; and Helmut Koester and Krister Stendahl of the Harvard Divinity School faculty, who knew Goodenough after his move to Cambridge brought him into association with them. I appreciate the information and perspectives provided by my telephone interview and correspondence with Jacob Neusner, Goodenough's friend in his last years and his literary executor.

I am grateful for the valuable contribution of Hazel Barnes, one of Goodenough's students and Evelyn's friend of many years, who read an early draft and offered her insights and advice. For his helpful suggestions on my work I thank Thomas Kraabel, Goodenough's research assistant during the years 1964–1965 and editor of a collection of his essays. I am indebted to Hope Hale Davis, who read and made critical comments on each chapter, and to Ellen Aitken, who during editing provided her expertise in the history of religion.

I appreciate the generous responses of the following in my requests for information: Frank K. Lorenz, Hamilton College's curator of special collections; David K. Himrod, assistant librarian for reader services of the United Library of Garrett-Evangelical Theological Seminary and Seabury-Western Theological Seminary; the archivist of Lincoln College, Oxford University; Richard P. Bowman, research assistant for the Commission on Archives and History of the Southern New England Conference, United Methodist Church; Virginia Washburn Kiefer, curator of special collections, Colorado College Library; Judith L. Arneson, assistant director of the Bryn Mawr College Alumnae Association, who provided materials by and about Phyllis Goodhart Gordan, a Bryn Mawr alumna; and Robert Elinor, who gave me his notes of the 1989 Society of Biblical Literature's section on Goodenough and other information.

I am grateful to Douglas Robbe. Having received from Cynthia Goodenough materials relevant to Robbe's research on Goodenough's agnosticism, Robbe placed them in my care, when he no longer needed them, with Cynthia's permission. I later added them to the Goodenough papers in the Yale University Library Archives.

For their assistance in my research, I thank the staff of the Andover-Newton Theological Library Archives of the Harvard Divinity School; the Manuscripts and Archives staff of the Yale University Library, especially Judith Schiff; and the staff of the Schlesinger Library, Radcliffe College, especially Sylvia McDowell.

I appreciate the help of Susan McArthur, who prepared the typescript for publication, and of Alan Clark, for essential assistance in obtaining permissions to publish.

I am grateful to the American Council of Learned Societies for permission to use materials from Goodenough's article "Religionswissenschaft" in the *ACLS Newsletter* 10; to the American Bar Association for permission to quote from an article by William Riddell published in the *American Bar Association Journal,* 16; to the *American Historical Review* to quote from a review by E. F. Scott; to *Archaeology* for permission to use material from articles by Harry Leon; to E. J. Brill for permission to quote from *Religions in Antiquity,* edited by Jacob Neusner, and *An Early Christian Philosopher* by J. C. M. Van Winden; to Cambridge University Press for permission to quote from *Justin Martyr* by L. W. Barnard and *St. Paul and the Church of the Gentiles* by Wilfred Knox; to Catholic University of America Press for permission to quote from a review by Abram Simon in the *Catholic Historical Review* 21; to the University of Chicago Press for permission to quote from a review by Ralph Marcus in *Classical Philology* 52 and reviews by Shirley Jackson Case and George Meyer in *The Journal of Religion* 15 (1935) and 46 (January 1966); to *Church History* for permission to quote from a review by E. F. Scott in *Church History* 4; to T & T Clark for permission to use material from *The Prophetic Gospel* by Anthony Hanson; to Doubleday for permission to quote from *The Power of Myth* by Joseph Campbell with Bill Moyers; to Augsburg Fortress for permission to quote from *The Opponents of Paul in Second Corinthians* by Dieter Georgi; to Hadnan Books for permission to quote from *Rebirth and Afterlife* by Sister Charles Murray, British Archaeological Reports Ltd., International Series 100; to Harcourt Brace for permission to quote from *Modern Man in Search of a Soul* by C. H. Jung; to HarperCollins for permission to quote from *Marching Off the Map* by Halford Luccock; to the *Harvard Theological Review* for use of material from "Symbolism in the Dura Synagogue: A Review Article" by Elias J. Bickerman; to Harvard University Press for permission to quote from *Philo on the Creation,* translated by F. W. Colson and G. H. Whitaker, and *Philo with an English Translation,* edited by F. H. Colson; to Hebrew Union College for permission to use material from *Logos and Mystical Theology in Philo* by David Winston; to the American Humanist Association for permission to quote from "Scientific Living" by Erwin Goodenough, published in the spring 1942 issue of *The Humanist;* to Iliff School of Theology to quote from an article by J. Josephine Leamer in the now defunct *Iliff Review,* 1966; to Jewish Publication Society for permission to quote from *Wolfson of Harvard* by Leo F. Schwarz; to *Judaism* for permission to use material from an article by Cecil Roth, reprinted with permission from *Judaism* 3, no. 2 (spring 1954), copyright 1954 American Jewish Congress; to *The Living Church* for permission to quote from a review by

Arthur Vogel in its 31 October 1965 issue; to W. W. Norton for permission to quote from *The Cry for Myth* by Rollo May; to Oxford University Press for permission to quote from an article by Arthur Darby Nock in *The Classical Review* 54, no. 3, *Essays on Religion and the Ancient World* by Arthur Darby Nock, edited by Zeph Stewart, *The Commonwealth of Lincoln College, 1427–1927* by Vivian Green, and *Philo of Alexandria* by Samuel Sandmel; to Philo Press for permission to use material from *The Theology of Justin Martyr* and *The Jurisprudence of the Jewish Courts in Egypt* by Erwin Goodenough (APA-Philo Press, Postbus 122, NL-3600 AC Maarsseu, Netherlands); to Princeton University Press for permission to use material from *Jewish Symbols in the Greco-Roman Period* by Erwin Goodenough; to the Putnam Publishing Group for permission to quote from *Landmarks in the History of Early Christianity* by Kirsopp Lake; to Regnery Publishing for permission to use material from *God and Man at Yale* by William F. Buckley Jr.; to Scholars Press for permission to quote material published in several issues of *The Journal of Biblical Literature;* to University Press of America for permission to quote from *Toward a Mature Faith* and *The Psychology of Religious Experiences* by Erwin Goodenough; to *Yale Alumnae Magazine* for permission to quote from the April 1959 issue; and to Yale University Press to quote from *Politics of Philo Judaeus* by Goodenough and Goodhart; *Yale: The University College 1921–1937* by George W. Pierson; and *Religion and Learning at Yale* by Ralph Gabriel.

I appreciate Cynthia (Mrs. Erwin R.) Goodenough's permission to use material from *By Light, Light: Religious Tradition and Myth* and *An Introduction to Philo Judaeus* by Erwin Goodenough, to which Mrs. Goodenough holds the rights.

Preface

Erwin Goodenough was not only a historian of religion whose writings on Philo Judaeus and Jewish symbols have had a major impact on the study of Judaism through their emphasis on the existence of multiple Judaisms, especially Hellenistic Judaism. He also pioneered in regarding sex as integrally related to the spiritual—a view currently reflected in Morton and Barbara Kelsey's recent book *Sacrament of Sexuality*.[1] His insistence on "the value of 'myth' for moderns" in 1937[2] anticipated Joseph Campbell's development of that thesis and his popular television talks on the subject with Bill Moyers.

To see how Goodenough came to these views, it is necessary to follow the course of his life, as it determined the directions his scholarship took and his conclusions. We gain insights as we trace his personal journey from the fundamentalist Methodist upbringing through his introduction to the Harvard Divinity School's empiricism; his first marriage and the years at Oxford; his relationships with Tom French, Carl Jung, and Erik Erikson; and his divorce and second marriage.

We can trace this journey through the rich store of his letters to his parents, his second wife, and his many friends. In addition to these, we have the insights of interviews with those who knew him—his boyhood associates, those who worked with and for him at Yale, his children, and those who were close to him during his last months. My friendship with him began in 1938, when I was a graduate student in English at Yale and an intimate friend of Evelyn Wiltshire, who became his second wife. It continued until I moved to St. Louis with my husband in 1955. During those years I knew him as a scholar, a counselor in my career choices, and a family man. My relationship with Evelyn and his son Ward gave me access to many letters, and I had conversations or correspondence with all six children.

All these resources throw light on a remarkable man whose life has an unusually close relationship to his work. Among the many aspects of this relationship, one is especially consistent: from his writings on Philo in the 1930s through the last volume of *Jewish Symbols,* published in 1965, the year of his death, Erwin Goodenough retained the belief of his early Methodism: that "so long as men are men, spiritual reality will always remain the most important factor in human life."[3]

Chapter 1

Early Life, Marriage, and Graduate Study at Harvard Divinity School

Erwin Goodenough once made a comment especially pertinent to his own life: that it is easier to understand the greatness of a genius "when we have heard the story of his early environment and youth."[1]

His lifelong conviction that he was destined to undertake and accomplish certain projects originated in his mother's devout Methodist faith. This led her to see particular meaning in his unexpected recovery from celiac disease, a wasting childhood illness. She had been delighted when he was first put in her arms, and she cried, "A boy! Perhaps some day he will go to college." But at two-and-a-half years old, celiac disease left Goodenough emaciated, weighing only ten pounds. One night his four-year-old sister, Ursula, was told that he would be dead by morning and the angels would take him away. Yet when day came, Ursula, finding her brother still there, cried, "Oh Erwin, the angels didn't take you away!" And he replied, "I ain't gonna be died. I'm gonna be a big man like Grandpa."[2] This was a turning point in his illness. He began to digest his food and gain weight, and his mother believed that his recovery meant he was marked for a special purpose.

Goodenough never became "a big man" physically, like six-foot Grandpa Erwin Ramsdell, but there were similarities. Grandpa Ramsdell had been a sickly boy and had had a troubled early life because of a stern father like Erwin's. Yet he had become successful, in spite of these childhood handicaps. When he married Anna Buckley, the village doctor's daughter, she helped him to educate himself beyond his fourth-grade schooling, and he studied law after his day's work in a shop. He passed the bar examinations; first clerked, then was a partner in a lawyer's office; eventually became a judge of circuit court; and was addressed as judge the rest of his life. Grandpa Erwin Ramsdell was a good model for his young namesake.

Erwin and his mother, 1895.

Mary Ramsdell, Erwin Ramsdell's only child, was born in Adams, upper New York State, in 1865. Her father, determined that she have the education he had missed, enrolled her in the Adams Academy; her son found in her papers a detailed account of the academy building and of the fire that destroyed it, which demonstrated her ability to express herself.[3] Very pretty as a young girl, she later developed a disfiguring goiter, which aggravated her sense of inferiority. Throughout her married life she always deferred to her husband, no matter how wrong his judgments might be. Her children found her loving and warm, in contrast to their father. She had a keen sense of humor, would recreate with animation any amusing incident she had seen, and led the children in laughing and crying as she read Dickens to them.

Mary's later years were happy. The distressing goiter was removed. She enjoyed her grandchildren, delighting in sewing dainty baby clothes for them. The oldest, Ward, recalls his pleasure in being "one to one with Grandma"[4] when she read *Under the Lilacs* and other favorites that gratified her sentimental tastes. When she was in her seventies, long widowed and afflicted with Alzheimer's disease, she surprisingly began to use crude, obscene words that shattered the image of a simple, pious woman. Mary Ramsdell obviously knew more of life than she had revealed while dominated by her proper, puritanical husband.

Erwin described her as "my sainted mother,"[5] and in *Toward a Mature Faith* he paid tribute to her "vivid faith in God's goodness and care for her." He stated that her example led him to find his deepest comfort, even in midlife, in the prayer "Thy will be done."[6] But an unpublished late memoir gave a more negative view of her influence: "My mother talked to me about the loving and forgiving Jesus, let my [*sic*] cry it out in her arms, until my destructive passion had been repressed, turned against myself, and coated over with a sickly smear of Christian sweetness."[7] She thus gave her son not only a lasting faith which he appreciated and retained, however changed in its understanding of faith, but also a view of Christian conduct that he came to consider unhealthy.

Erwin's father, Ward Hunt Goodenough, was born in Watertown, New York, in 1864 into a family that had come from England to Sudbury, Massachusetts, in 1638 on the ship *Confidence*. The seventh of thirteen children, he was the first to be given the chance to work his way through Hamilton College, where he was elected to Phi Beta Kappa. He then read law in the office of an Ogdensburg attorney and was admitted to the bar. When he married Mary Ramsdell in 1890, they went to live in Brooklyn, which, according to a *Harper's* article of 1893, the year of

Erwin's birth, was a town "where there is elbow-room and a hush at night, and where they see trees and can have growing flowers."[8] They later moved to Jamaica, Long Island, where Goodenough became the assistant manager of the Queens branch of Title Guarantee and Trust Company, at a yearly salary of $3,000 (as much as his son earned teaching at Yale twenty years later, when money had much less purchasing power). He also bought and sold real estate astutely and was very well off as a result, until later in life. He then went into a speculative venture with two partners, planning to become rich, and encouraged his friends and others to invest in it. The two partners absconded to Mexico with all the funds, and Goodenough was reduced to a very limited income because he conscientiously repaid those who had lost their investments on his advice.

Ward was a devout Methodist who served as the highly respected Sunday school superintendent of his church in Jamaica. A plaque in his honor at the YMCA expressed its appreciation of his generosity.

Goodenough preached the value of work and practiced it in his family as well as in his business life. His many manual skills included carpentry and making dresses for his wife, skills that complemented his role as patriarch. Because of his example and teaching, his son Erwin enjoyed refinishing and reupholstering furniture and crocheting, especially the edging for the baby bonnets of his children.

Erwin was born on 24 October 1893 at No. 329 Hoyt Street, Brooklyn, two years after his sister Ursula and three years before his sister Helen. He thus fulfilled his father's wish for a boy after the first girl, "and so on, first a girl and then a boy until—well we will stop on an even number." The last part of the plan did not work out, for there were no more children after the third, though not from any reluctance on the part of his wife, who, he commented, "envies the lot of an old she cat the most of anything for then she could have a good warm nest full twice a year."[9] Because there was no second boy, Erwin was the main focus of his father's expectations, and his mother's joy and pride.

Although Ward Goodenough was pleased that a boy had appeared in the sequence he had determined on, he was deeply disappointed to have a weakling for a son—one whom the boys at school teased and tormented physically. In an autobiographical chapter of *Toward a Mature Faith* Goodenough stressed that his father was kind and generous to many needy boys, several of whom he helped through college. He also contributed financially to Erwin's and his wife Helen's enjoyment of their three years at Oxford and on the Continent. But an unpublished late memoir describes the harsher side of his relations with his son: "My childhood consisted of problems with my father—along with his inspiration. . . .[10] As a little boy my father loved to humiliate me, to show his superior physical skill. We used to play at sparring, although it always ended with his backing us into a corner and crowing at our humiliation.[11] Once, at school, Erwin finally had struck back at a younger boy who was pushing him around while the older boys laughed. When he reported the incident, his father cruelly turned his triumph to shame by asking, "Was he smaller than you?"[12]

The oldest grandson, Ward, testifies to the taunting, cruel streak. When the boy recited "Hey diddle diddle" and came to "The Cow jumped over the Moon," his grandfather said, "The Cow wouldn't jump over the Moon. It's the Cow jumped over the Fence," bringing the little boy to tears as he insisted, "No, Grandpa. That's not the way it goes. It's the Cow jumped over the Moon!"[13] Another time, after Grandpa had put strychnine and quinine on his grapefruit to bring out the bitter flavor that he liked,[14] he urged Ward to try a spoonful. Then he laughed when the boy's mouth puckered with the biting taste.[15]

Excessive craving for mother love, to compensate for his father's harshness and his humiliation by other boys, made Erwin, by his own account, "the world's worst cry baby." But he overcame this at age seven, as he recalled forty years later. An old woman then living with the family was so tired of his bawling that she promised him ten cents if he did not cry for a month. Since that was a fortune to him, he worked hard at restraint for three weeks, suppressing all howls, no matter what the provocation. Then in the last week a boy stole his one and only marble, and he shrieked. After a moment he realized what he had lost, "Such a moment—I shall never forget it." But the old woman gave him another three weeks' trial. This time he succeeded; he got his ten cents, "& I became no longer a cry baby."[16]

His bond with his older sister, Ursula, was the only uncomplicated relationship of his early years. She, rather than his younger sister, Helen, was his playmate and remained his confidante and support to the end of his life. Her early devotion is seen in her first letters to her grandparents, in which "Brother" always figures: "Brother is well enough to play all day"; "We've got a snapping game and Brother can play Snap"; "I had a lovely ring with a carbuckle [sic] in it. . . . Brother had a ring too and his Pickinninny."[17]

Looking back on his childhood, Goodenough, in an attempt at self-analysis, recounted the psychological scars he received from his parents: "1. A repressed hatred of my father for his treatment of me, his ridicule of me, his preference for my sister Ursula (Dedy). All this I repressed making me feel guilty for having the hatred, but unaware of the source

Erwin and his sister Ursula, 1907–1908.

of my guilt. 2. A craving for mother love and attention which . . . made me feel more guilty, more dependent upon the mother-love [*sic*], and her approval, to ease my sense of guilt."[18] Whether he was describing the reality or his perception of it, he was stressing the Freudian aspects of the situation.

In the same letter that listed the psychological problems his parents created, Goodenough also complained of having a nineteenth-century boyhood, "surrounded by women's influence, my mother, women teachers, the old maids I went to Maine with, all of whom were the women of that earlier period."[19] But such a boyhood was not unusual. The mother was the major figure in the middle-class home, which was her sole domain, and there were mostly women teachers in the classrooms. Neither did the old maids who accompanied him to Maine make the Goodenoughs unusual, for single women without occupations or homes of their own often would attach themselves to a family.

His parents' strict, pietistic, and puritan practices were not so typical. Both Brooklyn and Jamaica were serene towns made up of single-family houses and green lawns, streets shaded by horse chestnuts for the carriages and an occasional automobile, and avenues with streetcars, which provided public transportation. Some of the residents commuted to work in New York City, but others, like Ward Goodenough, worked nearby. Most of these residents indulged without scruples in card playing, dancing, and drinking, expressing a repudiation of Victorian repressiveness that was fashionable in the early twentieth century.

The Goodenoughs, in contrast, lived by religious principles that Erwin later identified with seventeenth-century Puritanism. The family went to four church services on Sunday, read only religious literature, and played only sacred music on that day. Like all strict Methodists, they frowned on alcohol, tobacco, cards, dancing, and theater at any time. A large motto asking What would Jesus do? was hanging on the wall of Erwin's bedroom[20] and was a constant reminder of his parents' moral demands. Even as a grown man he never revealed that he had deviated from his parents' religious views or moral standards. He continued to dread their disapproval, and his son Ward remembers seeing his father hastily hide a cigarette under the bed one day when he was ill and his mother, who was visiting, surprised him by coming into his room without knocking.

Both his parents and the church emphasized what Goodenough later described as "repression and masochistic 'submission,'"[21] but, whereas all sexual urges and aggressive impulses were to be repressed, the

Methodists encouraged free emotional expression in worship. The minister might be so deeply moved by the service or his own sermon that he would shout, "Praise the Lord" or "Glory," to the congregation's delight. The congregation, in turn, sang with great feeling the hymns "Nearer my God to Thee," "Draw me near, nearer, nearer, precious Lord," "Jesus, lover of my soul," "Safe in the arms of Jesus, safe on His gentle breast."[22] They must also have sung, "Just as I am, without one plea" and "What a friend we have in Jesus," motifs deeply ingrained in American religious life, as Charles Ives emphasized by weaving them into his *Symphony no. 3, The Camp Meeting,* composed in 1904, a year when Erwin would have been singing them in the Methodist church in Jamaica. The appeal of this tender, warm Jesus to the young Erwin is clear from a poem he wrote when he was twelve.[23]

The Thought of Jesus

  I. I love to think of Jesus,
      When troubles 'round me grow,
      For He the seed of cheerfulness
      Will allways [sic] gladly sow.

  II. Tho' many be my sorrows,
      Tho' I give up to remorse,
      When I think and pray to Jesus,
      He makes me to rejoice.

 III. So let us think of Jesus
      Often, the whole day long,
      And he will make our hearts to seem,
      As light as a beautiful song.
        August 8, 1906[24]

He came to reject the stern father God, but throughout his life, even when he was intellectually an agnostic, he turned to his mother's gentle Jesus as a source of comfort and trust. And his appreciation of the emotional element in the Methodism of his childhood contributed to his later conviction that the erotic, however veiled or channeled into ritual, was an integral part of all religions.

Summing up the effect of his early religious experience in *Toward a Mature Faith,* he concluded: "There are always elements of truth in anything by which men have lived with even partial success. At the expense of logical consistency I have clung to those elements from my boyhood while I have gone into a different world, or a series of different worlds."[25]

Adolescence was emotionally painful for Erwin, just as childhood had been. At twelve he had a serious recurrence of the yet undiagnosed celiac disease, which left him frail and puny. Not in any way good-looking by peer standards—slightly stooped, with mousy brown hair and deep-sunk blue eyes[26]—he was also socially immature. He was further handicapped by having to honor his parents' strictures against dancing and the theater. The purpose was his "influence on others," but in reality it made him "a prize exhibit of a moral prig,"[27] he wrote, for such moral rigidity seemed ridiculous to his peers. The Jamaica public high school was as secular and socially oriented as many suburban schools of the early twentieth century. His fraternity consisted of the boys no other fraternity would pledge, and it was known, according to a schoolmate, chiefly for never giving good dances. His classmates saw him as "all brains,"[28] for he developed intellectual superiority, he later wrote, as "my revenge on the boys who used to twist my arm, on my father who never gave me any companionship or tenderness."[29]

He was a member of the Arista Club, made up of the high school's ranking students. Although he later regretted that his mind, "which should have been developing its innate critical tendencies,"[30] was held in check by his parents' insistence on submission and the lack of any critical training in the school curriculum, at the time he suffered only because he was not "one of the boys." There were other misfits, like Thomas French, who grew up to become an eminent psychoanalyst, yet in high school was "that funny little guy,"[31] as a fellow-student remembered him. But the presence of fellow oddballs did not lessen Erwin's problems.

Disdained by his peers and tormented by the total repression of any sexual urges, Erwin "retreated from society to God and music for consolation."[32] He had learned to play the piano as a child, and he continued to play it and the organ, often for five hours a day,[33] and also listened to phonograph recordings of what he later called sentimentalized renderings of the Romantic composers.

The one great experience of Erwin's teens was his initiation into mystical ecstasy. When he was fifteen, his family began to spend its summers in the Goodenough family home in Pierrepont Manor in upper New York, which was owned by "Uncle Charlie," an older brother of Erwin's father. Uncle Charlie had no formal education, had worked from the time he was a small boy, and was now supervisor of a large dairy farm.

Unmarried, Uncle Charlie found fulfillment in religion, in the ecstatic mystical experiences that set him apart as "sanctified." First, Goodenough reported, "He had been baptized by the Holy Ghost, for once the roof of the little meeting house had opened to let through a great flame of fire: the flame sharpened down to a cone whose point touched him on the top of his head."[34] Then he had experienced the death of self-assertion, giving up every symbol of pride, just as he urged a farmer to stop wearing his one personal treasure, his gold watch and chain. Uncle Charlie initiated Erwin into the mystical experience, and once, when his nephew went with him to a camp meeting, the boy gave himself so wholeheartedly to praying an old farmer "through" to sanctification that he was overcome, and two men had to help him from the meeting. Already deeply religious, Erwin learned from Uncle Charlie the desire and the way to become "part of a larger reality, in terms of which alone the individual can find meaning."[35] Because he knew what it meant to have a mystical experience, he later was patronizing to historians of religion who could not understand the nature and power of mysticism.

In 1911 Goodenough went to Hamilton, his father's college, one of the older small liberal arts colleges, in upper New York State, with an ample campus about a mile from Clinton. As he later looked back on his years there, he saw himself as still the complete misfit he had always been in school. He resented the accepted rituals: the initiation of freshmen by paddling them black and blue, which was his memory of that rite; the insistence that freshmen sit on the bleachers during every day of fall football practice. *Toward a Mature Faith* states that he tried desperately but unsuccessfully to enter into the "rah-rah" life of his fraternity brothers of Delta Kappa Epsilon, the Dekes, the least academically oriented of all the Greek houses.[36] They enjoyed card playing, which he had been taught was sinful, and they spent hours in what were to him mindless, boring bull sessions. But to offset *Toward a Mature Faith's* late picture of his unhappiness, his letters of the time include one to a friend in his freshman year, Wally Johnson, to whom he wrote much as any freshman might write. He reported that he had a summer job at the Twilight Inn in Haines Falls, New York, "one of the most exclusive and high toned places in the Catskills," as superintendent of a tennis and bowling club, and added, "Maybe I don't get good grub! . . . It is a bully place with very fine people, and a good bunch of fellows." He asked Wally for gossip about "the fellows he might pick up" and warned him not to introduce another student "to any girls for you don't know how very dangerous he is in that line"[37] — none of which suggests a total misfit.

In a letter of 1941 he complained that his Hamilton education was like that of Harvard back in 1850, "with courses in everything but what would make my own country a reality."[38] But Hamilton's curriculum resembled that of many small private colleges of the early twentieth century, in which there was little emphasis on American history and literature.

Three foreign languages and mathematics were required for graduation, along with public speaking, which was a requirement all four years. Freshmen had no electives. Two courses in foreign languages were required the second year, and one in the junior year.[39] There was no art or music department, and Goodenough regretted that, although he was the college organist for three years, he received no training in music theory or technique.

Goodenough majored in English literature and found in his independent reading an escape from the limitations of his parents' cultural perspective. Looking back in 1964 he wrote: "I was up late every night living in India with Tagore; in Russia with Tolstoi, Turgenev, and Dostoevsky; in Norway with Ibsen; in France with du Maupassant; in all times and places of England from Beowulf to Shaw; and the contemporary novelists of America took me into American ways that my father and mother never alluded to."[40] He developed some of his ideas for *The Hamilton Literary Magazine,* which include an article on the writings of Rabindranath Tagore; one on the individualism of Henrik Ibsen; and one praising New Criticism for its position that the critic is an artist—a view that became central to Goodenough's conception of his own role as a scholar.

A course in Shakespeare that was part of his major introduced him to what became a lifelong endeavor: "to explain the phenomena of life in terms of its basic sources."[41] He wrote several papers on the sources of Shakespeare's plays, his professor, Dr. Frank Ristine,[42] was so impressed with them that he suggested they might be the basis for a doctoral dissertation, and Goodenough decided to go to graduate school to study English when he left Hamilton.

He found no similar new directives for his religious life. The college requirements of daily Bible study and Sunday chapel left him without any fresh insights. The courses in the Bible and New Testament Greek were strictly academic disciplines. He did not fit into the YMCA group, which adjusted easily to the worldliness of college life, as he could not. His closest companion was still "the evangelical Jesus,"[43] and his ideal was David Livingstone, whom he described in *The Hamilton Literary*

Magazine as "a Christian soldier, an exemplar of the effacement of self and joy in the Cross of Christ."[44]

He did well in his studies, in part because he wanted to be elected to Phi Beta Kappa, as his father had been. He won the Clark Prize, the college's highest distinction, and at the commencement, where he was salutatorian, he delivered the prize oration, "Christianity and the War." In it he denounced both individualism and militarism, and its eloquent conclusion proclaimed that the power of Christ would triumph and peace be born—an assurance echoing the views of the peace organizations, which had some popular support even after World War I began in Europe.

In *Toward a Mature Faith* he referred to the summer of 1914, when war broke out in Europe, as "the dread summer," but did not mention the war's impact on him. Instead, he wrote of "a remarkable new . . . religious experience" during that summer, in which he "went through the gamut of agonies of guilt at certain peccadillos"[45] (probably masturbation).[46] This led him to resolve that if God "reinstated" him, he would enter the ministry, which ended the crisis.

His plan was both to prepare for the ministry and also to study for a Ph.D. in English. So in the summer of 1915, as a start toward the doctoral program Goodenough enrolled at Columbia University, probably influenced by Dr. Ristine, who had received his Ph.D. there. But he went no further than taking a summer course. In the fall he went to Drew, a Methodist seminary in Madison, New Jersey, where he appreciated the beautiful campus and wrote of the "fine fellows."[47] In the year he spent there he studied Biblical Literature, Biblical Theology, the New Testament, Church History, Religious Pedagogy and Psychology, Homiletics, and Music. In the fall of 1916 he transferred to Garrett Biblical Institute in Evanston, Illinois.

Before going to Garrett, he made another change in his life. On 5 September 1916 he married Helen Miriam Lewis, a young woman whom he had met in the Methodist Church in Jamaica. She was born in Westbury, Long Island, and when they met her father was a prosperous businessman and farmer in Jamaica. Helen was tall and beautiful, with brown eyes and hair, and men found her extremely attractive. We do not know what she saw in the physically unprepossessing, socially immature, priggish Goodenough. But she was over twenty-five. At that time many young women felt that twenty-five was a deadline for marriage, and, although she was a graduate of Normal School and had taught for several years, she was not committed to teaching as a lifetime career.

Until he knew Helen, Goodenough had had only "romantically idealized attachments to various girls," had repressed his sexual urges, had no erotic experience, and had been shocked when the specifics of sexual intercourse had first been described to him.[48] Helen was his ideal of beauty; he was drawn to what he perceived to be her fine character; and he believed that with her he would realize his dream of a fulfilling spiritual and sexual relationship. He loved her passionately and found his pleasure in pleasing her rather than in being pleased.

In a late memoir he stated that Helen never really liked him although she accepted him. He went on to describe how the situation was complicated by his father's falling in love with her after their engagement, "carrying on a violent courtship of her for many years. She loved this, for it was passion without overt sexual demand—beyond the most passionate hugging and kissing."[49] His father gave her a ring with two diamonds, inscribed "together yet separate,"[50] insisted that she think of him as her spiritual husband, and wrote her daily, long letters addressed to "My own dear darling sweetheart."[51] Hard as it is to see how Erwin could accept this relationship, he claimed that he repressed all resentment of his father's humiliation of him, as he had done when he was a boy.

Perhaps later, in retrospect, he exaggerated his father's relations with Helen, because when he wrote to his parents from Oxford he emphasized how happy he was in his marriage: "You surely never said a truer thing, Mamma, than when you said that the greatest thing I ever did was when I won Helen Lewis. The statement could be improved by only one correction—it is not only the greatest thing I ever did, but is at least the greatest thing I shall ever have done when I am become an old man."[52] And there is no outward evidence in their early married years of the tensions that developed later.

Goodenough entered Garrett Biblical Institute with his religious beliefs still largely those of his upbringing, and he found there a similar "conservative Methodist orthodoxy."[53] But he also encountered for the first time the Social Gospel. This popular early-twentieth-century Protestant movement held that Jesus' teachings challenge Christians to apply the law of love to a broad spectrum of social issues. It was eloquently expounded by Walter Rauschenbush in *Christianity and the Social Crisis* and *Christianizing the Social Order* and by his disciples in seminaries across the country. To many young Christians it was an exciting modern version of their "calling" to mission. Goodenough's background and inclinations had not prepared him for it, however. He "suddenly felt confused,"[54] and, although he always admired men who reached out to help others, he never believed that the social message was a central element of religion. This view led him to see his vocation as that of a seeker for historical evidence of religious beliefs. During the Great Depression years when the theologian Reinhold Niebuhr was writing *Moral Man and Immoral Society* he focused on the Hellenism of Philo Judaeus, and he consistently disassociated himself from his political and social-activist colleagues at Yale.

While at Garrett Institute, during weekends and the summers of 1916 and 1917, he served a small Methodist Church in Crescent City, a town on the corn plains of Illinois. He preached effectively, according to his later estimate of his efforts. Then, "in the second year I awoke to the fact that I was a most promising young preacher who both philosophically and historically had no idea what he was talking about."[55] He felt that he needed, instead of more courses in theology or philosophy, "a few facts about where Christianity had come from, how it became what it did and so what were its deepest and permanent values."[56] As he later explained his motivation, in an address to the Society of Biblical Literature, "Once one had found the historical Jesus, it was felt, one could recover the sense of certainty, find it through historical criticism itself. It was this desire which brought me into such studies. . . . It has not been the past for its own sake. . . . Pupils like us went to the masters to learn; it was the past in which we thought was the eternal present, the true social gospel or whatever was the problem of the day which most concerned us." He was impelled by "the hope that man would know better how to live in the present if he could understand the secret of early Christianity, because a man would have a basis of certainty for his judgments and hopes. . . ."[57] Stating his reasons somewhat differently in an autobiographical fragment, he wrote that he wanted to define the meaning of "Wesen des Kristentums," a term made popular by Adolf Harnack's book of that title.[59] This led him to look outside his denominational seminaries for further study.

Goodenough's credits in advanced Greek and Hebrew from Hamilton, in addition to the year of courses at Drew Seminary, had enabled him to receive the Bachelor of Sacred Theology degree from Garrett Biblical Institute after a year there. The Cook County, Illinois, draft board exempted him from the draft, as a minister. Thus, in the fall of 1917, having received a scholarship to Harvard Divinity School, he was free to go there. He found its graduate program a stimulating contrast to the conservatism of Garrett, for it emphasized a critical, historical approach to the Bible, and three of its distinguished teachers introduced him to this approach.

F. C. Conybeare was a visiting Lowell lecturer from England between

1919 and 1920. He was the author of *Magic, Myth and Morals: A Study of Christian Origins,* and Goodenough later described him as "one of the greatest critical historians in the field during his generation."[60]

George Foot Moore, regarded as the foremost American historian of religion and authority on Judaism, was a dynamic, demanding teacher, intolerant of any unproven assumptions, and difficult to disagree with. He was "indeed a scholar beyond scholars,"[61] and, according to Goodenough, "no one who had heard them will ever forget the great lectures on the history of religion"[62] he gave.

Kirsopp Lake, professor of early Christian literature and from 1919 Win Professor of ecclesiastical history, was Goodenough's supervisor and mentor. In 1911 Lake had published *The Earlier Epistles of St. Paul: Their Motives and Origin,* stating, "The study of the religious life of the Graeco-Roman world as a whole is now fully recognized to be absolutely necessary if we do not wish our notions about early Christianity to be a mere caricature of truth." A few lines down he continues: "To understand the history of religions we must understand the psychology of religious men," and in the next paragraph, "Our great need at present is the study of the living soul."[63] Lake must have shared these views with his student, for here were the seeds of Goodenough's own later interests: his lifelong concern with the problem of Christianity's rapid Hellenization, leading him to study Philo and Jewish symbols in the Greco-Roman world ("world" rather than "period" being the word he originally chose in his *Symbols* title);[64] the psychological focus that led to The *Psychology of Religious Experiences;* and "the study of the living soul" in *Toward a Mature Faith.* Forty-five years after sitting in Lake's class Goodenough remembered his phrase "the sacrament of the imagination,"[65] which Goodenough transposed when he affirmed in "The Mystical Value of Scholarship" that "scholarship is also a sacrament."[66]

An empirical approach to the study of religion distinguished the Harvard Divinity School at this time. Goodenough learned to verify every statement about historical facts and to distinguish between such facts and hypotheses. He was finally freed from the belief that one must not apply critical methods to matters of faith—from the counsel that "the best way to read the Bible was to read it when on my knees."[67] He came to realize that his procedures in tracing the sources of Shakespeare's plays were equally appropriate for examining the New Testament—that he could employ "creative understanding" in this examination. Conybeare had written in 1909, in *Magic, Myth and Morals: A Study of Christian Origins:* "Nothing is so contemptible as the facile orthodoxy which would fain raise no questions and plead that it is so much simpler to take every statement in the Bible at its face value. . . . We must face the problems of our age, and adopt the solutions which an enlightened criticism provides."[68] Goodenough came to agree heartily.

At the same time, he wrote in *Toward a Mature Faith,* "I by no means gave up the sense of reality of my spiritual experience. Jesus was still vividly with me. As I went to Harvard and had a little parish in Holbrook, Mass., I preached to my simple congregation more movingly than ever."[69] There was no reason to abandon Methodism in favor of another denomination, for when Lake learned that Goodenough was a Methodist, he said quietly, "Never mind. They're no worse than the others."[70]

At first Erwin commuted about seventeen miles to Cambridge from Holbrook, where he and Helen lived in a small upstairs apartment in an old, colonial-style homestead that they later thought of fondly as "the little Holbrook nest"[71] and their first home. But at the end of Harvard's first semester Erwin contracted a mild case of tuberculosis and had to withdraw for a year and a half. With his father's financial help they spent much of the time in Vermont so that he could be in the country and have good air, for which Vermont was especially noted at that time. He served a parish there in the summer of 1918. In the fall they moved to a large apartment house at 9 Fairfield Street in North Cambridge, about a mile and a half from the Divinity School. Soon afterward they came down with influenza at the height of the flu epidemic that was taking so many lives. They had no furniture and, sick as they were, had to sleep on a mattress on the floor, although Helen was a few weeks pregnant. But they recovered, and they gradually accumulated a bed and other furniture.

On 30 May 1919 their first child, Ward Hunt, named for his grandfather, was born, and Goodenough returned to Harvard for the 1919–20 school year. The only example of his work in the Divinity School archives shows him to be already meticulous and critical and having a sharp eye for interesting detail. This, a paper of May 1920 for Church History 3, is a careful description of the items in the *Liber Pontificalis* from John VIII to Honorius II. Goodenough notes that this section is the only part of the *Liber Pontificalis* catalogue deserving attention. He reviews the names and the lives of the popes that are included, pausing to comment that in the margin of the manuscript there is a recorded tradition of Popess John, a learned woman posing as a man, who was elevated to the papacy and disclosed her sex only when she died in childbirth. Having included this tidbit, Goodenough cautions that the account is "the product of too late a hand to carry any weight as history,"[72] thus balancing his sense of human interest with scrupulous concern to deny that the tradition is verifiable.

He was an eager learner, writing in *Toward a Mature Faith* that "here was an atmosphere which fired my enthusiasm as nothing since Uncle Charlie's mysticism had done. There was so much that was positive in it, the possibility of new discovery and evaluation, that I had no notion of the process by which my Faiths shrank to faiths as I learned to hold one or the other of them up to the light of facts."[73]

He was also an excellent student, and Kirsopp Lake, an Oxford graduate, urged him to go to Oxford to read for the Doctor of Philosophy degree in theology. Garrett Biblical Institute awarded him a Gustavus F. Swift Fellowship of $600. This was assigned to Garrett by American University to enable "young men of exceptional record in scholarship to continue their studies," thus helping "our choicest men to complete a preparation for widest usefulness." If they went abroad, they would come back "with the culture of sight-seeing in the world's most famous museums and libraries, and with the experience of travel giving new educational methods and new points of view."[74]

Lake, whose Oxford college was Lincoln, arranged for Goodenough's acceptance by that college, and Erwin's father was happy to supplement the Swift Fellowship money. Lake thus pointed the way, and the Swift Fellowship and his father opened the doors for the "man of destiny" to enter his lifelong profession of scholarship. The Harvard Divinity School had been instrumental in what he later described to Erik Erikson as "the struggle of a youth in an assured and dogmatic background to free himself."[75]

Chapter 2

The Years at Oxford
and *Justin Martyr*

Goodenough went to Oxford to begin his study of early Christianity by examinging the writings of Justin Martyr, a second-century theologian. But finding new personal satisfactions and broadening his cultural interests became equally important. At Oxford he was part of an impressively old, yet very alive, university, experienced the close companionship of peers as well as a warm family life, and had a base from which to explore the cultural riches of the Continent. In the three years he was there he fully met the Swift Fellowship's objectives that a fellow enjoy the opportunities for visiting the world's famous museums and libraries and gain new points of view. As a result he came to consider himself a man of the world—the Western European world—as his weekly letters to his parents make clear. Simultaneously, in developing his dissertation, *The Theology of Justin Martyr,* he came to see a relationship of Hellenistic Judaism to early Christianity, which led to his lifelong investigation of that relationship.

The Oxford of the early twenties was an exciting place. The Michaelmas (fall) term of 1920, Goodenough's first term, saw the largest number of undergraduates Oxford had ever admitted: 4,181 men and 549 women. There were former officers and noncommissioned men in the special short programs it provided for them. Some were bent on a good time, carrying over their "Eat, drink, and be merry, for tomorrow we die" attitude from the trenches. Others read for their War degree with grim determination. The nineteen-year-olds from the public schools (the English equivalents of United States private schools) were noisily eager to make the university, which was unusually full of older men, aware of their presence. In addition to the novelty of older male students, on 14 October 1920 the first awarding of degrees to women took place in the Sheldonian Theatre, with the five principals of the women's colleges

(which had up to then graduated women without degrees) becoming
M.A.'s and sitting behind the vice-chancellor.[1]

Lincoln, Goodenough's College, on short Turl Street off the main
High Street, represented both the old and the new Oxford. Built in the
churchyard of All Souls' Parish in 1429, it was one of the oldest and
smallest of the Oxford colleges, founded to train clergy to combat heresy
and "to overcome those who with their swinish snouts imperil the pearls
of true theology,"[2] according to Richard Fleming, then bishop of Lincoln. Both the first quadrangle and the Hall date from the fifteenth century, and most of the other buildings from the seventeenth. The Hall,
with its panelled walls and timbered roof, where the students dined by
candlelight, must have seemed very impressive to Goodenough, who had
known nothing older than Harvard.

The college maintained the traditions and mannerisms of the public
schools, and the rector, J. A. R. Munro, was reserved and stiff, although
an effective administrator and a respected scholar. A large number of the
undergraduates still came from families of the professional classes. The
major difference of the period was the greater number of them than at
any time in Lincoln's history. Among the candidates for a higher degree
there were also more graduates of foreign universities, some of whom
were married, living in their own quarters and relatively removed from
college life.

Goodenough, one of these, showed no awareness in his letters that he
sensed anything unusual about either Oxford or Lincoln College, perhaps
partly because most of his friends were fellow Americans. He reported to
his parents that "we are all very happy."[3] And he wrote an acquaintance
in the United States, "Oxford has been hospitable to me beyond my expectations. . . . I have found every don's door open to me which I wished
to enter for help in my work, and always an interested and helpful greeting. In such an atmosphere it is a true pleasure to work."[4]

The second year they settled in St. John's Road, near Lincoln College
and the Bodleian Library, and Goodenough wrote, "We are fitting into
things very much better because we know the ropes better and how to
adapt ourselves to conditions. . . . We get along easier with the servants,
we fit into national habits and life."[5] (Specifically, they had come to accept hearty English breakfasts, afternoon teas, and conventions in dress.)
That year he also found the Bodleian Library much pleasanter to work
in than previously because he was given a desk in the oldest part, Duke
Humphrey's fifteenth-century library, with the privacy of individual
desks between the seventeenth-century bookcases.

He played tennis regularly every afternoon in good weather. Punting on the Cherwell River was another, entirely new, activity that he enjoyed with his friends. For he now had close friends, which he had never had before. As a boy he had "passionately wanted the other boys to like him,"[6] but they did not. Now all that changed. Almost from the first the Goodenoughs were invited out for tea, for dinner, or for the evening. Erwin found Oxford an ideal place "to learn the gracious art of entertainment, by no means an easy thing to learn, and by all means one of the most important things in our work as teachers or ministers."[7] Thus tutored, they gave tea, dinner, and evening parties in return, and after bringing a pair of fine silver candlesticks back from Berlin Goodenough wrote, "We are planning now to give all our parties by candlelight."[8]

Among fellow Americans, Goodenough knew and entertained Amos Wilder and his sister. Like Goodenough, Wilder lived in town, with his mother and sister, while at Mansfield College as a divinity student. He was also a poet, and Goodenough admired his work, which was to appear as *Battle-Retrospect* in the Yale Series of Younger Poets in 1923. (Later Wilder became an eminent New Testament scholar.)

Three fellow graduate students, Edward Mason, Theodore Hatfield, and Robert Shaw, became the close friends Goodenough had earlier yearned for and lacked. Mason, a Rhodes scholar, had been a varsity football and basketball player, "a big heavy Kansas boy, powerful in body and mind, but very quiet and reserved," Goodenough wrote, the emphasis on Mason's build reflecting the same high value that his father placed on physique. Like Goodenough, Mason was spending 1920–1923 at Oxford. Hatfield was the son of a Northwestern University professor, "small, keen, a brilliant conversationalist, a writer of great merit, an artist in all his thinking and moving." Shaw, according to Goodenough, was "a round faced overgrown boy, whom everyone likes to have around."[9]

All three spent the Christmas vacation of 1921 with the Goodenoughs in Berlin, staying in the same hotel, sitting together at the theater, going to museums and shops, taking meals and trips together, and spending the evenings "chatting."[10] Erwin wrote to his parents, "In Ed and Ted I have found real men friends for the first time in my life, and you well know that the experience must be a beautiful one."[11] Again, a month later, "We never lived lives such as in this last term. . . . We are steeped in a fascinating friendship, and Sunday, being a day the boys took off for the most part, was devoted . . . to little excursions, or quiet gettings together which . . . have meant a very wonderful experience to us."[12]

Ed and Ted went to Jena with the Goodenoughs in the summer of 1922, when their second son, John, was born. Ed and Ted provided Helen with flowers, books, and their company while she was in the hospital with the surgery she needed after the birth. Erwin expressed to his parents his grateful dependence on their support during Helen's illness: "The boys will be here with me until the middle of October, so that I shall not be alone until all is well on its way to a new start."[13]

After they left, he wrote his parents: "We shall both miss them very much. They have been a wonderful help all through the ordeal."[14] When he and Helen went from Jena to Wiesbaden, "the boys" joined them for three weeks of the 1922 Christmas vacation, and, when they were alone again, "we had all four been together so much that we felt lost without them."[15] As Goodenough summed it up: "Certainly there must rarely have been a group of four people each one of whom loved each other more wonderfully. It is the finest friendship any of us have ever known, or are likely to know."[16]

He gave Helen full credit for "the boys'" intimacy, reporting with pride that they provided her with books so they could have her opinion on them. There was no hint of jealousy, although Ed and Helen were obviously very intimate. After returning to the United States Erwin and Mason remained good friends. Mason received an appointment at Harvard in 1923 and was a frequent visitor at the Goodenoughs' Woodbridge home.

Erwin had a very satisfying family life as well as friendships during the Oxford years. He describes sitting with Helen "cozily about the fire as I write with my paper on an old real Queen Anne gateleg table" while Ward was "having an ecstatic play . . . with the fine doll Aunty Dedy made for him."[17] When they were alone evenings he played his favorite piano music or refinished a piece of furniture. From Schongau he wrote that Helen was perfectly content reading English poetry and knitting suits for Wardie, being "deeply and wonderfully happy in this unplanted life I have asked her to lead since we were married."[18]

He was a devoted father. Sharing his own father's pride in manliness, he was delighted that there was "none of the molly coddle"[19] about Wardie; that he was "thick set and solid—ideal build" (unlike Erwin); that he "is a very real boy."[20] Later he writes, "He continues to be a joy unspeakable with his bright keen little face, eager, boyish, boisterous, but with a tender side."[21] The father delighted in playing hymns with a marching rhythm and seeing Wardie march around the room with a stick on his shoulder,[22] he was so pleased with Wardie's keeping in step that he gave no thought to the warlike aspects of the feat. Or he would play "jiggy" music, and Wardie would dance a jig "in perfect time . . . kicking and slapping his knees."[23] Erwin summed up his feelings in terms he habitually used with his parents: "God is good to us beyond our deserts to give us so sweet a boy, and yet so thoroughly alive and virile."[24]

The fond father thought the second son, John, equally remarkable. He wrote his parents; "I grow more proud of my two little boys all the time. John is certainly a beautiful baby."[25] Six weeks later, "He never cries, sleeps all night and is the best baby I ever saw."[26] Again, three weeks later; "Johnny is a little dear. I never knew a baby could be so good. He laughs and plays with his rattle and talks, or else sleeps."[27]

Because of the generosity of Erwin's father and the favorable exchange rate of the German mark, the Goodenoughs were fortunate in being able to travel. Their first summer abroad they spent in Schongau, a picture-postcard Bavarian town at the foot of the Alps, where they soon learned how inexpensively they could live in Germany. They had a similar experience in Jena, an old university town south of Leipzig. Thus they could enjoy the charm of these towns and also save money.

To spend so much of their time abroad posed no problem, for the Lincoln College year, like the rest of Oxford, had residence requirements of three eight-week terms. Erwin, Helen, and Ward could live and travel on the Continent between terms and during the long summer vacations. After their 1921 summer in Schongau they returned to Oxford by way of Heidelberg, Mainz, and a boat trip down the Rhine to Cologne, so as to see Germany at its most romantic, before going to Dover. They went to Berlin for the 1921 Christmas vacation, coming back to Oxford weighed down with beautiful books and etchings, silver candlesticks, and a great fondness for "the magnificent country."[28]

During the Easter vacation of 1922 they spent several weeks in Paris. From Paris they traveled south to the château country, visiting Loches, Chenonceaux, Ambois, and Blois. Back by way of Chartres, "ablaze . . . with the most marvelous old glass,"[29] they saw as well as heard the Angelus rung and were so caught up by the cathedral's spell that they had to run to the station to catch their train.

The summer of 1922 they spent in Jena, where John was born. Since Helen had to have surgery because of complications following John's birth, they stayed in Jena through the fall, since Erwin had fulfilled his residence requirements and could finish his dissertation in Jena as well as in Oxford, especially since the University of Jena had a fine library

Erwin in the summer of 1921 in Schongau, Germany.

and scholars Goodenough could consult. Then they went to Wiesbaden for the winter, to avoid the struggle with water freezing in the wash basins at Jena and to enjoy Wiesbaden's art, music, and opera.

Goodenough's experiences with the people in these countries gave him very definite opinions about the Americans, English, French, and Germans, which he continued to hold and express for many years. He tried to pattern himself on the men of the American Club at Oxford, "whose vacations are spent in ransacking every remote corner of the continent, and in picking up ideas and impressions."[30] He bristled at the presumption of a popular American writer who addressed these men, pouring out anti-German propaganda and pontificating that France was not imperialistic, for "'I have just been in France a month, and *I know!*'"[31] Goodenough also attacked the "fatuous self assertive ignorance of the American populace,"[32] who swallowed France's argument that crippling Germany was essential to French national security. By the end of his second year he had become the typical American living abroad, in his contempt for American crudeness. He sneered at a fellow train passenger from San Francisco who was loaded with jewels, "a thing which no continental woman of taste would dream of doing when traveling," and who told everyone how wealthy she was, then jeered at a German customs official, "Say, dearie, who won the war?"[33] He wouldn't go to Oberammergau to see the Passion Play because it was overrun by Americans, and he wanted his parents to tell their friends, if they asked about it, that "we don't like the American company they (the Oberammergauns) keep there."[34]

Early in his Oxford days he had written an American who asked for his impressions of England that "we do not wonder at the pride an Englishman takes in his native land."[35] He was also grateful for being at Oxford long enough to have the chance to appreciate the "positive"[36] qualities of the English. But he was disgusted by the excitement over the wedding of Princess Mary, King George V's daughter, and he wished the English people would "vomit up the Royal Family for good and all" rather than "vomit up only loyalty and patriotism."[37] More sweepingly, he contrasted the Germans with the "prejudiced, unreasoning, ignorant and passionate . . . English or American provincial society."[38]

After he and Helen had traveled through France, he wrote his parents: "France is a beautiful and wonderful country, and the French people everywhere treated us with the greatest kindness."[39] But he thought the French attitude toward German reparations ridiculously shortsighted, and he attributed France's help in the American Revolution to opportunism.[40]

In contrast to his criticisms of England and France, Goodenough expressed only warm feelings for the Germans. During the fall of the mark he wrote, "Germany, beloved Germany, her people are simply magnificent in this present appalling state—a people deep, art loving, courteous."[41] In the letters to his parents he praised the Germans' hospitality, their devotion to Ward, and their care of Helen during her surgery in the Jena Klinik after John's birth.

When he took an overall look at his European experience, he reflected more impartially: "I am glad that I am an American and love the English and Germans and Italians all at the same time";[42] and, again, "Isn't it strange how we find all peoples so fine and how we can love them all."[43]

His attitude toward dress reflected his new posture of sophistication. After having cared little about clothes, he became fashion conscious. He wore spats and sported a stick, like any English gentleman. He decided that England was the place to buy men's clothes: "The quality of the materials . . . is beautiful indeed."[44] Walking with Helen in the shopping section of Paris, he concluded that the French "are certainly more stylish a race than the English, but are by no means the galaxy of marvelous grooming and taste we had looked to find."[45]

He delighted in buying for Helen, especially hat after hat: a pink one trimmed with gold, one of white kid, one with a very large egret feather. The cost never seemed to be a problem; the favorable exchange rate of the mark made purchases in Germany irresistible, and Goodenough's father honored every telegraphed request for money, perhaps at least partly because he delighted in making Helen happy.

Erwin and Helen could take full advantage of the opera and theater in the cities where they stayed, for in the evening they could always leave Ward in the care of the landlady, boarding-house owner, or, later, the nurse-maid-governess Renée Tronchet, whom they engaged after John's birth. They decided to spend the Christmas vacation of 1921 in Berlin rather than Dresden because there were two opera houses in Berlin to choose from, and only one in Dresden. And Goodenough wrote to his parents that "opera and art will always be different words to us after this [European] experience."[46]

There were equally good theater opportunities. In London they saw *The Silver Box,* Galsworthy's melodramatic attack on social injustice. In Oxford they treated themselves to two contemporary Irish plays, "to get in touch with the very wonderful contemporary movement in literature."[47] They saw an Oscar Wilde play because they wanted to see "how he goes on the stage," and concluded it was "not the last word of decadence, but he is getting pretty well on toward it."[48]

They studied the history of art and modern art seriously, guided by Helen's judgment, which Goodenough described to his parents as the "sweetest and truest."[49] They bought books to help them, and he wrote, "We have made large progress in the appreciation and understanding of the very modern schools of art," adding ruefully, "We are still in the dark about cubism, however."[50] They visited every important art gallery and museum in the cities where they stayed. When in Paris they spent several days in the Louvre and visited the Sainte-Chapelle, a special joy. Goodenough was fully aware of their enrichment, and he wrote to his parents, "We wonder and wonder how our little traps and ornaments are going to look to us when we return to them, for certainly our taste in every line has developed out of all proportion to our 'station.' "[51]

The letters to his parents said less about Oxford's intellectual or cultural life, apart from its theater. He made no mention of the poets Robert Graves, John Masefield, or W. B. Yeats, all guests of Lincoln College's Fleming Playreading Society during Goodenough's years there. *Toward a Mature Faith* stated, "At Oxford I met no one so stimulating or formative as the great men at Harvard,"[52] and the only mention of the Oxford notables beyond his own Lincoln College was the comment, "When I was a student at Oxford . . . I remember hearing one of its great physicists, a Nobel prize winner, say that science had proved there was no God."[53]

Evangelical Christianity had less hold than ever on Goodenough. Lincoln College was dear to Methodism, for John Wesley was a Fellow of Lincoln for twenty-five years, preached some of his earliest sermons from its pulpit, and it was while he was there that his followers were given the name "Methodists." Yet Goodenough never mentioned this association to his parents. He attended an occasional service at the Oxford Wesleyan Church, and he and Helen had tea at the minister's house. In his first formal involvement with English Methodism he accepted an invitation to talk to the Methodist Men's club in Oxford on "Social Service in America."[54] But in the light of his current interests he considered it more important to be chosen president of the Theological Society of Lincoln, and more flattering to be asked to join the Oxford Society of Historical Theology,[55] where he was the only student among the theological dons.

His Sunday churchgoing was distinctly ecumenical. In Oxford he attended some church most Sundays. When in London he and Helen went to services in Westminster Abbey, and when in Canterbury to a sung service at the cathedral. In Paris they attended Palm Sunday Mass at the

Church of the Madeleine, and he wrote to his parents, "Helen and I get as much or more from such a service than from any service of any sort we know."[56]

During that Easter vacation of 1922 in Paris he arranged with the Methodist bishop Edgar Blake to be ordained in the Union American Church. In 1921 the Methodist New York East Conference had elected him to be ordained in Europe, and this was the delayed ordination, performed at the end of the Easter Sunday service, which, he wrote, "will always be a particularly choice memory."[57] The ordination was a means of fulfilling his parents' expectations and his own earlier promise to God to enter the ministry. But he clearly saw his future in teaching, not as pastor of a parish.

Goodenough had come to enjoy scholarship. The "inspiration" of Helen,[58] the warm family life, close friends, the freedom from narrow, pietistic restraints fostered the relish with which he worked on his dissertation, "The Theology of Justin Martyr," and his commitment to it. Wherever they were, Goodenough had a study and wrote persistently, chapter after chapter. When he and Helen were not traveling, he established a routine of hours in his "beloved study"[59] or in the Bodleian Library, working a long morning and again from teatime to dinner, which was usually at eight. By his second year he fully appreciated the Bodleian, for he found it had almost every book that had been printed. Then he found additional Justin Martyr material in Berlin and spent four weeks of the 1922 Christmas vacation reading in the library there, although that meant giving up much of the time he and Helen had planned to spend in the museums. He even hired a German student to help him take notes.

The whole process gave him great satisfaction. "The real excitement of my life now [is] the development of my theories of Justin Martyr's relation to Greek Philosophy,"[60] he wrote his parents. Somewhat later he expressed the same enthusiasm: "I never did any work quite so fascinating as this writing in my life. To organize my ideas and see the thing take shape and grow is a sort of joy I had never experienced."[61]

His supervisor, Dr. Darwell Stone, a shy, formal man who always wore a top hat, was a theologian knowledgeable about Justin Martyr's writings. Goodenough was his first student for such a supervision, and Stone liked his plans and his progress.[62] When Goodenough showed him the critical chapter containing his original interpretation, which was a requirement for the D.Phil., Stone was encouraging.

In Jena, where they spent the summer and fall of 1922, Goodenough could not find a typist to type English, and he always wrote only in longhand. After he failed to locate one even in Leipzig, he bought a type-writer there and came back staggering under its weight. He then hired a private secretary to live with his family while he worked. He dispatched the typed dissertation to his examiners by mail from Wiesbaden, where the family had gone. Then, in February 1923, just when he planned to go to Oxford to take his examinations, he was faced with the "great strike" in Germany. He could get no money from the banks. No trains were running, so he had to go to Frankfurt in a taxi paid for with French francs he had borrowed. There he managed to catch a train to Strasbourg the next day, then traveled via Luxembourg to Belgium, and, finally, to Oxford.

He took the two written examination papers required for the D.Phil., had a very pleasant oral examination on his dissertation, with only friendly questions, and was granted the degree. Still, he found the experience stressful and "took a good dose of Bromide" the night before,[63] so he could sleep. The whole procedure was quite different from the casual, easy acceptance he recalled when reminiscing to a friend years later. According to that later recollection, he handed the dissertation to his supervisor only after it had been completed; the supervisor hefted it, thoughtfully riffled its pages, and concluded, "Well, Goodenough, this seems substantial enough for a D.Phil."[64] Twenty years had erased all memory of the anxious waiting for comments each time he submitted a chapter. The supervisor had now become the stereotypical uninvolved Oxford don, and the degree process itself a formality, in line with Goodenough's professed scorn of many academic requirements and his feelings about the English.

At the end of what had clearly been an ordeal, he wrote his parents in conflicting tones of humility and conceit that some of his colleagues would see as characteristic and offensive. First he commented, "I some-how can not believe that so humble and unworthy a person as the little boy I always think of myself as being has actually achieved so outstanding an academic distinction." In the same letter, in quite a different tone, he went on to gloat, "At least I shall always now be in a position to express my very hearty contempt of degree chasing and the silly American insistence upon a Ph.D. before one can begin to do any teaching."[65]

He went back to Wiesbaden to bring Helen to Oxford for the 17 February ceremony in which he received the degree "in my gown of blazing glory" (the Oxford scarlet gown, which he always highly prized).[66] There was a celebration with his friends. Ted Hatfield helped him to correct the proofs of the dissertation to prepare it for publication. Helen and Erwin then returned to Wiesbaden, where the children and Renée Tronchet, the nursemaid-governess, awaited them.

Ed Mason, who had just received his B.Litt., joined them in Wiesbaden, and they all set off for Alassio, the little town on the Italian Riviera that Goodenough had chosen as the ideal spot for the weeks of rest and relaxation he felt he needed. Italy was more expensive than Germany, but he wanted Alassio's climate and seaside location to recuperate from his efforts, and his parents were happy to finance this luxury, as they had underwritten so many Continental trips. He, Helen, and Ed could sightsee from Alassio as they chose, and they went to Monte Carlo for a short visit. But mainly they relaxed and felt "the joy of mere existence."[67]

Goodenough managed to get a passport for Miss Tronchet, so that she could accompany them to the United States, and on 5 May the family sailed for home on the *Berengaria,* enjoying a luxurious voyage on the second-ranking ship of the Cunard Line. As he wrote to his parents of the three years abroad, " 'We have lived' and lived gloriously."[68]

Goodenough had also published his first scholarly work. *The Theology of Justin Martyr,* appropriately dedicated "To My Parents in Loving Gratitude," was privately printed in Jena in 1923 by Verlag Frommannche Buchhandlung. The German mark was so low in relation to the dollar that this was financially feasible, especially since his father underwrote the cost.

The choice of Justin Martyr may have resulted from a decision Goodenough later said led him to his study of Philo, as he described his reasoning to Professor Minear of the Garrett Biblical Institute. "When an historian finds a place where the evidence is not sufficient to construct a picture without a projection . . . the historian moves on to another field, just marking this one, like a good prospector, to be non-paying dirt. That is why I so early abandoned the synoptics."[69] Both Conybeare and Lake had cited Justin Martyr frequently in their lectures. And Goodenough found in Justin's writings the incorporation of both the Palestinian and the Hellenistic Judaism that Christianity drew upon "still strikingly intact"[70]—in other words, "pay dirt" for a study of Christianity's origins.

The subtitle of *The Theology of Justin Martyr,* "An Investigation into the Conceptions of Early Christian Literature and Its Hellenistic and Judaistic Influences," identifies Goodenough's primary interest in the early theologian. The preface makes this interest explicit, stating that the importance of Justin is "his transitional position":[71] one must know the sources of Justin's ideas before one can understand them and their meaning in second-century Christianity. Hence, a knowledge of Greek thought and the thought of Judaism, especially Hellenistic Judaism, which Goodenough has, is essential for understanding Justin. The preface thus indicates that in interpreting Justin Martyr's theology Goodenough will focus on what will be his continuing interests: the origins of early Christianity and the importance of Hellenistic Judaism as one of these origins.

His presentation is comprehensive and systematic. In the first chapter he gives a succinct summary of the key theories of the major Greek philosophers and the popular doctrines and myths in Justin's environment. In the second he describes Palestinian and Hellenistic Judaism and outlines the metaphysical system of the Jewish philosopher Philo of Alexandria as an example of Hellenistic-Judaic thought.

He then describes briefly Justin's *First* and *Second Apology* and the *Dialogue with Trypho*. In the *Dialogue,* Trypho is the leader of a group of Jews with whom Justin discusses the truth of Christianity, and Goodenough characterizes Trypho as typical of Dispersion Judaism and important literary evidence of Jewish religion in the Roman world. As Goodenough reads Justin, Justin's Trypho knew Scripture, had received rabbinic teaching, and believed in obeying the Law in the form of the reduced requirements of circumcision, Sabbath observance, and ritual washing that was followed by typical Jews of the Dispersion. But Trypho did not object to Justin's mystical view of justification. Goodenough therefore concludes that Justin created in the character Trypho what he saw as an ideal Jew, whose thought incorporated both Palestinian and Hellenistic Judaism.

When Goodenough proceeds to characterize Justin the apologist, he develops his original contribution to Justin Martyr interpretation—the originality required for a doctoral dissertation. He demonstrates that Justin was drawing upon the arguments of Hellenistic Judaism in representing Christianity as the true philosophy, and enhancing its authority by asserting that Moses was superior to Plato and that the Pentateuch was a profound philosophic treatise. In supporting this thesis Goodenough points repeatedly to the similarities of Justin's arguments to those in Philo's writings, although he also recognizes that Justin's spirit and purpose were very different from Philo's.

After chapters that develop each of Justin's main doctrines (of God, the Logos, the Holy Spirit and the lower powers, the Created World, Christ, Redemption and the Christian life, and eschatology), the concluding chapter affirms that Justin was a traditionalist, not an intellectual pioneer, and that he presents a body of thought already accepted as Christian doctrine. That body of thought, Goodenough states in his closing sentence, had drawn heavily not on Greek philosophy or Palestinian Judaism, but on Hellenistic Judaism: "In brief, the Christianity which Justin has described, with its foundation of primitive Palestinian Judaistic Christian beliefs, was almost entirely dependent for theory upon a Hellenistic Judaistic tradition which had been running in through the doors opened by St. Paul, and by the authors of the Epistles to the Hebrews and of the Fourth Gospel."[72]

This emphasis on Justin Martyr's large debt to Hellenistic Judaism not only made the original contribution required of Goodenough's dissertation. It was also his first development of the hypothesis that Hellenistic Judaism was a more important strand of Judaism than scholars had recognized and that it was a key element in the origins of Christianity. This was a hypothesis that he was to reiterate and expand upon for the next forty years in his writings on both Judaism and early Christianity.

Goodenough portrays Justin sympathetically as a Christian mystic whose interest in philosophy was prompted by his hunger for mystical experience—a portrayal that reflects Goodenough's own appreciation of mysticism. But he also consistently belittles Justin the thinker. He states that Justin's writings show "conviction rather than penetration"[73] and are the work of a "philosophic dilettante"[74] whose interpretations often obscure rather than clarify. "His was an inferior mind,"[75] according to Goodenough, and "while we honour the Martyr and revere the Saint the fact must definitely be admitted that Justin was in no sense a philosopher."[76]

In 1943, when Goodenough listed his achievements, he stated, "The book was well received all over Europe and America."[77] So it was, considering that it was the first work of an unknown scholar, published by a small press in Germany. There were favorable reviews in *The Journal of Religion, The Literary Review of Today, The Anglican Theological Review,* Aberdeen's *Expository Times, Revue des Sciences Philosophiques et Théologiques, Theologische Blätter, Nieuw Theologisch Tijdschrift,* and *Theologische Literaturzeitung.* These reviews as a whole described Goodenough's treatment as able, careful, comprehensive, exhaustive, temperate, and valuable.

Since those early reviews there have been mixed estimates of the work. J. C. M. Van Winden, in *An Early Christian Philosopher: Justin Martyr's Dialogue with Trypho, Chapters One to Nine* (1971) described it as "one of the best works on this author."[78] But he and other critics have challenged some of Goodenough's main points.

B. W. Barnard, in *Justin Martyr His Life and Thought* (1967) questioned

Goodenough's evidence that Justin's thinking reflects Hellenistic Judaism and rejected his arguments for Justin's dependence on Philo. He saw what Goodenough ascribed to Philo and Hellenistic Judaism as rather in the system of Albinus the Middle Platonist.[79]

Robert Joly, in *Christianisme et philosophie: Études sur Justin et les apologistes grecs du deuxième siècle* (1973) disagreed with Goodenough's portrayal of Justin as a Christian mystic, terming his arguments "feeble."[80]

Barnard, Van Winden, and Daniel Bourgeois in *La sagesse des anciens dans le mystère du Verbe Évangile et philosophie chez Saint Justin philosophe et martyr* (1981) all challenged Goodenough's description of Justin as a philosophic dilettante, a simple Christian whose writings were uncritical and reflected an inferior mind. For Barnard this was "wide of the mark."[81] Van Winden insisted that Justin had a well-balanced and organized mind.[82] Bourgeois concluded his general disagreement with Goodenough by wondering why he lost so much time studying someone whom he valued so little.[83]

Goodenough may well have been influenced in his negative judgments of Justin and in his patronizing tone by his Harvard teacher Kirsopp Lake. In *The Stewardship of Faith,* Lake had stated that Justin's "powers of distorted exegesis are almost incredible."[84] In *Landmarks in the History of Early Christianity* (1922), Lake's criticism was more comprehensive, asserting that Justin's only claim to the title of philosopher was his dabbling "with little profit in many schools"[85] before his conversion and, finally, that "Justin was not a man of commanding intellect."[86]

The attitude of intellectual superiority to Justin Martyr that Goodenough probably adopted from Lake, and the supercilious tone which he may have picked up at Oxford, ruffled the scholarly Christian community's feathers. They resented his belittling the intelligence of a highly valued early theologian. It was the first of Goodenough's challenges to accepted Christian positions.

The Oxford letters and this departure from traditional Christian views in his first publication give a clear picture of Goodenough approaching thirty and ending his three years abroad. In spats and stick he patterned himself after an English gentleman. Yet he had no use for the British sense of superiority, finding the Germans, who were struggling with a nightmarish economy, far more admirable. He took great pride in his Oxford scarlet gown with its blue-ribbed silk facings, but could sneer at the American degree chasing. His contempt for his fellow Americans' "self-assertive ignorance"[87] abroad and the arrogance the letters often expressed went hand in hand with an occasional, if infrequent, awareness of this arrogance, as in his report that baby John's daily increase in beauty was as obvious as the daily increase in his "marked resemblance to his god-like Papa."[88] He still had a deep religious sense and wrote of his ordination in Paris as a "particularly choice memory."[89] But he had become impressed by the social values to which Oxford had introduced him and emphasized the importance of gracious entertaining in the work of a teacher or minister: "To combine dignity with cordiality and homely warmth is a real art."[90] The letters also repeatedly express the satisfaction he found in his relationships. Yet they make it clear that, while these relationships sustained him, scholarship was a priority, for he wrote with great enthusiasm of the Justin Martyr dissertation.

Chapter 3

Finding Himself: Goodenough as a Teacher and Scholar at Yale

Goodenough landed in New York City in May 1923 with his wife, the two boys and their governess, his D.Phil., and the need of a job. They went directly to his parents in Jamaica, Long Island. While Ward and John thoroughly enjoyed the special attention they received as grandchildren the elder Goodenoughs had never seen, their father explored the job market.

He had originally planned to teach in one of the theological seminaries that had encouraged him to hope for an appointment, for he could thus combine his early religious commitment with his later satisfaction in scholarship. But after the years abroad he was "so far left (in theology) that none of the seminaries . . . wanted me."[1] For he had come to believe "there is nothing too sacred for the human mind to question,"[2] an early step in his movement toward agnosticism.

His Oxford D.Phil. made him "nobody's baby," since it was not considered an equivalent to an American Ph.D. He had no teaching experience and no mentor to help in placing him. "I packed my grip," he recalls, "and went all through New England from college to college, applying in first one department and then another."[3] A teachers' employment agency could offer only a position without stipend at an "unheard of" college in central New York, teaching education twelve hours a week and philosophy in whatever additional hours he could find. He wrote in the late memoir describing this period: "To have taken such a job would have meant that I had stretched out in my grave and pulled in the dirt on top of me."[4] So he considered a temporary job as a caretaker at the Wayside Inn in Sudbury, Massachusetts.

At this low point, when he was in New York City about to board the train for Jamaica, he met a young graduate of Union Theological Seminary who had been looking for a position in church history. The young man told him that there was an opening in freshman history at Yale, for which he had been rejected, he thought, because he did not seem to be a gentleman. He looked Goodenough over and was encouraging, "Perhaps you would pass. At least you could try."[5]

Goodenough hurried to catch the next train for New Haven and applied. With his Oxford and Continental sophistication he was clearly a gentleman, and, after an interview with a "wise old professor," who glanced through his dissertation, he was appointed instructor in history. This appointment, which he saw as the work of "the mysterious hand," one of the "special providences that have occurred in every great emergency in my life,"[6] opened the door to what became his lifelong career at Yale.

He and Helen rented a house in New Haven for a year. Then, in 1924, Erwin's father bought them a handsome house at 28 Amity Road in Woodbridge, a popular suburb.

While they appreciated this gift, the father's financial help, which Erwin had drawn upon heavily and gladly during the Oxford years, became galling now that he wanted to feel independent and was especially irritating to him in the form it took, although Helen may have looked on it as a game. His father, instead of sending them a monthly sum regularly, when he visited would leave money hidden around the house for them to come upon when they opened a bureau or desk drawer. The father no doubt saw himself providing delightful surprises without making any commitments, but Erwin resented this sporadic help when he was struggling with heavy expenses.

The upkeep of the Woodbridge home was a burden. He was obliged to retain the former owner's caretaker until he learned how to maintain the house and the grounds. Renée Tronchet, who had stayed with them while they were in New Haven, left in 1924 to be married, but they had a maid intermittently until the late thirties.

Their new life was a great change from that of the Oxford years, especially for Helen. After they no longer had Renée Tronchet, they could not leave the children for long stretches, and in the early years there were few trips to enjoy museums and operas, although New York City was a center for the arts. Erwin and Helen became part of a well-to-do Woodbridge set with expensive social and liberal sexual standards—a less flamboyant version of the 1920s lifestyle in F. Scott Fitzgerald's portrayals of the Jazz Age. Dinner parties meant a white damask table cloth, olives and celery in cut-glass dishes, and an elaborate meal served by the maid. The Goodenoughs entertained often, had Erwin's family and friends as house guests, and Ed Mason, now teaching at Harvard, as a frequent visitor.

Two years after the move to Woodbridge, in June 1926, another son, James, was born, and in November 1928 a daughter, Hester.

The Yale Goodenough came to in 1923 was less impressive physically than it would be ten years later. There were as yet no Sterling Memorial Library or Hall of Graduate Studies on High Street, and none of the nine residential colleges to be built in the thirties. The Divinity School was still at the corner of College and Elm Streets, for the Sterling Divinity Quadrangle, up the hill on Prospect Street, enrolled its first class in 1932. But the Harkness Memorial Quadrangle, a Gothic-style granite complex, was completed, overshadowing the brick, brownstone, and limestone buildings of the older quadrangles.

There were twice as many students after the end of World War I than before, with more drinking and drunkenness under Prohibition and with newly liberal sex standards. Many students came to college to learn how to succeed, not how to become scholars. The stereotype of the average Yale undergraduate was that he was rich and content. Upton Sinclair wrote in 1923 in *The Goose-Step,* his diatribe against American higher education, that Yale is "a place where the sons of millionaires draw apart and live exclusive lives" and "the secret societies permit you to get drunk and to acquire your due share of venereal disease, but they do not permit you to wear the wrong color tie, or to use the wrong kind of slang, or to smoke the wrong tobacco."[7] Professor Chauncey B. Tinker was equally scornful, on different grounds, complaining, "No captain of industry is busier than the modern undergraduate. The whole state of affairs is an accurate reflection of our national indifference to the things of the mind, a phase of democracy which was not foreseen by the clergymen who founded Yale solidly, as they supposed, on books."[8]

Other faculty members had different views of the students. George Pierson, who wrote a history of the Yale of those years, saw the undergraduates as "serious and idealistic, and more than ever determined to think for themselves."[9] Pierson said that he saw the college as dedicated to both the intellectual and the spiritual in a predominantly materialistic age. He identified a conflict between the college faculty and the Yale Corporation, which was dominated by financiers and industrialists: "Here a belief in the arts and a longing for a more intellectual, cultivated, spiritual society did battle against American materialism—against the overwhelming success cult of our giant society."[10]

Yale obviously no longer subscribed to its original aim of preparing its graduates "for Publick Employment both in Church & Civil State"; but compulsory daily and Sunday chapel continued until 1926, in spite of undergraduate and faculty opposition. Then, when Battell Chapel could no longer hold the increased number of students, chapel became voluntary. The college temper was increasingly secular. A member of the class of 1926 wrote: "I defy a youth of average intelligence . . . to have even a cursory knowledge of Biology and Geology and to be a fundamentalist,"[11] and there was popular assent to the slogan in the *Saturday Evening Post* of February–May 1923: "The beginning of Doubt is the beginning of Wisdom."[12]

James Rowland Angell had become president of Yale in 1921. He held a B.A. from the University of Michigan, not Yale, but his emphasis on excellence was entirely in line with the intellectual ideals of Yale. He wanted a more scholarly and hard-working student body whose members also were men of good character, physically fit and with well-rounded personalities.

Angell defined a good college teacher as one who was stimulating, with broad learning, and interest in the students. He also wanted his faculty to be scholars. In his inaugural address he placed great emphasis on research: " It will always be true that where the great investigators and scholars are gathered, thither will come the intellectual elite from all the world."[13] He wanted them to be concerned with publication, for "only by publication can the scholar expose his intellectual powers to the critical evaluation of his peers."[14]

Goodenough met all of Angell's criteria for a good college teacher. During the years he spent at Oxford and on the Continent he developed a wide knowledge of art and an acquaintance with opera and the theater, as well as proficiency in his own fields of classics, history, philosophy, and religion.

Especially in his early years at Yale he felt "the deep pleasure which giving and teaching has."[15] Some doctoral candidates found him intimidating and coined the saying that if he were on an examining committee there should be a sign over the examination room door saying Abandon all hope, ye who enter here.[16] Others felt that as a dissertation adviser he gave them too little attention. Many, on the other hand, became his admirers and friends. Perhaps because of his ministerial training, he took great satisfaction in counseling students who came to him with psychological or religious problems, or just to talk. And he wrote to McGeorge Bundy, class of 1940, in November of that year, "I shall never forget our hours together. . . . Contact with you has been as important an experience for me as it could ever have been for you."[17]

The students in their turn responded, as he reported in describing a last class of the year, "When I got done I saw that the boys had dropped all pencils, were sitting as though enchanted, and they got up afterwards and just walked out in silence. One boy stayed afterwards and walked out with me. He had told someone a week before that his future was in my hands—that what he wanted was to try to find such an integration of scholarship and life as I had found. He told me as we walked out together that it was useless to try to tell what the course had meant to him. But this he knew—that he and a number of others were just dedicated to the task of spreading my conceptions."[18] Norman Holmes Pierson, who became a professor of English at Yale, affirmed appreciatively to Goodenough that he was "my first history teacher when I was a freshman and helped to open my eyes to the world I have since lived in."[19] And McGeorge Bundy, when he was special assistant to President Johnson and deeply involved in the Vietnam War issues, wrote to Goodenough, upon learning of his final illness, "Your teaching has been one of the permanent components of my education. There are things I think and do all the time that would be different if I had not worked with you. . . . It is so, I think, with hundreds of your students."[20]

Goodenough phrased the relationship between teaching and scholarship very pragmatically when he said, "After all, if you're a scholar, it's because you have people to teach."[21] But in his later years research and publication became his priorities as he became increasingly committed to presenting his interpretation of Hellenistic Judaism, the role of symbols in this Judaism, and ultimately Hellenistic Judaism's relevance to early Christianity. He also came to share the general academic view that the measure of a university is the publications of its faculty. When a young instructor in biblical literature at Wellesley consulted him at an American Academy of Religion meeting about some materials the instructor had, Goodenough, in a deep voice, said gruffly, "Young man, my advice to you, publish like hell. No university was ever built on good teaching."[22] He also came to insist on the religious nature of scholarship at its best, stating in the *Introduction to Philo Judaeus* that "the goal of scholarship should be not knowledge, but wisdom,"[23] and in "The Mystical Value of Scholarship" that scholarship can be "a sacrament."[24] Thus the teacher who came to Yale in 1923 had all the qualities Angell required, and in the thirty-nine years he spent there came to find in scholarship a commitment that met his emotional as well as his intellectual needs.

Charles Seymour, chairman of the history department, was a graduate of King's College, Cambridge, as well as Yale. He was a member of the

Paris Peace Conference after World War I, had lectured at Stanford and Cambridge, and at Yale was made Sterling Professor of history in 1922. He was a popular teacher and suave, shrewd, and persistent as an administrator.

Goodenough as a junior faculty member found most of his colleagues congenial. He was drawn to Ralph Gabriel, professor of American history, because of his learning in many fields, combined with a deeply religious spirit, and they became and remained close friends until Gabriel's early death. He especially valued Michael Rostovtzeff, who came to Yale in 1925 as professor of ancient history and classical archaeology, and dedicated *The Jurisprudence of the Jewish Courts in Egypt* to him, as "Eruditissimo, Benignissimo," who "puts his knowledge and himself at the disposal of anyone who comes to him for guidance."[25]

His relations with Wallace Notestein, the popular professor of English history, were more strained. Notestein was an ardent Anglophile, whereas Goodenough was highly critical of the English and had very warm feelings for the Germans. At first Notestein was a good friend. But a late memoir of Goodenough states: "Notestein cast me out because I refused to join in the worship which he and the socially prominent New Englanders lavished upon all things English."[26] In looking back, he may have exaggerated the tension, but the comment indicates that Goodenough was not one to defer to views that differed from his own.

Teaching the required course of History 10, The Development of Western Civilization, to freshmen soon made Goodenough restless. In 1925 he was giving a course on the history of the Renaissance and Reformation, "taught it very well,"[27] by his own estimate, and was promoted to assistant professor in 1926, at a salary of three thousand dollars. He felt, however, that he could not teach the course and continue working on what he considered his own project, Philo, especially since when he did Renaissance and Reformation research and focused on Melanchthon, he found that Melanchthon's deductions about the Ten Commandments could all be traced to Goodenough's "fatal figure Philo." So he went to Seymour, his chairman, and said, "I have to stop it. . . . I can't go on for the rest of my life giving these same lectures. . . . I must not get away from Philo, I must not get away from the work I was destined to do." The memoir goes on to report that Seymour only warned him, "Of course you understand that this threatens your tenure at Yale. The only place that we in History could use you is in the Renaissance and Reformation." Goodenough continues, "I said, 'I'm sorry. I have got to carry through.' "[28]

The memoir also states Goodenough learned, "in strange ways I need not divulge," that Seymour "carried on propaganda to have me dropped from Yale."[29] He gives no reasons for Seymour's hostility. But as an administrator Seymour no doubt resented both Goodenough's defiance and the loss of a popular course. Their basically different points of view on college affairs may also have been a factor. Seymour, as a conservative on university issues, had favored the retention of compulsory chapel, which Goodenough opposed.

However, Goodenough's friends on the faculty, members of the classics department and Rostovtzeff in history, "rallied" to prevent his removal and arranged for him to give up the popular Renaissance and Reformation course for a graduate course on church and state in the Roman Empire for three students.[30] In 1928 he was able to drop that course and give one on Hellenized Judaism in the religion department, also one in the classics department on Greek philosophy, so he was finally close to Philo in his teaching.

Why this feeling that work on Philo, the Jewish philosopher who lived in Alexandria, a center of Hellenism, during the time of Jesus, was "the command of destiny,"[31] as Goodenough told the unsympathetic Seymour? There were many reasons.

Goodenough gave a very pragmatic one when, in a letter of 1941 to Professor Paul Minear of Garrett Biblical Institute, he explained that he turned to Philo because as a historian he could not find "pay dirt"—sufficient evidence—in the Gospels for a picture of early Christianity and would have to fall back on his personal preconceptions. "That is why I so early abandoned the synoptics, etc., for Philo and the possible Hellenistic Jewish influence in the origin of Christianity. I had to have some fairly fresh dirt, or at least a new process for gold extracting, or I would be doing what I feel the students of the Synoptics and Jesus are constantly tempted to do—look so long into emptiness that I should see my own face as Jesus Christ come out of it to greet me."[32]

F. C. Conybeare, the guest Lowell Lecturer at Harvard Divinity School when Goodenough was there, might have introduced him to Philo. For Conybeare was "a great Oxford authority on Philo,"[33] according to Goodenough. G. F. Moore, another of Goodenough's Harvard teachers, at one time gave a seminar on Philo, offering a very different interpretation from the one that Goodenough would develop. Goodenough said that it was E. Bréhier's *Les idées philosophiques et religieuses de Philon d'Alexandrie* that led him to begin his study of Philo,[34] but Conybeare or Moore may well have acquainted him with Bréhier's work.

The conviction that work on Philo was "the work I was destined to do" went far deeper than any sense of finding "pay dirt" there. The idea of destiny permeated Goodenough's understanding of his accomplishments and reversals. He attributed the origins of the belief that he "was a tool and instrument being used to work out certain plans" to his mother's early faith that his recovery from celiac disease at age two and a half was a "miracle of God,"[35] who had a special purpose for baby Erwin.

But why Philo?

As Goodenough mentioned to Minear and stated more explicitly in an autobiographical fragment, Philo represented both the Jewish and the Greek elements that were, from Goodenough's reading of the evidence, the sources of Christianity and was an "incredulously [sic] neglected figure."[36]

As early as in his work on Justin Martyr, Goodenough found in Philo what was essential to him: "He was trying to do what few people have done so well, to join, in some degree of consistency, his philosophy with his religious impulses."[37] Goodenough never totally abandoned the comfort of the caring God of his Methodist childhood, while adopting agnosticism philosophically. He perceived Philo as emotionally needing a personal, loving God, while as a philosopher he saw God as the absolute; and Goodenough valued Philo's ability to reconcile these two aspects of deity.

He also found in Philo a mystic longing for union with the divine like Goodenough's own adolescent and occasional later experience, and he perceived this longing to be "present in a profound mind which was not content without a tremendous effort at grasping and thinking through the intellectual problems arising from his mysticism."[38]

Finally, he saw in Philo the kind of philosophy he felt was needed for his own time, "a philosophy which gives a possible answer to the demand of human hearts that we square science in some way with human experience and . . . the hope that the universe is not indifferent to human values."[39] For Goodenough found it imperative, as an intellectual of the twentieth century, to reconcile his religious beliefs with the generally accepted scientific theories of his time. Science was the authority that held all the answers according to many educated people in the twenties, and Ivan Pavlov, the famous Russian physiologist, expressed a view generally held by intellectuals when he said, in 1923: "Only science, exact science about human nature itself, and the most sincere approach to it by the aid of the omnipotent scientific nature, will deliver man from the existing darkness and will purge him from his shame in the sphere of inter-human relations."[40] Goodenough could not give that role of absolute authority to science, and Philo spoke to his sense that there is a need for religion, but a religion compatible with the science of the time. As he later wrote, "In Philo, and what I project into Philo, I am trying to solve the problems of adjusting that boy [who] was so devout a Methodist . . . to the world he grew up to discover."[41]

With this regard for Philo's religious position and for his role in the origins of Christianity, Goodenough, influenced since childhood by his mother's sense of his special purpose, could understandably announce to Seymour that he was "destined" to work on Philo.

From 1925 through the years when he was working on *By Light, Light: The Mystic Gospel of Hellenistic Judaism,* which was primarily an interpretation of Philo, Goodenough wrote various articles related to Philo's philosophy and also a book, *The Jurisprudence of the Jewish Courts in Egypt.*

The first article was "The Pseudo-Justinian 'Oratio ad Graecos,' " published in 1925.[42] His purpose was to show that this early, anonymous "oratio," written in the first fifty or even twenty-five years of the Christian era, represented a stage of Hellenistic Judaic thought contemporary with Philo and similar to his mysticism. Then the study of Philo's concept of the Law led him to an article on "The Political Philosophy of Hellenistic Kingship" in 1928,[43] and in 1929 to another, "Kingship in Early Israel,"[44] on the early Jewish view of kingship. In these studies Goodenough followed a pattern that was to characterize his teaching and writing: he made his specific historical or philosophic point, then showed its relevance to his day.

"The Political Philosophy of Hellenistic Kingship" describes the concept of the true king as ideal law embodied in a human being, a concept which was developed in the Hellenistic Age. Goodenough points out how this philosophy of kingship is related to Philo's thought, especially to Philo's view that the patriarchs, particularly Moses, were ideal kings before there were actual kings in Israel. And he concludes that the Hellenistic view of the king as the representative of God and his law persisted in European political thought until the present day.[45]

His study of Philo led him by chance to Philo's interpretation of Jewish law in its relation to the Greek and Roman law administered in Alexandria. His preface to *The Jurisprudence of the Jewish Courts in Egypt,* published in 1929, recounts that he was organizing material for a study of Philo's concepts of the Law when he came on notes that showed

Philo's expert legal knowledge. So he interrupted what he was doing, reread Philo's *The Special Laws,* and realized that he had the makings of a book.

The Special Laws is "one of the most comprehensive pictures of a legal practice which we have of any people of that period,"[46] Goodenough says. But he argues that Philo's purpose was quite different from a survey: Philo was trying to reconcile current Greek and Roman legal practices in Alexandria with the Ten Commandments and their rabbinic interpreters. Thus he holds that his review of Philo's *Special Laws* has an interest for more than legal scholars and students of Jewish law under Roman rule. The student of religion can find that Philo's struggle in *The Special Laws* to reconcile his Judaism with his Greek eclectic idealism resembles the contemporary liberal theologian's attempts to reconcile Christian tradition with the principles of modern science.

In *The Jurisprudence,* Goodenough first introduces Philo the many-sided man who will interest the general reader. He relates Philo's account of being at chariot races where the excitement was so great that some of the spectators rushed onto the course and were trampled. He notes that Philo described the crowd's enthusiasm at a play of Euripides. He completes the picture of Philo's enjoyment of worldly delights by quoting his comment that at banquets he would often "become a helpless slave to the pleasures of food and drink."[47] And he makes it clear that these enjoyments and appetites conflicted sharply with Philo's ascetic contempt for his lower nature.

The chapters after the introductory portrayal of Philo the man review the main points of *The Special Laws,* following Philo's order of development from the First through the Tenth Commandment. In discussing these points Goodenough presents what are for the general reader some of the most interesting aspects of Philo's thought.

Goodenough notes in detail what he considers Philo's rationalization in justifying circumcision by "some hook or crook,"[48] as Goodenough terms it, a rite that the Greeks and Romans ridiculed. Philo argued that circumcision was practiced by the Egyptians, whom he usually belittled but here described as "the most ancient, and populous, and philosophic of races."[49] He pointed out its sanitary aspect. He stated that the operation makes the penis look like the heart, which creates thoughts as the penis creates life. He asserted that it makes men prolific. Then he cited its symbolic value as "a gesture of contempt for merely human powers."[50] For Goodenough this last argument illustrates Philo's characteristic use of allegory to defend a practice of the Alexandrian Jews that non-Jews criticized.

In reviewing Philo's treatment of the statutes derived from the Commandment forbidding adultery, Goodenough points out that Philo's discussion of the laws concerning marriage and sexual relations stressed the sanctity of the family, and that his discussion of adultery reflected Jewish sexual standards much stricter than those of their Hellenistic environment; for both partners must rise and wash after sexual relations; prostitutes must be lynched; adultery must be punished by death. When he reviews Philo's comments on the laws governing marital difficulties, Goodenough injects his own sympathy with the husband in his support of Philo's view of the law that when a man has unjustly tried to divorce his wife and she is vindicated he must keep her: "This forcing of the husband to keep the undesired wife Philo quite accurately calls the worst punishment of all which the man is called upon to undergo."[51]

When discussing Philo's accounts of court procedures and what he held to be the qualities required of a judge, Goodenough asserts that Philo was indebted to Hellenistic thought on the subject, but he considered this thinking consistent with, if not derived from, Jewish Scripture. For throughout, as Goodenough interprets Philo, he was arguing that there was a basis in the Law of Moses for the Alexandrian laws of Philo's days.

In this, his earliest work on Philo, Goodenough introduces two controversial interpretations of Philo's intentions. The first he would develop more fully in his next study of Philo, *By Light, Light.* In *The Jurisprudence of the Jewish Courts in Egypt,* Goodenough argues that Philo's interpretation of the laws concerning the temple, priests' duties, and festivals turned "the whole ritual and priesthood, customs, garb, rites, and seasons, into a highly developed mystery religion, in which the High Priest was an incarnation of the Logos in symbol . . . who was the mediator to God, not only for the Jewish people, but for the whole human race, and indeed for the entire cosmos."[52]

The second interpretation is specific to *The Jurisprudence.* A main thesis of this work is Goodenough's insistence that Philo was describing the Jewish laws that were actually administered in the Alexandrian courts. As he concludes by summarizing the system of Jewish legal procedure in Egypt that Philo described, he emphasizes that Philo ignored, misquoted, or even refuted the Torah in order to present a system that Jews in Alexandria would have been allowed to use under Roman rule. Philo insisted throughout, according to Goodenough, that the Mosaic Code, when read correctly, prescribed the same general principles and procedures as the Greco-Roman laws. His primary purpose, as Goodenough reads him, was to describe not what was written in the Mosaic Code, but what was administered in the Egyptian courts. And for Goodenough it was because Philo accomplished this so ably that *The Special Laws* is valuable as a picture of the actual legal procedures in the Jewish courts of Alexandria in his time.

"In *The Jurisprudence* Goodenough . . . shows a true lawyer love of accurate perception and tersely scientific statement," wrote William Riddell when reviewing the book for *The American Bar Association Journal.* "This work . . . will cause no few, as it has caused me, to read Philo again and with a new appreciation."[53]

Ralph Marcus in his 1935 review in "Recent Literature on Philo" was more critical. He described *The Jurisprudence* as "high-spirited and persuasive (but not convincing)"[54] in its argument that Philo in *The Special Laws* was commenting on a system of law actually in force in the Jewish community of Alexandria, not an ideal reconstruction of Mosaic Law for apologetic purposes.

F. H. Colson, the translator and editor of the ten-volume edition of the Loeb *Philo,* was equally critical in his 1937 introduction to volume 7, which included *The Special Laws.* He praised Goodenough's "fresh and illuminating way of treating the many problems which these treatises suggest."[55] But he had two basic disagreements with Goodenough's conclusions. First, there was too little evidence that when Philo departed from the Torah he was describing what was actually administered rather than what he thought appropriate—a variant of Marcus's objection. Second, Colson argued that Goodenough exaggerated Philo's "alterations and denials"[56] of the Jewish laws, for Colson held that Philo presented a fair and accurate account of these laws. Samuel Sandmel, in his 1979 *Philo of Alexandria,* repeated Colson's objection to Goodenough's view that Philo described what was actually administered in the Jewish courts in Alexandria, stating, "The thesis is virtually everywhere rejected."[57]

Thus, in his first volume on Philo, Goodenough's interpretation differed from those generally accepted and led to challenges. This putting forth of controversial theories, already seen in *The Theology of Justin Martyr,* was to mark Goodenough's work throughout his scholarly career.

Chapter 4

Family Life, Relations with Religious Leaders, and *The Church in the Roman Empire*

Goodenough's involvement with his family complemented his commitment to Philo. The English translation of the Greek dedication of *By Light, Light* is "To my household," continuing, "for the household is said to be a combination of wife and children. These have filled my wants." He never took his research home with him but kept the evenings free for family and friends. He and Helen played word games like "a third of a ghost" at the dinner table with the children. Then, if they did not have a maid at the time, he did the dishes, saying that Helen had done her part in making the meal. When a piece of furniture needed reupholstering he went to work on that, for, having been well taught by his father, he enjoyed using his manual skills.

Evenings at the piano were a favorite relaxation. He liked composing, writing the music for *Children's Songs,* which was published with lyrics by Bill Adams, L. R. Jackson, and others. He was a fine pianist and especially enjoyed Bach, but also Mozart and Beethoven. His son Ward remembers lying in bed listening to his father's music, then years later hearing Bach's Toccata and Fugue in D Minor at a concert and recalling that early experience with a shock of recognition. And his daughter Hester has fond memories of sitting beside her father at the piano as he played Bach preludes and fugues.[1]

Although he hated the sand and the bugs at the beach, he organized family outings to nearby Hammonasset, a large state park ocean beach, where they all had a picnic and swim.[2]

He was a master at telling stories to the children when they were young. Then, as Ward and John became old enough, he and Helen taught them to play bridge, and the boys and their parents made a foursome in the evening. Later, when Ward and John had gone away to school, Erwin and Helen played Michigan rummy and other card games with

47

Jimmy and Hester, having, since their Oxford days, disregarded the Methodist strictures against card playing.

Ward came to feel that his father's high expectations for his oldest child made him unduly hard on him. But the younger Jimmy was "an adoring son" and saw Erwin as "the perfect father. In comparison to other fathers, he seemed to me to be the best."[3]

In the late twenties they took into their home Helen's sister's son, William D. West, whose father, a Methodist minister, had died, leaving his family almost destitute. Bill, who was fifteen and a sophomore in high school, came to live with the Goodenoughs for a year, while his grandfather was getting a house ready for the family. According to his cousin Ward, who was about nine at the time, Bill deeply appreciated that experience and, particularly, how kind Erwin was to him.[4]

Erwin and Helen played bridge regularly with their next-door neighbors, the Thompsons, and Erwin's colleague Ralph Gabriel and his wife. They also often danced in private homes and occasionally at the Assembly. But Erwin took most delight in gracious entertaining, which he had first experienced at Oxford. He often said there was nothing he liked more than giving a good party, for "I always have so much better a time at my own parties than at almost anyone's else."[5]

Goodenough's relations with the Methodist Church were "not so happy" in those years, he confessed to American University President Douglas, when describing his ministerial involvements since he had been a Swift Fellow. He had entered the New York East Conference in 1919, while at Harvard, and after his ordination as an Elder in Paris was accepted as a full member of the conference in 1924. He was assistant pastor of the Jamaica Methodist Church the summer before he went to Oxford, and also the summer after his first year at Yale. But he complained to President Douglas that he could never "make a real connection"[6] with the conference. He attended its meetings for a few years and regularly volunteered for supply preaching. Since he was never called upon, he decided that he was considered an outsider, and in 1928 he withdrew from the conference, giving up the ministerial office. That ended his official church connections. Yet in 1937 he wrote to Fay Campbell, the director of the Yale Student Christian Association, "I shall never stop being a Methodist, little as the Methodists are aware of it. To me a religious ethic is only possible as it comes from a personal religious experience."[7]

He had cordial relations with the religious leaders in town. He preached in pulpits of clergy friends, was the supply minster at the Woodbridge Congregational Church when it was awaiting a new pastor, and his children went to Sunday school there. New Haven Rabbi Sidney Tedesche read *The Jurisprudence of the Jewish Courts in Egypt,* discussed it with Goodenough, and made welcome suggestions. When Stewart Means, a rector emeritus of St. John's Episcopal Church, wrote *Faith: An Historical Study,* he expressed in the preface his gratitude for the "wise and generous criticism of two dear friends,"[8] one of whom was Erwin Goodenough. Goodenough in turn, in his introduction to *Faith,* paid tribute to Dr. Means's gifts as a thoughtful student of history and a pastor whose studies helped him to "live more fully himself, and to respond more sensitively to the lives of others,"[9] for Goodenough firmly believed that scholarship enriched one's own life and one's relationships. He "dearly loved" Means, and when he talked with him as Means was dying, tears ran down Goodenough's cheeks.[10]

Although Goodenough taught a course in early church history at the Divinity School in 1929, the Divinity faculty was, on the whole, unfriendly. When Paul Minear was working on a Yale doctorate between 1930 and 1932, he saw Goodenough as "already a more or less permanent antagonist of the Divinity School";[11] and Goodenough delighted in telling a friend, "When I was with a group of the New Testament people I shocked them by remarking I thought it highly unlikely that Jesus was a virgin."[12]

Goodenough had given a course on church and state in the Roman Empire in the graduate school since 1928, and in 1930 he was asked to write *The Church in the Roman Empire* for the Berkshire Studies in European History, a series designed as background material to accompany a course in European history. Goodenough's survey exhibits the qualities that marked him as a fine teacher. The account of the Christian church's rise and expansion into an early medieval institution is clear, comprehensive, and very readable. It explains complex issues in simple language with apt turns of phrase and the voice of authority, as his summary of early Christian morality illustrates: "It was a Jewish-Greek morality, Jewish in its patient steadfastness, Greek in its flouting of external goods, but still uniquely Christian in its emphasis upon love and humility, and in the abandoned enthusiasm with which it was practised."[13] He often concludes sections with a dramatic climax, as in his closing comment on the Eucharist: "For what rite has ever been devised more magnificently appealing than the breaking of the sacred bread together, the sharing of Christ's life in common, as it was done in prisons by little groups of Christians, with no ritualistic appurtenances, just before they went out singing into the arena to be torn by the wild beasts for their Savior?"[14]

In his portrayal of early Christianity he points repeatedly to Christianity's appeal, as in the statement: "It promises rich rewards of the spirit to those who honestly follow the orthodox chart of life. And legion have been the witnesses to the fulfillment of its promise."[15] But he is scornful of doctrines of the Trinity, asserting that these solutions to the problem of one divine nature represented in three distinct persons had "little . . . to offer to an intellectual seeker for truth."[16]

Goodenough's account also develops two highly controversial hypotheses as to the origins and nature of early Christianity.

The first he states in the foreword: "Christianity . . . was a summation of various religious ideas of the environment inherited from the past, with some new added force to give it distinctness."[17] He makes a similar statement about the church as the state religion of the Roman Empire: "She adopted, one by one, the essential ideas and rites of paganism as her own."[18] Then he devotes a subchapter to "this assimilation of paganism."

The second hypothesis is the earliest expression of his thesis about the nature of early Christianity, which he was to develop in various allusions in *Jewish Symbols in the Greco-Roman Period* and explicitly in his last, fragmentary statement, "Paul and the Hellenization of Christianity." In *The Church in the Roman Empire* he refers briefly to Paul's description of Christianity as "the perfect mystery religion".[19] He writes of its "change from a Palestinian sect to a mystery religion of salvation."[20] Finally, concluding his emphasis on pagan borrowings, he states, "Many scholars are convinced that the sacrament of the Eucharist, even as celebrated in the early Church, was a direct borrowing from the mystery religions," and, while other scholars disagree, "there can be little doubt that once the rite had begun in the Church, the example of heathen rites profoundly modified the Christian attitude toward it."[21]

Both his references to Christianity as a mystery religion and his conclusion that it was so successful in the Roman Empire because it assimilated pagan elements already familiar to the converts challenged traditional Christian teaching.

Father Lawrence T. Riggs, the Roman Catholic chaplain at Yale, immediately attacked Goodenough's interpretations. He had already protested, in the *Yale News,* against Goodenough's teaching of religion from the historical point of view. Now he used the *Yale News* again to criticize "The Rise of the Christian Church" chapter of *The Church in the Roman Empire* as "inaccurate, biased and misleading," and asserted, "Professor Goodenough has reached the conclusions he set out to reach, quite regardless of the facts or a sound analysis of the facts."[22]

Father Riggs's attitude was an extreme expression of the general disapproval of Goodenough's approach to religion among his colleagues in the Divinity School and some other faculty. This approach contrasted sharply with Karl Barth's neoorthodox concern with Christian doctrine. It also struck a very different note from the evangelical statement of the 1928 International Missionary Council of Jerusalem that Fay Campbell, Yale's representative at the council, brought back to the campus. But many undergraduates had a different approach to religion. As one student wrote, in an editorial "Godless Places," in the March 1932 *Yale News:* "Very few realize that there is a real, deep religion in an American university, that young men who boastfully claim to have no religion are often following the most progressive religious minds of the era. . . . Reverend Sidney Lovett, 1913, newly appointed chaplain, comes . . . to a 'godless place,' where enthusiasms, hope, and especially open-mindedness reign supreme."[23] Goodenough's teaching and *The Church in the Roman Empire* called upon this open-mindedness, which was to remain one of his professional goals.

Chapter 5

Goodenough's "Fatal Figure," Philo

Goodenough, sharing his mother's faith in his special destiny, in 1934 again felt the touch of the "mysterious hand" that had led him to Yale. In 1933 he had been made a Fellow of Jonathan Edwards College, one of the new residential colleges built with the Sterling bequest, which opened that year. He became editor of *The Journal of Biblical Literature* in 1934. As early as 1933 he wrote to a colleague that his promotion from associate professor to professor was "in the works."[1] Yet, looking back in a late memoir, he saw the professorship which was offered him in 1934 as a special act of Providence, "a succession of doors . . . miraculously opened up when need arose."[2] As he recalled the situation in this memoir, after the Divinity School became a separate entity, there was just one professorship in religion left in Yale College, "essentially for the Christianizing of the Yale undergraduates."[3] The man who held this professorship was nowhere near retirement; but, in 1934, at just the right moment for Goodenough, he resigned to become president of a college in Canada. Who would succeed him? Seeing a chance to change the "Christianizing" aspect of the position, which many faculty considered inappropriate, Goodenough's friends in the history and classics departments proposed him. "And so the only professorship in the United States of America which would have allowed me really to have carried on in my free way was suddenly given to me. . . . I was all the more committed to carrying on my work"[4] — with Philo.

The first result of this commitment was the publication of *By Light, Light: The Mystic Gospel of Hellenistic Judaism* in 1935, which he had been working on during the previous ten years. This study focuses primarily on what Goodenough interprets as the mystic writings of Philo. The title comes from Philo's account of how the mystic comes to his experience of God: "Those men are on the way to truth who apprehend

God by divinity, a light by its light."[5] The subtitle reflects Goodenough's thesis that Judaism in the Hellenistic period, after Alexander's conquest of the East, had become a mystery religion before Philo's time; that it grew out of the desire in the Hellenistic age to experience emotionally what had been learned intellectually from the Greek philosophers; and that it resulted in a complete transformation of Judaism. Philo is the primary literary evidence for this Judaism; hence the importance of his work and Goodenough's focus on him, with only two chapters on other mystic writings.

According to Goodenough, previous students of Philo who described his philosophic system had interpreted his writings primarily in accordance with their own interests. Goodenough claims that he, in contrast, has tried to read Philo "to understand what Philo himself thought he was driving at in all his passionate allegorical labors"[6]—what he wanted to say to the reader. So *By Light, Light* is a much needed new interpretation of Philo's thought.

This interpretation would help to explain the unexpected nature of the Jewish art in the synagogue that Yale, together with the French Academy of Inscriptions and Letters, had excavated in 1932, in the ancient trading city of Dura-Europos on the Euphrates River. For Goodenough saw the literary sources of Hellenized Judaism as a first step in understanding the mystic character of the Dura paintings and planned *By Light, Light* as the first in a series of studies to be followed by one on the Dura art. But, much to his resentment, Yale assigned the right to publish the authorized description of the synagogue to Carl Kraeling, professor of New Testament and curator of Gerasa antiquities. Kraeling's account did not appear until 1956, so *By Light, Light* could have no immediate sequel dealing with the Dura synagogue, as Goodenough had hoped.

However, this interpretation of a key literary expression of Hellenistic Judaism would throw new light on the role of its "mystic Gospel" in the origins of Christianity. Goodenough therefore saw the present volume as the first of a series devoted to developing what was for him "an inevitable thesis"[7]—that "Judaism in the Greek-speaking world . . . had been transformed into a Mystery."[8]

The Philo whom Goodenough presented in *By Light, Light* as the chief source for our knowledge of this Mystery was a fellow spirit. Goodenough saw in Philo's view of God all the elements he himself sought in deity. Philo's God was both "the Absolute, and the Prime Cause, a God who was the source and sanction of ethical idealism, and the goal of . . . mystical aspiration."[9] He therefore conformed to

Goodenough's philosophical conception of God. He also incorporated Goodenough's deeply ingrained Methodist commitment to morality. Finally, he satisfied the mystic's need for identification with deity that Uncle Charlie had awakened in Goodenough. Of these three aspects of Philo's concept of God, as Goodenough read him, Philo's mysticism was the primary focus of *By Light, Light*.

For his time Goodenough was unusually perceptive in recognizing the subjective aspects of a historian of religion's work. In *By Light, Light* he wrote, in explanation of Philo's primary concern with religion rather than metaphysics, "We are all solving in our work our deeper emotional problems and it may or may not be apparent to ourselves or to others what we are ultimately doing."[10] In *An Introduction to Philo Judaeus* he explicitly states, "As I project myself back to Philo's age it must always and only be myself that I project. . . . My own emotional life as well as my preconceived ideas will make me stress what seems quite inessential . . . to others. . . . To me no religion is more than intellectually comprehensible which does not include the mystic longing for inner completion by participation. This is bound to affect my understanding of Philo. Unquestionably I shall respond as many others would not to the passages where he expresses a mystic longing."[11] This subjectivity does not trouble Goodenough as a historian. He sees different groups and different generations finding different meanings in the same works and values these other points of view for their role in coming closer to the truth.

The first thesis of *By Light, Light* is that the Jews of the Diaspora, in their encounter with the Hellenistic world, were profoundly influenced by the mysticism of the Pythagoreans, the Orphics, and their vision of complete assimilation with the nature of God. As a result of this encounter, many of these Jews transformed their Judaism into a mystery religion, which, according to Goodenough, included initiations, sacraments, robes, and a mythology. In *By Light, Light* Goodenough often conflates mysticism and the mystery religion Philo described, and clearly "The Mystic Gospel of Hellenistic Judaism," *By Light, Light*'s subtitle, is a Gospel of the Mystery.

Goodenough traces the development of the Hellenistic Jews' mystery religion by showing that these Jews, especially in Alexandria, the heart of Hellenism, were attracted to their neighbors' religion. Since they could not be initiated into the cult of Isis or Orpheus and still be Jews, they interpreted the Torah allegorically so that it became "the greatest, the only true, Mystery,"[12] with Moses a priest as well as giver of the Law. Goodenough then asserts that these Hellenized Jews believed that the philosophic and religious ideas of the Greeks had already been best expressed in the revelation Moses received and in his example. Thus he concludes, "A great mystic conception of Judaism and of life was thereby developed,"[13] although he admits there are only "shreds of literature"[14] as evidence, and that all vestiges of the way in which Judaism developed into a mystery are lost.

According to Goodenough, "The objective of this Judaism was salvation in the mystical sense."[15] Release from matter and union with God was its aim. God was the Absolute, joined to the world by his "light-stream," the figure of speech for God's emanation, like the beams of light and heat responsible for the creation and the means of God's relation to humankind. Humanity sought to leave material concerns behind and rise to true life and immortality by ascending the ladder of the light-stream. The Law, which deals with material matters, was reinterpreted, by what Goodenough terms "a clever solution,"[16] to be merely the physical copy, in the medium of nouns and verbs, of the true, unwritten Law, the Logos. The written Law was thus of secondary importance. It was the unwritten Law that was the true Law of Judaism. And the true Jew received his Law through the example and mediation of the patriarchs, who had risen by the light-stream and were God's means for others to obtain through them the same vision the patriarchs had and thus identify with the mystery.

Although Goodenough affirms that Philo was not alone in his thinking but represented many Jews in the Greek world, his study focuses on Philo because Philo was the first to describe the mystery. And not only is he the key to explaining it; the mystery is, for Goodenough, in turn the key to understanding Philo, "for all his writing is oriented about it"[17] — a highly controversial claim.

He concludes his introduction with an equally controversial linkage of Hellenistic Judaism with Christianity, stating that "both religions came to be predominately expressions of that powerful genius, the Greek genius as it survived in the Hellenistic and Roman world."[18]

Having stated his position, Goodenough moves systematically through the chief points he has chosen to develop his interpretation of Philo's teachings about the mystery. According to Goodenough, as the title suggests, Philo sees the light-stream as the most adequate image of God. The light-stream had two types of formulation. One was that of the female principle, in which the mysticism of sex was central. The other concept, which Goodenough states to be more important, is the concept of the light-stream as a *pleroma,* a Greek word meaning "fullness," which Goodenough identifies with the Persian idea of the solar rays God sends out. For Philo, according to Goodenough, there is an elaborately schematized descent as the various manifestations of God radiate from him, and Goodenough charts the descent from τὸ ὄν (being) to the world of form in one diagram, and to that of God's creative and royal powers in another.

He develops Philo's view of the higher law as the Law of Nature. As Goodenough interprets him, Philo saw the Torah, the Jewish written law, first formulated in the Decalogue, as a textbook of specific commands for beginners; but when fully understood it was a symbolic expression of the Natural Law, revealing God's nature and the mystic way to him. Thus, for Philo, according to Goodenough, the Torah has the answers to the mystic seeking of the Hellenistic age.

Goodenough states that Philo's concern with the Torah as the revelation of higher truth was central to all his nonpolitical writings, and he proceeds to two conclusions, which were to be sharply challenged. First, Philo could be a loyal Jew without stressing the literal meaning of the Law that "normative Judaism"—George Foot Moore's term—demanded. Second, it was Philo's purpose to show both Jews and those Gentiles sympathetic to mysticism that the real meaning of the Torah lay in "its mystic teaching."[19]

For Philo, as Goodenough reads him, the mystic teaching of the Torah is most fully expressed in its account of the lives of the patriarchs, who with their wives each demonstrated ways to approach God. Goodenough summarizes Philo's portrayals of these lives, following Philo's order of their importance: the lesser triad of Enos, Enoch, and Noah; then the higher one, Abraham, Isaac, and Jacob; and finally Moses, the greatest of all. This summary includes details that would have disturbed some of Philo's Christian readers, but no doubt delighted the iconoclast Goodenough, as, for example, that the Torah made it clear to initiates that Isaac was begotten by God, not by Abraham: he was "the direct child of God through Sarah,"[20] who conceived after she was miraculously restored to virginity.

Philo's Jacob is of special interest to Goodenough. Philo's description of Jacob's mystic encounter with God was the source of the title *By Light, Light,* for Jacob had a vision of God by way of his light-stream, like the sun's. Furthermore, Goodenough finds an example of that blending of morality and mysticism he valued in Philo's interpretation of the shrunken thigh Jacob suffered after he wrestled successfully with the angel. For the shrunken thigh meant to Philo, according to Goodenough, that "the Mystery was not complete until the glorified soul had been so

brought back to face the problems of fleshly control and ethics, that in
the end the Mystery solved, not hindered, the development of a fully
rounded life in the flesh."[21] Finally, as Goodenough reads him, Philo saw
that for Israel, as a people, following the experience of its prototype
Jacob, who became the "See-er,"[22] "the frustrations of philosophy have
been done away, its dreams fulfilled."[23] For philosophy, according to
Goodenough's reading of Philo, cannot derive from the evidence of
phenomena the vision of the Divine Being that Jacob has revealed to Israel.

Goodenough's portrayal of Philo's Moses then provides the preparation for his summation of the Mystery. First he describes the Moses
Philo's presented to the Gentiles: the ideal king, legislator, priest, and
prophet. He then pieces together from various treatises the picture of
Moses that Philo gave to Jewish initiates and his allegorical version of
Moses' life. In this version Moses' chief function was to lead men from
bodily enslavement into immaterial reality by the flight from Egypt and
the passage through the Red Sea, in which the Israelites' lower passions,
exemplified by the Egyptians, perished.

Goodenough concludes that Philo's Moses was "a type of the perfect
mystic," but also the "Logos itself."[24] He once provided spiritual sustenance to the Israelites in the manna and the stream he brought forth from
the rock in the desert and is now an ever present mediator between God
and men, the "Savior-Sage"[25] interceding with God to have compassion
on all humanity. Goodenough then draws the kind of analogy between
Philo's Hellenistic Judaism and Christianity that appears throughout this
work: "Philo sees in Moses an active and present power, and the prayer to
Moses for guidance, light, and annointing [sic], is precisely such a prayer
as Christian mystics have for centuries been addressing to Christ."[26]

Goodenough then summarizes what he sees to be the Mystery that
Philo read into the Torah: "It is the philosophy of an eclectic Neo-
Pythagorean Platonist . . . fused with mystic notions from the Orphics,
Persia, and Isis."[27] And he states that Philo's assured presentation of this
combination, that is, without any sense of the need to justify it, implies
that he did not invent it, but that Jews in Egypt, especially Alexandria,
had encountered it in their environment "ready made"[28] for at least two
centuries.

But mystic Judaism is more than a philosophy, Goodenough asserts.
For Philo states that through its saviors, the patriarchs, especially Moses,
"not only could Mystic Judaism point the way: it could give men strength
to walk along it, or to run along it as a fugitive from the allurements of
matter and sense to the peace and safety of immaterial reality."[29]

He then presents evidence that Philo was describing not merely a mystic reading of the Scriptures, but also a type of Jewish cult, with initiations, cult robes, and secret doctrines. Goodenough explains that Philo distinguished this as a lower mystery, which he contrasted with the higher Mystery, the Mystery of Moses, which had its own sacred Laws and as its high priest Moses, who was "less than God, but greater than man."[30]

Goodenough's description of the further details about the Mystery found in Philo's various treatises contributes to his final conclusions, which largely repeat or assert more strongly points he has already made or implied. They are: Philo's main writings deal with the Mystery. For Philo this Mystery was a higher Judaism than George Foot Moore's "normative," Palestinian Judaism, which Philo saw as meaningful only for those who could not enter into the Mystery. As Philo allegorized Judaism and made it into a mystic philosophy with borrowings from the Greek mystic philosophers, according to Goodenough, it must be read as "a Judaism so thoroughly paganized that its postulates and its objectives were those of Hellenistic mysteries rather than those of any Judaism we have hitherto known. For all its passionate Jewish loyalty, it was not fundamentally a Judaism with Hellenistic veneer: it was a Hellenism, presented in Jewish symbols and allegories, to be sure, but still a Hellenistic dream of the solution of the problem of life by ascent higher and ever higher in the Streaming Light-Life of God."[31]

This conclusion sums up Goodenough's view of Philo's Judaism, in which he sees the primary resource for our knowledge of Hellenistic Judaism. Both the subtitle, "The Mystic Gospel of Hellenistic Judaism," and Goodenough's thesis that Philo's development of his points assumed he was drawing upon an accepted body of beliefs, required that Goodenough give some examples of this mystic Judaism other than Philo's. This he does in two chapters that describe the mystery in *The Wisdom of Solomon,* the writings of Aristobulus, Alexander Polyhistor, and Ezekiel, and the anonymous *Oratio ad Graecos.* He closes his account of these writings with a vivid picture of their aim, "All alike were trying to become Jews in the highest sense by repeating the mystic experience of the Jewish Saints, that is by racing like them from matter toward God along His Royal Road, the great Stream."[32]

His examples of reference to the Mystery in other than Philo's writings, as supplements to Philo's views, bring Goodenough to the fulfillment of his purpose: to have "made clear the existence of the Mystery, and given an acceptable presentation of its points of view."[33]

Although *By Light, Light*'s use of Greek terms and citations of little-known philosophers was clearly meant for scholars, the press highlighted the aspect that would have immediate appeal to a wide audience. A 9 April headline read: "Yale Professor Offers New Interpretation of Origins of Christianity." The article then affirmed: "He sets forth a new solution to the problem of how, within Paul's lifetime, Christianity changed so easily from the simple teaching of Christ into an elaborate doctrine of salvation through Christ."[34]

The scholarly reviews ranged from high praise to praise with reservations and to sharp criticism, and it soon became evident how controversial his interpretation was.

Ernest Scott, a New Testament scholar at Union Theological Seminary, concluded in one review: "Dr. Goodenough has come nearer, we believe, than any previous writer to the inner meaning of Philo's message";[35] and in another states that he "has given us perhaps the most illuminating of all modern studies of Philo. His theory is a wholly original one, but is the outcome of prolonged study and genuine philosophical insight. . . . The reader continually feels that much that was perplexing to him in the thought and purpose of Philo has now been made intelligible for the first time."[36]

Rabbi Abram Simon praised Goodenough's book in *The Catholic Historical Review*: "This is a book of solid scholarship. Well documented, the entire field of Hellenistic Jewish literature has been traversed with wise discrimination."[37] Ralph Marcus of the Jewish Institute of Religion and Columbia University wrote, "Goodenough's book is well worth reading and will long remain as a valuable collection of material on this fascinating . . . theme [of Philo's mystic teaching]."[38] Kirsopp Lake, Goodenough's former teacher, stated, "It is delightful to find in Goodenough's *By Light, Light* a book remarkable for its addition to understanding, though it also adds to information."[39] Shirley Jackson Case of the University of Chicago Divinity School asserted, "This type of book has long been needed, and its production could not have fallen to the lot of a more appropriate author."[40]

There were also moderately or strongly dissenting opinions concerning specific points, especially Goodenough's emphasis on the centrality of the mystery in Philo's and Jewish thought. Marcus doubted that Philo went as far beyond "normative" Judaism as Goodenough assumed and questioned whether there was an organized Jewish mystery cult in Alexandria, as Goodenough supposed. Scott thought that Goodenough pressed his idea of a "mystery cult" within Judaism too far.

Other, broader negative criticisms followed. Harvard's Arthur Darby Nock, in *Gnomon,* described *By Light, Light* as one of the most stimulating of recent books, then insisted that Goodenough did not provide enough evidence that Philo's writings really are describing a mystery, although he used "mystery language."[41] Wilfred Knox in *St. Paul and the Church of the Gentiles* (1939) expressed complete agreement with Nock and stated flatly, "I am quite clear that his [Goodenough's] attempt to read a 'Light-mystery' religion into Philo's writings entirely misconceives the whole aim of Philo's work."[42]

In 1939 Goodenough came across a book about Paul by a Cambridge high-church "Father" he did not identify, who completely disapproved of *By Light, Light.* This led Goodenough to a characteristically lively expression of his strong anti-British, anticlerical sentiments as well as a defense of his purpose: "His whole attitude is as provincially English as though he were at a Dionysian festival in his flat hat, carrying a Thyrsus in one hand and an umbrella in the other. He never once dreams of trying to see any religious value or motivation in any of this material."[43]

Philo's political thought was, for Goodenough, an important aspect of this many-sided man, and in 1938 he published *The Politics of Philo Judaeus,* describing "Philo's relations with the Roman government, his personal attitude toward society, and his political theory."[44] This companion volume to *By Light, Light* was financially feasible through the support of Howard Goodhart, who collaborated with Goodenough on a *General Bibliography of Philo,* which formed the second two-thirds of the volume.

Goodhart, a Yale alumnus, 1905, and in the 1930s a member of the New York Stock Exchange, was a collector of rare books, including those by and about Philo: first of all fifteenth-century books that mention him, then early editions of Philo's writings, then secondary works and later editions and translations of Philo's books.[45] Wishing to publish a catalogue of this collection, he turned to Yale for advice. Yale consulted Goodenough, and Goodhart got in touch with him. They decided to work together on a classified Philo bibliography, to be published in a single volume including Goodenough's work on Philo's politics.

The friendship with Goodhart meant a great deal to Goodenough both personally and professionally. Goodhart often entertained Goodenough or the family in New York City at the Hotel St. Regis, where he lived.[46] There was professional advantage for Goodenough in the opportunity to publish what he termed the "concluding section" of his work on Philo, which by itself would have been a less than book-size companion to *By Light, Light.*

Yale also benefited from the friendship. Goodenough convinced Goodhart that it was important to acquire as complete a collection of Philo material as he could, and in 1940 Goodhart gave this Philo collection to the Yale Sterling Library, making it, according to Goodenough, the best place in the world to study Philo.[47]

Goodenough opens *The Politics of Philo Judaeus* with a dramatic account of the only documented incident of Philo's life. He relates that Philo was chosen to lead a commission that the Jews of Alexandria sent to Rome to urge the mad emperor Gaius Caligula to exempt them from setting up his statues in their synagogues and worshipping them. After the difficult journey to Rome across the Mediterranean, the commission's task seemed hopeless, for they had to trail after Gaius from place to place, without a proper audience. When they finally were summoned, they had to follow him as he strode through gardens and buildings, instructing contractors about alterations. As he walked, he suddenly demanded that Philo describe the Jewish ideas of justice. Philo had to do this on the run, addressing the back of the emperor, who was all the time talking to the builders. The crowd that had gathered jeered at the Jews and even struck them, so that they had to maintain their dignity while fearing they would be killed. The outcome was a total surprise: Gaius stopped, stated, "These men appear not so much wicked as unfortunate and fools for not believing that I have been endowed with the nature of deity,"[48] and dismissed them.

This incident of Philo's success as a diplomat supports Goodenough's opening contention that Philo's political ideas should not be neglected or treated inadequately, as they have been; hence the need for his volume.

He divides Philo's political statements into three types. First he describes the openly political treatises that he wrote for Roman readers, which Goodenough characterizes as the work of a "fearless and experienced politician"[49] who knew exactly how to veil his criticism of the Romans. Next he explains how Philo expressed himself to his Jewish readers in codelike allusions[50] that concealed the Alexandrian Jews' hatred of their Roman masters and showed their willingness to be conciliatory so long as they could preserve their religious identity. Goodenough illustrates Philo's third method of political statement, that of "innuendo," by his *Life of Joseph*. He explains that Philo retells the Genesis story of Joseph to portray Joseph as the model ruler, in order to imply that the current Hellenistic ideal of kingship actually originated in the Torah and that Egypt had once been ideally governed by a Jew.

From these descriptions of Philo's different modes of political writing,

Goodenough moves to a profile of Philo as statesman and philosopher and to a systematic account of his political theory. He highlights Philo's emphasis on the need to reconcile the claims of the civic and the contemplative life, for Philo's solution—that the mystic returns from the immaterial realm to be a responsible leader in his society—was congenial to Goodenough, who felt that his own mystic aspirations were compatible with his work as a teacher and scholar.

He sees Philo's view of the struggle between citizenship in the heavenly and the worldly city as the likely origin of Augustine's idea of the heavenly and the earthly cities, since Goodenough states that Augustine was Ambrose's pupil, Ambrose had initially taken the idea from Philo, and Augustine took it from Ambrose. Thus, Goodenough concludes, Philo was the source of what he describes, with a characteristic flourish, as "one of the most influential interpretations of life and society ever to sway the human mind."[51]

Goodenough ascribes a similar historic importance to Philo's view of kingship: rulership ideally represents God's rule, and the king is in a special relation with God, imitating God in giving order to the state and equality to all, though not in himself divine. This view, Goodenough asserts, which had been "worked out by the forgotten Jews of the Diaspora as they struggled to adapt their Jewish heritage to the daring claims of hellenistic and Roman royalty,"[52] was taken over by the early Christian apologists, then became "the official philosophy of the Christian Empire . . . and so set the pattern of royalty down into the Twentieth Century".[53] His emphasis on the contribution of Hellenistic Judaism to Western political theory concludes the work.

Both Christian and Jewish scholars took note of *The Politics*. Arthur Darby Nock of Harvard praised both *The Politics* and the *Bibliography* in *The Classical Review*. He wrote, "His is a remarkable study, highly suggestive and in the main convincing, and above all not a book only for specialists in Philo"[54] and, "The bibliography of Philo . . . is well arranged and eminently serviceable."[55] *The Living Church* reviewed it with a summary, though not a critique."[56] Rabbi Louis Finkelstein, chancellor of Jewish Theological Seminary, wrote to Goodenough on 31 May 1938, "You have placed in your debt all those who are interested in Philo and the history of his time."[57]

Goodenough concluded his work on Philo with *An Introduction to Philo Judaeus*, published in 1940. Developed from a series of lectures he gave at Jewish Theological Seminary in 1938, the book had two purposes: to help the beginner read Philo intelligently,[58] and to demonstrate

Philo's importance as a representative of Hellenistic Judaism, which was a major source of early Christianity, according to Goodenough. So the reader could judge the validity of his arguments as to this bridge aspect of Hellenistic Judaism, he planned the work so that the writings would speak for themselves.

From the outset Goodenough encourages his readers. He takes them by the hand and systematically outlines the procedures to follow in order to know Philo and decide whether he was indeed the Hellenistic Jew and the mystic that Goodenough portrays. His use of "we" gives readers a sense of sharing in a joint exploration, but his structure skillfully moves them in the direction he intends.

He opens by introducing Philo the man, much as he had described him in *The Jurisprudence of the Jewish Courts in Egypt:* a wealthy Jew of cosmopolitan Alexandria, devoted to philosophy and public service, but also fond of the theater, athletics, and banquets.

Then he describes the proper method of studying Philo: to read all his writings, examine the context of the passages in which he makes important points, study the backgrounds and the connotations of his language for his contempories, and, finally, be aware and wary of one's preconceptions.

This caution leads Goodenough to list his own preconceptions, most of which restate those already expressed in his earlier interpretations of Philo. He believes that Philo was divided in his loyalty to Judaism and to Hellenism; that Philo's frequent allusions to predecessors imply a long tradition of Hellenized Judaism like his own; that Hellenized Christianity arose out of a Hellenized Judaism like Philo's. Finally, Goodenough considers the mystic's longing for oneness with God to be a key element in religious experience, so he is especially responsive to Philo's mysticism, while he understands that others may disagree with his emphases.

When he proceeds to discuss Philo's writings, Goodenough's enthusiasm leads him to declare, rather naively, that the student who has conscientiously read them all will become "a Philo addict."[59] He may well seem to exaggerate in describing the rewards the student will reap from studying the works of this little-known figure who wrote at a time when Judaism was generally seen as playing a minor political and religious role, "He will have come to know the great leader of a great people in a great period of their history."[60]

Goodenough's review of the different facets of Philo's thought for the most part restates briefly interpretations he has previously developed. He recounts Philo's political views as outlined in *The Politics*. He describes

Philo the Jew as a man who "in accepting the abstract Pure Being of the Greek philosophic deity . . . never lost the personal and merciful God of the Jews,"[61] illustrating the point by drawing a parallel with the twentieth-century Christian who believes in both the loving Father of Jesus and the abstract God of the creeds. And he concludes: "The true Judaism of Philo is . . . shot through with just as true and genuine hellenistic conceptions and ideals.[62] For in "the living person . . . the two were a triumphant unit."[63]

In describing Philo's metaphysics he repeats the conclusions of *By Light, Light,* stating that the key to both Philo's philosophy and his mysticism is his conception of God as light, giving forth a stream of radiation manifested in the Logos and his creative and ruling powers. Goodenough commends Philo's view of the universe, that is, that it conforms to the laws of arithmetical numbers, time, and space, but that it derives its ultimate meaning from God, whose providence is beyond matter. And he commends its contemporary relevance: "Such a view of the universe . . . is a serious and sensible philosophy of nature . . . a philosophy which gives a possible answer to the demand of human hearts that we square science in some way with human experience and hope, the experience that man is living in a world where order becomes intelligible ultimately in mathematical terms, and the hope that the universe is not indifferent to human values"[64]—very much Goodenough's own view.

He has less praise for some specifics of Philo's ethics, criticizing his acceptance of slavery, his view of women as weak and incomplete, and the fact that he had one ethic for the Jew dealing with Jews and another for the Jew dealing with Gentiles, although he attributes to him the first concept of conscience. Goodenough concludes that Philo focused on the individual's relations with God rather than with society. He closes by drawing a parallel with early Hellenistic Christianity, which also stressed personal salvation and inner purity rather than humanitarianism and the social virtues. It was an emphasis similar to that in his own background, which had made him uncomfortable with the social gospel at Garrett Biblical Institute, and he described with obvious sympathy Philo's view that ethics is primarily a matter of one's relations with God.

Philo the mystic of *An Introduction* is the same Philo whom Goodenough had portrayed in *By Light, Light.* Goodenough commends his view that the real is the immaterial and that the scientific education of his day had value only when introducing "true knowledge and virtue."[65] To him, Philo was "saying in his figurative way what we have been saying very much to each other during the last twenty years, that attention to, and development, of scientific knowledge is no guaranty . . . of increase in our spiritual growth or perception."[66] Philo, according to Goodenough, held that salvation lies in the mystical approach to immaterial reality, through the Mystery revealed by Moses in the story of the patriarchs, and in Jewish rites. Goodenough maintains, as he had in *By Light, Light,* that Philo believed his mystical interpretation of Judaism had the answers to the questions pagans asked about how to come to reality, that only Judaism had these answers—"the only true Mystery"[67]—and that allegorization of the Bible revealed this Mystery in the lives of the patriarchs, who showed the way to it.

The work concludes by stating that the Judaism of Philo—the Law and rituals that Philo interpreted as ways to partake of the Logos and attain a new birth—was adopted as a major element in Christianity, although, Goodenough points out, scholars of his day had failed to recognize this, and Philo himself could not have imagined that his Hellenistic Judaism would be a basis for the doctorines of a new religion and its civilization.

Thus *An Introduction* acquaints the general reader with the main aspects of Philo's thought and restates Goodenough's two key points in his earlier studies of Philo: the centrality of mysticism in Philo's thought and its importance for understanding the development of Christianity.

An Introduction had the same mixed reception as Goodenough's earlier interpretations of Philo. He was delighted with a review by Ralph Marcus,[68] who praised *An Introduction* highly, writing, "Goodenough has a talent for making ancient thought and institutions come alive. . . . It would be difficult for any scholar to state so clearly, accurately, and eloquently, and in such brief form, the essential points of Philo's metaphysics and mysticism."[69] Samuel Belkin voiced a counteropinion in *The Journal of Biblical Literature,* stating, "This new book is not an important introduction to Philo by Goodenough, but *according to* Goodenough."[70] Yet Union Theological Seminary included it in the library's shelf of new books to be called to the special attention of students.[71]

Goodenough felt obliged to return to Philo in 1947 when Harry Wolfson offered a radically different view of Philo's thought in *Philo: Foundations of Religious Philosophy in Judaism, Christianity, and Islam.* Wolfson had been a young instructor in Hebrew literature and philosophy at Harvard Divinity School when Goodenough was a graduate student, and had continued there as a professor. In 1934 he published a study of Spinoza's philosophy, which led him to work backward from Spinoza to Philo and classical Greek philosophy and to plan a series of studies beginning with *Philo.*

Wolfson portrayed Philo as a Jewish philosopher who demonstrated that Greek philosophy was anticipated by the basic teachings of the Hebrew Scriptures and who was the first thinker to subordinate the guidance of reason to that of direct revelation and so became the founder of medieval philosophy.

He disagreed with Goodenough's view that Philo was not an original philosopher; instead he saw him as the dominant figure in European philosophy before Spinoza. He also challenged the position of *By Light, Light* that Philo's writings presented Judaism as "the greatest, the only true Mystery."[72] Furthermore, contrary to Goodenough's whole interpretation, Wolfson affirmed that Philo believed in the literal Law and the importance of obedience to it, as did medieval Jewish philosophers.

In a long review of Wolfson's book in *The Journal of Biblical Literature*, Goodenough, in 1948, took issue with Wolfson's key positions. He insisted that Philo used allegory to identify the religion of Scripture with the mystery religions of the times. He demonstrated that Wolfson ignored "Philo's mysticism and mystical conceptions."[73] He gave counterarguments to Wolfson's thesis that Philo was a systematic philosopher who combined rabbinic Judaism with Plato and Aristotle to produce the model for medieval philosophy. And he concluded: "The book should be called *a Philonic System,* for this it is. The mistake is to call it simply *Philo,* for I found little of Philo himself or his spirit in it."[74]

Yet many scholars accepted Wolfson's *Philo* as definitive, provoking Goodenough's complaint that later interpreters of a passage in Philo felt obliged to check whether Wolfson had discussed it. Wolfson's biographer, Leo Schwarz, writing in 1965, said that Wolfson's interpretation of Philo was generally recognized as "an event in intellectual history."[75] And by going on to state: "Wolfson had retrieved Philo from the catacombs of scholarship and restored him to a place of honor among the great philosophers,"[76] Schwarz implicitly dismissed Goodenough's writings on the subject. His only specific reference to Goodenough, without mention of any name, was the scathing comment: "The portrait that suffers most from Wolfson's Philo is the one which makes of him the purveyor of a paganlike mystery religion and of a mystical gospel that paved the way for Christianity. If ever such a mystic existed in Alexandria, he is as insubstantial as Banquo's ghost."[77] This comment expressed essentially the same disparagement as that of Ralph Marcus, who in his 1949 review, "Wolfson's Reevaluation of Philo," had written,

"Philo qua systematic philosopher is fortunate in having found a more appreciative interpreter in Wolfson than he seems to have found in Goodenough."[78]

Samuel Sandmel, in *Philo of Alexandria: An Introduction,* published in 1979, included a chapter "Goodenough on Philo" in which he discussed Wolfson's "rejection" of Goodenough and concluded that "those who regard Philo as thoroughly Hellenized are right, and . . . Wolfson is wrong. But I believe also that Goodenough represents a viewpoint that is guilty of excess and that, fascinating as his views are, they are all too often insubstantial."[79]

David Winston, in *Logos and Mystical Theology in Philo of Alexandria,* published in 1985, pointed out that although Goodenough and Wolfson were both sympathic to Philo, they were, nevertheless, "poles apart." For Goodenough saw Philo as a mystic in the Greek tradition whose Hellenistic Judaism met his emotional, existential needs, whereas Wolfson saw Philo as critical of all Greek thought and as the creator of an original system that dominated European philosophy for almost seventeen centuries.[80]

In the Brown Classics in Judaica Series' reissue of Goodenough's *Introduction to Philo Judaeus* in 1986, Jacob Neusner, the editor, describes in his introduction the "two great, and conflicting theories of Philo" that culminated the nineteenth-century Jewish interest in Philo's writings and concludes: "Both scholars may rightly claim to have offered monumental and enduring contributions to the interpretation of Philo"[81] in a debate that he later termed a "key event."[82]

Neusner then focuses on Goodenough's "power" in *An Introduction to Philo Judaeus,* which, he claims, "lies in the clarity of presentation and in the massive grasp of Philo and his writings. He was one of the great teachers of his age, and, happily, because of this work, he teaches still."[83] Neusner concludes that with his *Introduction* "he attained the rank of premier American historian of religion of the twentieth century"[84] and that he and George Foot Moore in their works on Judaism showed other scholars "how to describe, analyze, and interpret religious systems, contexts and contents alike."[85]

For Neusner *An Introduction to Philo Judaeus* belongs in the Brown Classics in Judaica Series because, beyond Philo's historical importance, he spoke with such relevance to the issues faced by the contemporary American Jew. Neusner states that Philo, as Goodenough portrayed him, provides a model for this American Jew, "who thinks and lives in English and yet draws on the spiritual resources of the Hebrew language,

Scriptures and later Judaic writers."[86] This tribute to his success in presenting Philo's continuing relevance would have delighted Goodenough, who sought what the Brown Series commended: to "confront the record of the past as an on-going encounter with an enduring condition and an on-going human reality."[87] It would have confirmed his belief that it was his destiny to interpret his "fatal figure" for his own day.

Chapter 6

Summer at Colorado College and *Religious Tradition and Myth*

After completing his first two works on Philo, Goodenough had a chance to see the West and also to offer his first account of the various elements that contributed to early Christianity as he read it.

President Thurston Davies of Colorado College in Colorado Springs invited Goodenough to give a summer school course in 1935, the year *By Light, Light* was published. Colorado College is a small, coeducational liberal arts college at the foot of Pikes Peak in the Rocky Mountains, established in 1874 "upon a broad Christian foundation"; it was to be marked by "thorough scholarship and fervent piety, each assisting the other,"[1] and was nonsectarian. President Davies had been secretary of the graduate council of Princeton until 1934 and obviously knew of Goodenough's reputation as a teacher and scholar.

The course was to be of general interest: humanity's need for religion and the religious values that modern intellectuals can still have. This was a subject of great appeal to Goodenough because of his belief both in the continuing importance of religion and in the need to reinterpret it so that it would be compatible with current scientific and psychological theories. He therefore gladly accepted and suggested as a specific topic one that was related to his longtime concern with the origins of Christianity: "The Contribution of Greek Culture to Christianity," touching on "the social, ethical, philosophic, governmental ideas of the Greeks and the importance of these for later Christian developments." He was also to give four public lectures, choosing as his subjects: "The Religious Ideas of the Jews in the Time of Jesus," "The Established Religion of the Greek People," "Greek Mysteries," and "The Religion of the Philosophers."[2]

The Goodenoughs went out to Colorado in style. Hester, their six-year-old daughter, was still suffering the aftereffects of a ruptured appendix, so Erwin and Helen went by train with her. Erwin engaged a Yale

71

student to drive out with the three boys and their maid, Ruby Russell. This provided them with their 1928 Buick sedan in Colorado. They rented a house on Ute Pass, on the outskirts of Colorado Springs, in the shadow of fourteen thousand foot Pikes Peak.

President Davies and Charles Mierow, the summer school classics professor, formerly president of the college, and his family were extremely hospitable. The Mierows took the Goodenoughs on drives to the foot of Mount Harvard and Mount Princeton in the collegiate range of the Rockies, where they picnicked and swam in the Mount Princeton hot springs. The Mierows also entertained them at their woodland cabin outside Crystola, a nearby town. There they became part of a group including the superintendent of schools and an Episcopal rector. They played charades and danced to "The Moon Comes over the Mountain" and other records of that vintage, played on a wind-up Victrola. Sometimes Lloyd Shaw, a well-known square dance authority, would call a square dance.[3] Although Erwin later said that the "low years" with Helen began in 1921, the exhilaration of mountain trips and the enjoyment of these friends must have temporarily alleviated the difficulties of which he would complain.

In 1937 Goodenough published *Religious Tradition and Myth,* based on the lectures he gave at Colorado College and dedicated "To my friends in Colorado Springs."

Spiritual needs and problems received new attention in the 1930s. Earlier in the century, after the challenges of Darwin's evolutionist successors and Freud's theories, it was fashionable to question the relevance of religion. Dorothy Thompson, the distinguished journalist, is a typical example of the intellectuals' attitude during the 1910s and 1920s. Born the same year as Goodenough, the daughter of a Methodist minister, at college she outgrew her Methodist beliefs, told her father that she saw more value in science than in churches, and "was beginning to think that 'man had invented God and not the other way around.'"[4] But the Depression at home and Hitler's ruthless, unchallenged aggression abroad led many to question whether society was as self-sufficient as people had assumed and whether religion was the illusion Freud claimed it was.

The thirties produced a flood of Bible-thumping preachers and Father Coughlin, the radio priest, who ranted against "Christ-haters." But there was also the thoughtful voice of the theologian Reinhold Niebuhr, who pointed out the social relevance of Christianity in *Moral Man and Immoral Society.*

In *The Religion of Yesterday and Tomorrow,* Kirsopp Lake, Goodenough's Harvard teacher, had in 1925 argued that Christianity was "possible for educated men and women of the next generation" if its institutions "assimilated science."[5] Goodenough in *Religious Tradition and Myth* develops his own version of Lake's position. The title points to his thesis that the religious traditions of our civilization, incorporated in Christianity, still can meet modern man's spiritual needs and are "the fundamentals out of which the religion of the future must largely be built"[6] when they are understood to be myths expressing religious experiences. He demonstrates the continuing need for religion. Then he describes the key elements in Christianity, which, he concludes, are "the religious constants of humanity"[7] and still of value for the intellectual if he reads them as mythical descriptions of the life-enhancing encounter with "the inexplicable Greater Thing."[8]

The introduction opens on the informal note of autobiography: "We grew up in economic certainty,"[9] and "we were still nourished on the classics."[10] Then it brings the reader to the spiritual "predicament strictly of the intelligent men of our day."[11] According to Goodenough, in the vacuum left by discarding their religious traditions "the thoughtful men of our day are in a trouble of their own making, the trouble of having nothing left which they can honestly feel makes life and effort have meaning and objective."[12] Like everyone else, they need to feel that they are "not alone, lost in a meaningless and indifferent universe."[13] Implicitly challenging Freud's view that religion is a childish neurosis and Jung's confidence that focus on the psychic life will guarantee spiritual health, Goodenough affirms that people are "incurably religious."[14] For he defines religion as "what a man does . . . in response to his convictions, or possibly to his unconscious assumptions, as to the nature of the forces which really control himself and his environment."[15] He argues that this continuing need for religion points to a renewed study of "the religious history of our civilization,"[16] because, he concludes with the passion of a preacher, "The loneliness and inarticulateness of the modern intellectual's religious life is robbing our civilization of one of its deepest needs, the spiritual contribution we can give it."[17] The chapters that follow describe "the religious constants of humanity,"[18] indicating what is outmoded in their traditional form and what has continuing value.

In "Traditions from Judaism" Goodenough looks at Judaism primarily in terms of what it contributed to Christianity. He portrays the God of Judaism as one who inspires awe, who revealed correct conduct by giving men the Law, who is both a stern Father watching over our every act and also forgiving and loving, and, finally, as the God of the prophets, who demands that men practice both justice and mercy. Goodenough asserts: "We owe to the Jewish genius for religion the strength of our priceless tradition that religion is inseparable from our conduct toward our neighbors."[19] Beyond that, he affirms, "the greatest contribution of Judaism to Christianity . . . is Jesus himself, his life and teachings."[20]

In "Contributions of Greek Philosophy" Goodenough contrasts Judaism with the more mature philosophy of Plato and Aristotle, making it clear that this is no disparagement of Judaism, because men must never outgrow their childlike virtues. Then he describes the later, Hellenistic writers' view, which he had identified as Philo's in *By Light, Light,* that God, the self-contained and invisible, discloses himself in a great light-stream or, to use another figure, the stream of his utterance. Goodenough states that these concepts of light and utterance, rather than "Word," represent what he considers would be an accurate translation of the Fourth Gospel's opening, namely, "In the beginning was God and his Utterance. . . . It was light, and its light was the life of men."[21] Thus, he asserts, "the Fourth Gospel brought the God of the Greeks, with his streaming radiation, into Christianity, or shows it already brought in."[22]

In his summary Goodenough affirms that the God of the Jews has been the God of most Christians, but the Greek God has been the God of the creeds. He then concludes that, with the challenge of modern scientific developments, "if there is room for any deity in our new world it is deity as the Greeks, not as the Jews, conceived it."[23] He sees the Greek philosophers, rather than the Jews, as men who "had tried to make themselves intelligent citizens of an intelligible universe, and had adapted their religious aspirations to what seemed reasonable to their minds."[24] Christianity learned from them that an adequate religion must fit a man to live in a world of science, he states, but its solution, he regrets, was to keep science static by ecclesiastical censorship. Now, freed from that censorship, men have abandoned their childhood belief in a Father who counts every hair on their heads. Yet few can find adequate religious satisfaction solely in the philosopher's concept of an Absolute. What, then, will give such satisfaction? he asks.

Before answering this question, Goodenough outlines what Christianity owes to two other elements of our religious tradition, Greek religion and Hellenistic Judaism. After describing the worship of Zeus and Apollo, he proceeds to Orphism. Orphism, as he portrays it, taught that a man must strive for escape from his material body into immaterial life and that through its rites he could be purified to live a life of the spirit. Goodenough sees this asceticism and mysticism as one strand in early Christianity.

Next he stresses the contribution of Hellenistic Judaism, which he posits as the final element adopted by early Christianity from other religions. Restating much of what he had developed in *By Light, Light,* he characterizes Hellenistic Judaism, the religion of Jews who lived in the new city of Alexandria in Egypt, as "Jewish in its literature, Greek in its mystical hope and philosophy, and universal in its appeal."[25] Stating that it is preserved primarily in the writings of Philo, he briefly outlines Philo's allegorical reading of the Old Testament, in which Philo portrayed the patriarchs, especially Moses, as men who had found the mystic way of salvation and who, by their lives, showed later generations the way. Goodenough concludes, as he had suggested in *By Light, Light,* that the Christianity of the church fathers was the "marvelous child"[26] of Greek Jews. This Christianity took from Greek religion, as modified by the Hellenistic Jews, "its idea of salvation, and learned to think that the lowly Jesus of Nazareth was its heavenly Savior, the Logos, Son of God."[27]

In the final chapter Goodenough describes briefly the essence of Christianity, which he had gone to Harvard Divinity School to ascertain. He sees it as the composite of the elements it adopted from Old Testament Judaism, Greek philosophy and religion, and Hellenistic Judaism. Therefore, "the mystic and the man to whom religion was primarily ethics have worshiped and lived in mutual understanding."[28]

He then enumerates the individual features that have contemporary "usefulness." Goodenough sees the attitude to life and the ethics of Jesus, though not his literal instructions, as still important and the Christian theological concept of God as the Absolute, based on Greek metaphysics, as being still philosophically sound. And he affirms that all the elements he has described "are as valid as ever when they are regarded as mythical accounts of an experience still as open to us as to our fathers, one in which we escape from the littleness of ourselves into a larger personal and social life."[29]

Finally he proposes what he sees as a viable contemporary religious position. He states that modern science has made it impossible to believe that one can know God. But one can still have "a purely pragmatic and agnostic religious experience based upon the fact which was behind all these myths, the fact that whatever may be the nature of the universal Ultimate, man can and does in prayer seem to himself to communicate with something or someone greater than his normal personality."[30] He affirms that the object of this experience can be represented only in mythical language, which, as he uses the term "myth," is a means to "clarify our experiences to ourselves and convey them to each other in a way otherwise impossible."[31]

Among the myths held by modern individuals he lists not only God the Father and the "convenient"[32] myth of a mediator between humans and the Ultimate, but also "the myth of psychoanalysis, by which the personality we experience is called the super-ego."[33]

"A Reconciliation," the title of the last chapter, has a double meaning. It refers to Goodenough's insistence that the "sense of reconciliation, an experience of union, with the 'Power-not-Ourselves,' "[34] is still the means of attaining the values modern individuals seek. It also refers to Goodenough's argument that it is possible to reconcile religion and the modern world—that people can be both religious and intelligent. Examining the many elements in Christianity, he seeks to indicate what beliefs have contemporary meaning for intellectuals, so that they may continue to have the religious experiences that Goodenough insists they need, as long as they recognize their mythical character. As he explains his objective in a letter of 1939, he tried to make clear in the book that the religious life "was based upon human experience which could be accounted for only by some myth or other, but which was real as real experience in spite of the mythological expression we had to give it."[35]

His account of the various traditions that early Christianity drew upon enabled Goodenough to give a brief, popular summary of his views on Christianity's origins. His emphasis on the need to regard Christian beliefs not as ultimate truths but mythical accounts of religious experiences was his first statement of a position he was later to develop more fully. The book also had a place in the long-term program he identified in *Toward a Mature Faith* as making use of information "while I slowly transformed what was best from my whole heritage into a pattern which seemed to me to make some sense for living in the new age."[36] The reviewer in the *Journal of Bible and Religion* praised Goodenough's success in accomplishing this objective, stating that "here is an impressive and, it is hoped, a fruitful plea for a rediscovery of those valid 'basic notions,' those essential values, which have ever been at the heart of effective religious experiences, and which even in this scientific age may be found by those who truly seek them. . . . Addressed to those modern intellectuals who have abandoned religion, this little book carries a vital message of practical value. Others also . . . may read it with profit." [37]

Chapter 7

Middle Age and a New Love

Goodenough was in the New Haven Hospital in October 1938, suffering from the still undiagnosed celiac disease that had recurred about every ten years since childhood. With *The Politics of Philo Judaeus* published, he had a half-year sabbatical leave to work on his "picture book"[1] (*Symbols*). Before his illness he had applied for a research assistant from the National Youth Administration (NYA), the academic wing of the Work Projects Adminstration (WPA), which gave graduate students who needed financial aid a stipend to help faculty in their research. Evelyn Wiltshire, in her second year at the Yale English Graduate School, had decided that she wanted to be financially independent of her parents and applied for an NYA position. She was assigned to Goodenough and told to meet him in the New Haven Hospital.

Being very shy, Evelyn persuaded a friend to come with her and wait outside the hospital room to give her unseen support, while she faced the interview alone. She found Goodenough propped up in bed, his usually pale face now as white as his hospital gown and his blue eyes deep-sunk, but piercing. He was no doubt disconcerted to see that the prospective research assistant was a beautiful young woman with large brown eyes who gazed at him apprehensively, and his manner was brusque. When Evelyn stressed the second syllable as she used the word "harass," he quipped, "Young lady, that's something we don't mention in public." This intimidated her, as she confessed to her waiting friend.[2] But she was also attracted, even at this first encounter, in which Goodenough dealt mostly with details of the work she was to do, but also spoke briefly about his unconventional religious and other views. She later reported to him only that she thought him "an incredible person with a hairy chest."[3]

Evelyn was the only child of parents who lived in Turtle Creek, a small town outside Pittsburgh. They had little education and introduced

77

her to a world totally foreign to them when they sent her to Wilson, a small Presbyterian women's college in central Pennsylvania. After graduating in 1937, with no job prospects because of the Depression, she decided on further study in English literature at the Yale Graduate School, accompanied by her closest college friend and roommate, Hazel Barnes, who was continuing her studies in the classics.

She came to Yale with a receptive, wide-ranging mind. Wilson College had some stimulating faculty and with the attraction of its generous Curran scholarships brought many first-rate students. Evelyn was enthusiastic about the new ideas to which she was introduced while there and also enjoyed much of her reading in the graduate school at Yale. But both the seminars and her fellow students—especially the men, who made up the large majority—were disappointing. The seminars consisted largely of student reports that summarized rather than critiqued the works considered. The students seemed to her to have no interest in art or music and no love of literature, viewing the Ph.D. primarily as the prerequisite for college teaching. She also dated several undergraduates, but found them callow. The men she knew in Turtle Creek had even less to offer her, beyond the opportunities to go to dances, movies, and parties and to receive expensive gifts. Erwin Goodenough's ideas fascinated her, and invited her into a cultural world she had never known. As their work relationship developed into friendship, he read Plato to her; he discussed art, literature, music, the meanings of the symbols he was studying. He represented the kind of father figure her own, nonintellectual father had never been. At the same time she appreciated the fact that Goodenough valued her ideas, drawing out a perceptiveness she did not know she had, and she was flattered that he inscribed a copy of *Religious Tradition and Myth* that he gave her "To an interesting critic."

Evelyn came into Erwin's life at a time when he found no sexual or spiritual satisfaction with Helen. In the Oxford years he had written to his parents, "Helen is dear as ever, grows dearer all the time."[4] He acknowledged her guidance in their studies of European art, and he praised her as a thoughtful reader and keen observer. He recognized that she was "the attractive force"[5] in the intimacy with Ed Mason and Ted Hatfield that gave Goodenough his first real male friends, and his letters to his parents express only appreciation of Helen.

But there was a gradual change from the devotion of those years. He wrote Evelyn in 1940 that even as an undergraduate he had longed, without knowing what he wanted, for "[kalos] in sex . . . , καλος which is so far beyond sex, but yet . . . is to be found only through sex."[6] (He used the

Greek word for "beautiful," "fair," "good," following Plato's identification of *kalos* with ideal beauty in *The Symposium.*) And he claimed that he did not find this *kalos* with Helen.

Toward a Mature Faith, published in 1955, describes a dream Goodenough had had "some twenty years ago." He was in school, translating a passage from Greek, when he was at a loss for a key word. Awaking from the dream-nightmare, the Greek word *eleftheria* (freedom) had come to him. He interpreted the dream as expressing his passionate desire for freedom and concluded, "It was really a dream of a childish situation in which . . . a part of my nature was revolting against my parents and the religious life for which they stood." But he preceded this interpretation with the explanation "provoked by my problems at the time"[7] — the mid-thirties.

1935 was the year *By Light, Light* appeared with its dedication in Greek "To my family." It was also the year of the seemingly happy summer in Colorado Springs. Both Ward and Jim state that the children did not sense any discontent in their parents' relation to each other,[8] but Ward and Jim were away at school during much of the time. And in a memoir of 1962 Goodenough identified the years 1929–1937 as the "low years" with Helen,[9] that is, beginning well before the *By Light, Light* dedication. So one cannot pinpoint precisely when he began to experience marital malaise.

His increasing understanding of psychology contributed to his restlessness. He talked frequently with his boyhood friend, now the distinguished psychoanalyst Thomas French, when French and his wife, Erwin's sister Dedy, lived in Elmont, Long Island, and Erwin stated that their conversations provided him with "as fine a course of lectures on the subject as the world had to offer."[10] After Dedy divorced French and he moved to Chicago, Erwin continued his psychological discussions with Dedy, a doctor, as well as with his psychiatrist friends in New Haven.

Erwin and Helen early in their marriage had a liberal attitude toward sex. Erwin admired D. H. Lawrence's *Lady Chatterley's Lover* and his other fiction for their emphasis on the validity of finding sexual fulfillment outside marriage. And when he wrote *Politics of Philo Judaeus,* published in 1938, he criticized Philo's views on chastity, commenting that Philo was "in that deplorable but historically important line of ethical development which came ultimately to associate the word moral in a unique sense with sexual repression."[11]

At this point, when he was forty-five and discontented in his marriage Evelyn met Erwin's needs in several ways. He was physically attracted to her beauty. She provided a contrast to the coldness he felt in Helen at that time. And she satisfied what he later generalized as the mature man's "craving . . . for the young girl, the virgin whom he can protect, and to whom he can play the ruling father."[12] Whereas in their Oxford days Erwin had welcomed Helen's leadership, he now enjoyed being the teacher, introducing Evelyn to art and philosophy, initiating her into exciting sex and spiritual ecstasy. She was his devoted admirer, saw him as "a symbol of the potentialities of mankind,"[13] and went so far as writing, "To me you are God."[14] In what became an increasingly important role to him, she listened while he talked—of his work, as well as of his love.

Their meetings were limited mostly to Erwin's office, room 708 in the Hall of Graduate Studies. For he felt the need to be very secretive, since he claimed that Helen, in spite of their profession of sexual freedom, would become jealous. Thus, if she were to suspect his feelings for Evelyn, he was sure that she would be impossible to live with, and he did want to live with her for the children's sake.

At Christmas 1938 they only exchanged Christmas cards. But by March 1939 they were lovers, with Erwin managing a weekend in New York with Evelyn after she left Yale on her way to spending spring vacation with her parents.

In room 708 Erwin held Evelyn spellbound when he read Plato's *Symposium* to her and explained Plato's belief that the power of physical love enables one to become *kalos* and obtain a greater life. They had a special trysting place in a corner by the right-hand window.[15] When apart, they wrote passionate letters almost daily. Goodenough made a practice of carrying one of Evelyn's letters in his left hip pocket where he could touch it when he was with others. "I find it a real help, though when I take it out to file it is often badly crumpled from my clutching it so violently."[16] He used extravagant superlatives in describing her "beauties of character and loveliness"[17] and what she meant to him: "Never did a woman give such love to a man,"[18] and, "God bless you, my darling. I cannot thank Him enough for giving me the infinite inspiration of your love,"[19] and, in yet another letter, "You are as perfect a mate for me as my wildest imagination could picture. You are everything I have ever desired, and how I do love you! The future I just refuse to face!"[20]

But it had to be faced.

With her M.A. completed, Evelyn left Yale in June 1939, first for the Ogontz Camp in Littleton, New Hampshire, then in the fall to teach at the Ogontz School outside Philadelphia. Erwin and his family spent their usual vacation at Squam Lake, New Hampshire, where their friends the

Gabriels and the Baumers had cottages. Erwin could not get away to visit Evelyn in Littleton. At first he thought he could not even have her letters: "God! I wish you could write me here. But please don't."[21] Then he hit upon the plan of always being the one to pick up the mail in town. In August, when he did arrange a meeting in Brattleboro, Vermont, he instructed Evelyn to sign herself "Edward" if she needed to telegraph him, and he would sign "Edith Graham." He hated the sneakiness and having to write looking over his shoulder to see if anyone was coming into the room, even though "there is no eye over my soul's shoulder."[22] But he felt he must keep up appearances with Helen "so that all will be fine and sweet for the children."[23] "I must keep this family together in sweetness or break it up," he wrote. And the only way it can be kept in sweetness is to act in such a way as to arouse no suspicions."[24]

He was deeply rooted in his family, his work, Yale. "And you would not want me if I came to you an uprooted plant,"[25] he wrote Evelyn; later, "I am a guiding power as an ideal, and the very fact that I am so influential in their [the children's] lives would make my moral 'collapse,' as they would view it, all the more disastrous for them."[26] Again, expressing his sense of obligation to both his scholarship and his children, "I cannot see but that for the sake of the possibility of my saying what I must say to the world, for the sake of the children, I cannot become the object of a cheap scandal."[27]

He was a "fond fond pappa," as he termed himself. He insisted on a preparatory school for all four children. He chose Groton for both Ward and John, not because it was an Episcopal school dedicated to educating "Christian gentlemen," as it advertised, but for its academic excellence and prestige. Goodenough, who was very ambitious for his sons, had observed that Groton was a sure steppingstone to the Ivy League colleges and that its graduates at Yale were well prepared and socially mature. So Groton was the school for Ward and John.

When Britain declared war on Germany on 5 September 1939, Goodenough was not only distressed because of his sympathy with the German people, but also concerned about the safety of Ward and John, who were both in different parts of Scandinavia for the summer.

A letter from Ward, from England, saying that in Copenhagen he had managed to get a berth on an American passenger freighter as a waiter and was on his way home, made his father very happy. On Ward's arrival Erwin wrote to Evelyn, "My soul is singing for joy this morning. . . . For Ward came home Saturday night! What happiness! . . . We have done nothing but talk talk talk ever since."[28]

There were tensions, of course. Ward thought that his father was harder on him than on the younger children. Certainly, when he was a baby, Goodenough had used harsh measures to keep him from sucking his thumb, tying his arm to a board so that he could not get the thumb to his mouth. Ward wrote to his father from Cornell, where he was a senior, accusing him of pushing him. This so troubled Erwin that he took the letter to his psychiatrist friend, Clement Fry, who assured him that it was a typical expression of youthful rebellion from an intelligent, normal young man.[29]

And he was still "a *very* dear boy, sweet and kind."[30] Erwin approved of Ward's girlfriend Ruth when Ward brought her home with him, and he was delighted to hear from her that "no one has ever had any influence upon him comparable to mine."[31] When Erwin talked about his work with Ward, he wrote that Ward "was thrilled, transfixed. He said he saw himself, his relations with Ruth, the Good Life, and all the rest, as he had never seen it."[32] This delight in Ward's admiration was capped by his pride in his son's election to Phi Beta Kappa, "the third generation of Goodenoughs in that society."[33]

John, like Ward, came back safely in September 1939 from a summer in Finland. Erwin had the joy of meeting him at the boat in Brooklyn and finding him "more mature and finer than ever."[34] A later visit with him at Groton led Erwin to write to Evelyn, "Great 6´ boy, powerful and tender as a child . . . Quiet, reserved, he is the most loved and loving boy I ever saw. . . . Three boys are competing to room with him at Yale. . . . To have a boy who has everything, magnificent physique, brilliant mind, and holy spirit is so much to me."[35] When John was graduated from Groton with the Latin prize, a shared prize for the boy who did most for the school, and a *magna cum laude,* it was "a very exciting honor for the old man."[36]

"Little Jim" had gone to Woodbridge Country Day School, then to Westminster. When Britain declared war against Germany and Jim's long exposure to Erwin's anti-British, pro-German sympathies made it hard for him to understand why the United States sided with Britain, his father spent an evening carefully explaining it to him.[37] When Jim did poorly at Westminster, he cried as he told his parents about it, and "no one," Erwin reported, "can help him in this but me."[38] He talked with the headmaster and dorm master about Jim's inadequate performance there, apparently with good results. For he was delighted that Jim took two prizes at commencement, "one as leading scholar of his form, and one for the best student in Bible."[39]

Hester, the youngest, "another wonderful child,"[40] had also gone to the Woodbridge Country Day School and at eleven was sent to the Putney School. Before leaving, her father reported, "she clings to me every night, insists that I kiss her last after she is in bed, and looks at me as though she was getting all her life from me. Her going will be more of a personal loss to me than the going of any except Ward, for she is the little girl, and so sweet."[41]

Devoted as Goodenough was to his children, he was also deeply committed to his work as a scholar and his place in the Yale community. In 1940 he was about to publish his fourth book on Philo, was senior editor of *The Journal of Biblical Literature,* a member of the Yale Board of Permanent Officers, director of graduate studies in history, professor of the history of religion, and a professor in the classics, Oriental studies, and philosophy departments as well. To jeopardize his professional status was the most difficult part of making a break with Helen. He talked with Ward about his feelings for Evelyn, found him sympathetic, and believed that Ward would help the younger children understand the situation, so that, given time, their father would not have to worry about hurting them. But, he wrote to Evelyn, "I cannot imagine Helen's giving up her position without a struggle, and struggle means scandal. . . . Could I do my work, get a hearing for my books, if there were such a scandal?"[42] Everything he knew about Yale and the academic world led him to answer "no," and friends among his colleagues who were in his confidence agreed.

His financial situation was an added problem. In 1936, his father had died a poor man after repaying the losses he felt he had brought upon his friends by urging them to invest in a project bankrupted by his partners' embezzlement. He left the Woodbridge house he had bought for Erwin's and Helen's use to his wife, who deeded it to them. But there was an eight thousand dollar mortgage; it was expensive to maintain; and they kept a maid most of the years through the thirties. Already in debt and without any means to provide for Helen's independent upkeep, Goodenough seemed to his psychiatrist friend Clement Fry "just stuck."[43] He therefore concluded, to Evelyn, "I cannot so lose myself in the delight and glory of your love that I forget the practical problems of our relationship."[44] For, he asked despairingly, "if I throw up everything, cease 'prostituting' myself (as you quite *correctly* call it), try to forget the children, my career, the message of my research, still how would we live?"[45]

The idealistic standards he set for himself made his situation even more difficult: "I do wish passionately to make myself subservient to the Good that is greater than I am, because only so can I come to share in it."[46] And again, "I am determined that my love for you shall not swamp my whole obligation to God and myself."[47] Commenting on Emerson's "Self-Reliance," he wrote, "Little was said in his essay about a generous feeling of recognition toward others."[48]

He was convinced that Evelyn's love would enable him to realize what he had come to regard as a hopeless ideal: to have someone with whom to share his inner life, but after twenty-three years of marriage he felt obligated to Helen for what she had contributed. "She has cooperated with me in my early years of work to make my career possible; in bringing up the children. . . . Whenever she has got a little inheritance it has at once gone to Ward and John for schooling, or into the quicksand of my current bills, and it has gone, obviously at the cost of struggle, but freely and entirely."[49] So, he explained to Evelyn, while he could no longer love Helen with Eros, "a love of Agape, a tolerance, a kindliness, has taken its place."[50]

He was torn between his love for Evelyn and his responsibility to everything it threatened. He asked, "Can these two rights never be reconciled?" and was "constantly searching . . . to reconcile them in some higher vision of right." He was frustrated in this search, concluding, "I see no future barring an 'act of God,' and that is the hideous truth."[51] Yet at the same time he tentatively questioned whether his sense of obligation to "duty"[52] was a rationalization for timidity and a perpetuation of his longtime deference to Helen as his conscience.

Evelyn had no such conflict of loyalties. When she had been concerned that she was breaking up a marriage and Erwin had urged her to see the psychiatrist Clement Fry, Fry assured her that she was not responsible, that Erwin had been "living with the throttle on"[53] for years. She was baffled by Erwin's need for self-sacrifice. In her bitterest moments she accused him now of enjoying the role of martyr, now of prostituting himself "for a family, security, settled fortune."[54] She understood, yet resented that she must always come to him, at his convenience, traveling from the Ogontz School to New Haven to be with him for whatever hours he could steal from his family and professional commitments.

The friends who knew her situation tended to see it from her perspective. Hazel Barnes, her closest friend, was the exception; as a matter of principle she offered no judgment and refrained from pressing Erwin either to break off the relationship with Evelyn or to divorce Helen. Jean Swauger, Evelyn's Turtle Creek friend and confidante, urged her to insist on a commitment. I, as a fellow student of Evelyn's in the English graduate school program, had known Erwin since they first met, and I shared with her vicariously the raptures and frustrations of their relationship. Having entered Union Theological Seminary in New York City in 1939 to study for a B.D., I saw them when Erwin had professional meetings in New York, and I opened my mother's home in Leonia, New Jersey, to them. Although it was not "conventional morality"[55] that motivated me, as Erwin assumed, I felt that Evelyn should press for a divorce because I saw her as desperate for more than the fragments of a life she had with Erwin. But I came to the conclusion: "He is such an exceptional man, and such a rare spirit, you mustn't regret anything.' "[56]

Evelyn's parents objected strongly to the relationship when they learned of it, for Erwin was two years older than Evelyn's mother, and the father objected to marriage with a divorced man, who would find it hard to support both Evelyn and his first family.

While wrestling with all these issues, Erwin continued his customary domestic and social life. He celebrated the children's birthdays, played Michigan rummy, and went shopping and to the movies with them when they were home. He and Helen dined and danced or had an evening of cards with their friends. They visited Ward at Cornell, John at Groton, Jim at Westminster, Hester at Putney, and Howard Goodhart in New York. Erwin's mother visited them in Woodbridge. There were no outward signs of marital problems.

At the same time, Erwin was making Evelyn's graduate school friends his own after she went to the Ogontz School. He helped Ivria Adlerblum through the ordeal of her oral examination for the English Ph.D. and counseled her in her difficulties with a domineering mother, writing to Evelyn that he "wanted to punch her mother in the nose."[57] He was Hazel Barnes's dissertation adviser in her classics Ph.D. program, became her friend, and reported to Evelyn, "I shall be keenly on the watch for any opportunity to help her"[58] with personal problems. In return, when he read Hazel the manuscript he was working on, "I get a great deal from her encouragement, for she is the only one now who really knows what I am doing, and her comments and faith in it are very helpful."[59] His relations with me were ambivalent at first. We differed sharply in our religious views. But he became my friend and counselor, as he was Ivria's and Hazel's, writing me, "You and I have taken sometime to get acquainted. I think the barriers are pretty well down by now, and may I say that if at any time or in any connection a de facto brother-in-law would come in handy, you may be sure you have one in me."[60]

When Evelyn had gone to Ogontz, he wrote to her, "I had such a feeling that there was a reality in the group—Hazel, Eleanor, Ivria, and

ourselves. . . . I shall always have a very close feeling to them all—would
be glad to have them write me if I can ever help them—or if they would
like to perpetuate what was to me so lovely a thing as the feeling in that
group was."[61] These friends brought him closer to both Evelyn and her
generation, while at the same time he could be their counselor.

Evelyn decided to leave the Ogontz School at the end of her year there
and take a position at the Gateway School for Girls in New Haven in the
fall of 1939. In the summer she and Erwin had two weeks together at
Lake Bonaparte on the western edge of the Adirondacks. For Helen, not
suspecting Erwin's involvement with Evelyn, had suggested that he go
off by himself to have a change.

This time with Evelyn was decisive. When Erwin came back, he
brought himself to tell Helen that he didn't love her and would rather not
live with her. She was hysterical and crushed, but he didn't waver,
buoyed by the prospect of eventually marrying Evelyn. While he and the
family were visiting Howard Goodhart in New York, supposedly enjoying the wonders of the world's fair, he wrote to Evelyn, "These are
among the most horrible days of my life."[62] When in New York he went
to see his sister Dedy in nearby Elmont, Long Island, and she gave him
very helpful advice as to how the children would be hurt by the break
and which ones would feel it most.

When Tom French came East from Chicago, he talked with Erwin
about whether Erwin should undergo analysis. Tom said that analysis
was not in order, that Erwin should rather "hold on and try to break away
from Helen at the earliest possible moment."[63] But when Erwin was in
New York at the Conference on Science, Philosophy, and Religion, he
met a friend, Bob Casey, who disagreed with French. Casey, who had
been analyzed, said that an analysis would give Erwin an understanding
and mastery of his motives before he broke up his home. Such an analysis would cost at least two thousand dollars. But, although he had no luck
in trying to sell his house to raise the money, he decided: "I must be
analyzed to be fair to everyone else, and to myself. I have blundered
along long enough, and now I must know myself before I ruin everything. . . . I see no other way of saving my life."[64] He would raise the
money somehow, somewhere. When he consulted a New Haven analyst,
Edith Jackson, she said he must be analyzed "*at once*,"[65] and he agreed,
for his recurrent diarrhea, which he attributed to his psychological
problems, had been much worse in the last months. So he shopped
around for someone who would charge the minimum, which he would
have to request from the university as a loan.

The analysis never materialized. Goodenough continued to feel the urgency of his problem, writing to his friend Andy Morehouse, "I cannot string along Evelyn, the children, and Helen, to say nothing of myself, much longer."[66] Then, toward the end of 1940, a crisis, an "act of God" he had earlier seen as his only hope, moved him toward a resolution.

One night in late November, after a talk with Helen in which she revealed that "she hates my guts,"[67] then some bridge with the next-door neighbors, he went to bed and took a Seconal. When it did not put him to sleep, because he was wrestling with ways to get rid of the house and be free, he took a bromide. He was still as wakeful as ever, and there was no more Seconal. So he went to Helen's room for a drug her doctor had given her to induce sleep, took half of what she had said was the pre-scribed dose, went back to bed, and was almost instantly asleep. In the morning Helen could not rouse him and called their family doctor, Dr. Brown, who took him to the hospital. Although the interaction of the three drugs was no doubt responsible for his coma, he was put in the psychiatric clinic of the hospital (probably because it was assumed he might have attempted suicide) in what he called the "disturbed ward" and "the insane asylum,"[68] where "patients are not allowed to have even forks"[69] to eat with. But he was soon moved to a convalescent wing, where he spent more than two weeks, at first having no activity and no visitors, then gradually being allowed short visiting hours, gym workouts, and other exercises.

Dr. Brown prescribed a three-month recuperation in a warmer climate, and Goodenough received a semester's leave of absence from Yale. He decided not to go back to the Woodbridge house but to have someone bring him what clothes and other items he needed for a trip, so that when he left the hospital he could get his car and drive out of town. His family would be provided for, as Helen would receive a monthly sum from his salary. When he left the hospital, Christmas was only a week away, but he was in no physical or psychological shape to regret not sharing Christmas with the children.

On 21 December Goodenough headed for sanctuary with his friend Professor Rudolph Willard in Austin, Texas, as advised by Dr. Brown and with the medical leave from Yale. Evelyn went with him as far as Washington, D.C. Then she took the bus to Pittsburgh and her home. After wistfully watching her face recede as he stood on the bus platform, he went on alone. For company on the road he picked up hitchhikers, and when they had no money he bought their meals. One, a freshman at West Virginia University, was "unspeakably dumb";[70] another Goodenough took to be a low-grade moron. But outside Knoxville, Tennessee, he found a lively companion who could share the driving all the way to Texas, which more than repaid Goodenough for the cost of the young man's meals.

Christmas Day he arrived at his friend Willard's house, "with a pile of Bach scores in the trunk of his car,"[71] and he celebrated by a letter of greeting to Evelyn. In a few days Willard helped him to find long-term lodgings 120 miles from Austin, in Kerrville, rolling ranch country at two-thousand-feet altitude. Goodenough arranged to room in one house and board in another, there being a piano in each and horses nearby.

At the end of December he had only eighty cents in his pocket and planned to pawn his watch if he did not receive the check due from New Haven soon, but to compensate he found new, rewarding experiences to which Willard and Willard's friends introduced him. With one of these friends he went to a black church in Austin. The minister rose to preach, but was too ill with the flu to carry on. Goodenough sent up word, offering to take his place, and did so. He told a story of sparrows who flew toward the sun and thus, through light, glorified themselves. The congregation entered into the spirit of his preaching, singing out "O Lord" and "Amen."[72] "It was a great success," he reported to Evelyn. "They loved it, and I had a swell time."[73]

Chapter 8

Kerrville, Texas: The Decision to Seek a Divorce

Goodenough settled in Kerrville on 2 January 1941. His first impression was of "streets full of cowboys in costume, like a movie scene."[1] When he had a closer look, he described it as "just a typical Texas town, a few business blocks, one hotel which is beyond my purse, and otherwise a city of bungalows."[2] He expected the winter climate to be like a New Haven May,[3] but in the three months he spent there he experienced both snow and many cold, wet days that he spent by the fire.[4] His lodgings were on Main Street, two blocks from the post office and the business section. He ate his meals down the street. The food was good, if heavy. But he winced at the crudities of fat Mrs. Paul, the boarding-house owner, who introduced "a fellow feeder" with: "This is Mr. Anderson, oil and gas: oil on the hands, gas on the stomach"[5] and, when Goodenough asked for a napkin, said, "My other boarders eats neat."[6]

At first he saw himself as an exile and a broken man, lacking even the drive to find amusement. Besides being lonely, and weak from his stay in the New Haven Hospital, during the first weeks in Texas he had to have a serious sinus operation in a hospital in San Antonio, and his recovery both there and in Kerrville was slow.

But he soon found ways to pass the time. Although he had never done any horseback riding, he began to ride at a nearby ranch. He was very awkward at first and stiff after each outing. But he found Tony, a horse that he came to love, although he was not usually drawn to animals. At first they rode on the ranch of Tony's owner, which was used for a garbage dump and sewage disposal plant, with "great half wild hogs rooting in the garbage, and the smell of the sewer coming ever and anon across the whole." Then he discovered a gate to an adjacent pasture, and "Tony and I explored and explored to our hearts', and noses', complete content."[7]

He played the piano regularly and soon found two fellow musicians who liked to sing and fiddle while he played. He attended various churches: the Roman Catholic, the Episcopal, the Presbyterian, and the Methodist, where he enjoyed singing "Blessed Assurance" and "I Love to Tell the Story," although "the minister was an utter ignoramus."[8] And he read whatever he could lay his hands on, starting with Henry Adams's *Mont-Saint-Michel and Chartres*. At first he thought it Victorian in its sexual distinction between the masculine Christ and the feminine Virgin; he also saw his own "interpretation of life in terms of art . . . more thrilling."[9] But Adams's passing allusion to "the Virgin acting . . . under as many names as Artemis or Aphrodite had borne"[10] may have suggested his later association of Aphrodite and her symbols with those of the Virgin Mary. And when he finished, he judged it "a marvelous book."[11]

He happened on Paul Leicester Ford's *The Honorable Peter Stirling*, "a classic of American Litt.," published in 1894, which he had never read, although in his childhood it was considered a great book, and found it "an amazing mixture of wonderful writing . . . with drivel."[12] Of the two main themes, the strategies of the hero, an honest politician, and his love for a woman only half his age, the second must have appealed to Goodenough. But the book's outmoded ways of thinking especially struck him, and he recommended it to Evelyn because "the morality, the whole view of life of Ford, sugared with piety and self-righteousness, was the quicksand on which I started out to build my life."[13] He quoted specifically from a paragraph expressing what he called its "utterly hopeless attitude toward sex": "No young girl, however much she loves a man, is quite ready for that first kiss. A man's lips upon her own are too contrary to her instincts and previous training to make them an unalloyed pleasure."[14] His repudiation of the attitudes of Ford's generation led him to conclude that "thanks to you, I think I am coming through all the way to your generation. Certainly I am far more at home with it now than with my own."[15]

Goodenough was one of the supervisors of Hazel Barnes's dissertation on Plotinus. Hazel felt somewhat deserted by Goodenough in her final semester, and he, too, felt it was "desperately hard"[16] to help her from such a distance. Yet he made some suggestions, and working through her ideas gave him intellectual stimulus.

He wrote off the nearby Schreiner Institute, a military preparatory school-junior college, as "a place of appalling mediocrity."[17] But he found some bridge players there to make up a foursome. And he was pleased to be invited to a typical Texan dinner party, with all the heads of the institute for company and venison in many different forms for the "Texan spread."[18]

Dwight Knapp, Goodenough's doctor, and his wife, Mary Lou, were especially congenial and supportive. She had just been through a divorce, before her present marriage. Dwight became a friend as well as his doctor, urging him to feel free to go to his home at any time "whether anyone was there or not, just as a place to go and get cookies out of the jar."[19] As his doctor, Knapp helped him pinpoint his psychological logjam, which Dr. Brown in New Haven had failed to do. Knapp, who had, because of his conscience, remained married for years to a drug addict, showed Goodenough that conscience, not Helen, enslaved him.

He often went to Austin for dinner with Rudolph Willard; Johnny Faulk, then a young folklorist at the University of Texas, and his wife, Hally, and sometimes went with them to concerts. He even arranged to do the entertaining he loved, inviting Rudolph, Johnny, and Hally for a weekend with him in Kerrville. They went to the Knapps for dinner, listened to sermons by black preachers that Johnny was collecting, and Goodenough played for Hally to sing, while Dwight Knapp played the violin. Then, back at his lodgings, he put the Faulks in his bed, and he and Rudolph slept in a tourist-camp room Erwin had rented.[20]

Goodenough also became the friend of a wealthy rancher and his wife, Paul and Rita Raigorodski, who lived eight miles outside town. He thought Mrs. Raigorodski very formal, observing the rules he had come to resent in his life with Helen. But she was interested in Jung and the history of religion, so he found with her the kind of conversation he craved.[21]

At first he worried about the children. He felt that Ward had "kicked" him.[22] For Ward had let him know how he felt about being left as the male head of the family, with his mother emotionally distraught and the children excluded from their father's new life. Ward could not ignore how his father's action had pained him or continue to feel as he formerly had about him.[23] Although Ruth, whom Ward married in February, wrote a "dear note" that brought tears to Goodenough's eyes, Ward's defection "has hurt me more deeply than I have allowed myself to admit or face."[24]

John, who was a freshman at Yale, wrote to his father after meeting Evelyn, accusing him of running away to escape his problems and of leaving his finances in terrible shape, saying that all the family except Erwin had been sacrificing, and that he should break with Evelyn and "get back to sanity."[25] There was, however, a later letter from John, saying that he had written too hastily and that he actually understood his father's position and loved him.

Jim was shocked when Erwin wrote that he was planning to get a divorce and gave the reasons for it, since Jim had not sensed any marital unhappiness.[26] But in a fine letter he convinced Erwin that "his love for me is too deep to renounce me."[27] And there had also been a "sweet" letter from Hester.[28] Erwin did not want to hurt the two younger children—to have them feel that "the man they both so much admire seems to them to have turned out a despicable creature."[29] But there were fewer years of involvement with them than with Ward and John, and he saw less difficulty in continuing to give them love and support in a new relationship.

Goodenough's finances were still a serious obstacle to a complete break with Helen. He owed the university nearly four thousand dollars[30] and could not afford to pay the interest on that loan and keep up the big Woodbridge house and grounds while dividing his income with Helen and the dependent children in a divorce settlement.

But he was gaining new psychological as well as physical strength. Dr. Knapp told him that his dreams showed he was bringing his subconscious into line with his reason, that he was working out his whole life pattern, and was on the way to becoming "an integrated personality . . . and a strong personality such as I have never been."[31] He felt that Evelyn's love had brought this new strong personality into being, that it was "God's own will, who gave you to me, and has joined us forever,"[32] and that his earlier sense of duty to his family was one of his irrational "old hangovers of childish teachings."[33] He wrote to his lawyer in New Haven, asking him to see if the university would buy his house to avoid the delay of a commercial sale.[34] His psychiatrist in Austin approved the move, and Evelyn's daily letters applauded it and assured him they could become financially solvent.

He began a reevaluation of his whole life, encouraged by the belief that God had a purpose in bringing on the break and forcing him to find "a new perspective in this isolation."[35] He found this new perspective in analyst Karl Menninger's *Man Against Himself,* which Dwight Knapp had recommended. For, he wrote, "it has made me see myself as never before, and while the first shock was very distressing, I am at last beginning to get myself adjusted to it, and am greatly helped by the experience. It . . . describes the conflict between the death urge in man and the life urge. The death urge is usually a guilt complex, which makes one, if not a suicide, then a chronic invalid, in which the body actually picks up infections more readily . . . because the person wants the sympathy and mother-love which illness brings. It makes him want to be a martyr, etc. . . . The weakness of my present condition seemed something I was not fighting as I should. . . . Now that I see it I have a new will to live, an abhorrence of my old masochism, as never before. And I feel that a load was lifted from my heart. I am simply going to get strong, and get strong quickly, and come up there and smash those old patterns."[36]

He traced the problem of his conscience to its religious origins in his early Methodist training and its psychological sources in his repressed hatred for his father, his craving for his mother's love, his resentment of his father's love for Helen, and his resultant repressed anger against Helen, for which he substituted idealization of her. He complained of his early upbringing among and by women and criticized his nineteenth-century-type education at Hamilton. He condemned the HenryJames-like sense of expatriation that made him hate to have to return to the United States after the years abroad. He saw the need to repudiate his contempt for his country for, as he looked back on the importance of this change, "my gradual break from the expatriation, my discovery of America, was necessary for me to become a man."[37]

Man Against Himself led him to interpret his years of thinking only of Helen and the children as a "death urge," and to decide he must become completely free of the whole family. He repudiated his "old loyalties and childish sense of duty."[38] As he looked back, he felt that all his life he had tried to live through other people and to get them to live his life for him—first his mother, then Helen, then the children.[39] He rejected his earlier insistence that he could not pull up his roots, "that the old oak could not be transplanted. That was the old. Now, the roots are out, and *the tree is still alive. It could* be done, is being done."[40]

He rejected Plotinus's, Philo's, and Paul's position on the need to subdue the flesh to achieve the life of the spirit. He had been reading Hazel Barnes's dissertation on Plotinus, in which, as she discussed Plotinus's view of katharsis, she reviewed his emphasis on the need for the soul to repudiate the body. He could not accept this or Philo's view that "bodily pleasure . . . is the beginning of wrongs and violation of law, the pleasure for the sake of which men bring on themselves the life of mortality and wretchedness in lieu of that of immortality and bliss."[41] These views were sharply challenged as he read Aldous Huxley's *Point Counter Point,* with its attack on "Jesus diseases"[42] of hatred of the body and sex and Huxley's denial that asceticism was essential to the mystical experience. From his new perspective he wrote, "Plotinus, Philo, Paul, all wanted us to purify ourselves of the flesh to go into a spirit world. Well, I find that the error of my life has been taking that all too seriously. I do want the world of spirit . . . but I know now that whatever the monks could do, my way is the road to the spirit through the flesh–your flesh, and that nothing else can make either matter or spirit real to me any more."[43]

Goodenough continued to value Philo and Paul for other aspects of their thought, but his rejection of their insistence on transcending bodily desires marked a major confirmation of his thinking as to the meaning of many of the symbols he had been examining at Yale. His current experience of the relation of the sexual to the spiritual, and his reading of Freudian psychoanalysts, led him to focus increasingly on the sexual significance of symbols. He reported to Evelyn that his Austin friends Johnny and Hally Faulk "got me going on sex and symbols . . . just ate up all our idealism and true realism."[44] Thus, when he interpreted early Jewish and other symbols, he saw many more of them as sexual than did other scholars and read these sexual symbols as expressions of the spiritual aspirations of those who used them.

Having reevaluated and reoriented himself, Goodenough was ready to return to New Haven at the end of the three-month absence Dr. Brown had prescribed. He left his rooms in Kerrville with some regret and would have liked to buy the house, for these rooms were "profoundly symbolic"[45] to him—the fireplace chairs (in which he imagined himself sitting with Evelyn), the desk on which he wrote and "sat so many hours pouring out my heart to you."[46] But he closed "this chapter of *Texas* correspondence"—the exchange of daily or twice-daily letters—with words paraphrasing 1 Corinthians 13: "When this reaches you the next stage will be to have . . . the perfect love that has put away childish things though not put away the children who have become adult; that casteth out fear; that leadeth to vision face to face; that having endured all things, suffered all things, now abideth as the transcendence of faith and hope. This is before us—yet let not the solemnity obscure the joy of the Lord."[47]

Chapter 9

Jacob Serving for Rachel in Wyoming

On his return to New Haven in the spring of 1941, Goodenough made arrangements for the divorce from Helen.

Throughout the month he spent there, he felt he had the support of his children. John, at Yale, sustained him with his acceptance as Erwin worked on the divorce settlement. John talked to Jim at Westminster School, and this reassured his father, for he felt that John knew how to handle the situation.[1] He was equally pleased with "little Hester: "A more completely intelligent, sane, and loyal reception of the news I could not ask."[2] So, blind to or refusing to recognize the children's unexpressed anger,[3] he could write to Evelyn, "Thus is cleared up the last family obstacle to my going."[4]

He planned to apply for the divorce in Wyoming, which lacked the sensational connotations of Reno, Nevada. Although he dreaded going out there to establish the necessary two months' residence, he repeated to himself the title of the fourth-grade story of Christopher Columbus's voyage: "Going East by Sailing West." Thinking as he did in symbols, he saw the trip as his "last and greatest coming to life through death"— "going West"—and as leaving Evelyn to find her.[5]

It was a two thousand, three hundred-mile drive to Laramie, his goal. After days of flat stretches he was exhilarated to come to the high plains, then the mountains. "The great fertile plains of Nebraska began soon to tip up magically before my eyes," he wrote Evelyn, "and for hundreds of miles it kept steadily up, each town higher than the one before. . . . Always it was the plains until near the end of Nebraska, when we were 3000 ft elevation, it began to roll in long sweeps, but each sweep higher. Then on into Wyoming . . . climbing and climbing until we were 8,000 ft up. . . . I stopped and looked—and looked, just limp with it all. Then down and down an endless hill into Laramie . . . "[6]

Needing a job for the evidence that he was a *bona fide* Wyoming resident, he made many inquiries and was finally hired at St. Michael's Episcopal Mission to the Arapahoe Indians at Ethete, more than two hundred miles northeast of Laramie. In exchange for room and board in the home of the mission school principal, Clifford Wilson, and his family, Goodenough was to be their general handyman and tutor. He swung a scythe, pitched hay, mowed the grass, learned to irrigate, hoed and weeded the bean patch, and trimmed trees. Between garden chores he cleared the manure out of the chicken house, swept the mission buildings, cleaned the toilets, and helped construct the new church at the nearby town of Fort Washakie. Afternoons and evenings he gave Wilson's children and their Indian maid piano lessons, tutored a child in algebra, helped Wilson with theological questions related to the ordination Wilson was studying for, and took tickets for the movies that the mission showed in the gymnasium.[7]

His mood at Ethete swung from elation to depression and finally to quiet satisfaction. At first he was delighted with his capacity for physical work and saw the project as a symbol of his labor of love for Evelyn, resembling "Jacob serving for Rachel."[8] He also enjoyed the chance to observe Indian ceremonials and study their religion and symbols. For symbols had now replaced Philo as what he saw to be his destined work, and he wrote to Evelyn, "There seems a fatality about me and these symbols."[9] He saw the examination of Indian religious symbols as part of his larger project of symbol interpretation. He talked with anyone knowledgeable about Indian symbols, read whatever was available, and began to see the meaning of symbols in Indian life.[10]

The rodeo and other activities of Memorial Day bored him, but "the very tedium and disorganization was a good insight into the way of life of the people." So he concluded that early letter from Wyoming, "Think of me as very happy in this soothing atmosphere and with these kind people."[11]

By the next week his tune changed. "The people here are kind and sweet," he wrote, "but quite dull, and there is nothing in the weeds and grass I spend hours in cutting to put into letters. I feel I am just becoming a loving animal."[12] Again, "All the things I used to live in and by, and which I would take for granted, are cut away from me; not even this wild strange country seems real to me, often, and in waking states I feel lost in a nightmare of delusion."[13]

When he wrecked his car he felt completely marooned and dependent on an unknown "someone"[14] to get away from Ethete. After he developed an arm infection, he admitted that he hated the work: "I crave a good time, a giggle, and hate myself for the craving when I am working out this time for *you*."[15] Among the factors that kept him from gaining weight he listed "inner friction at the kind of work which has always been distasteful to me, and remains so subconsciously in spite of my efforts to put poetry into it. . . . Lack of fun in these surroundings."[16]

His complaint over lack of fun was an exaggeration prompted by a low mood. He played the piano regularly, both for his own pleasure and for others, and he delighted in playing hymns for a group to sing.[17] There was badminton, which he enjoyed, and he often found partners for bridge. He was excited by a trip north, which meant crossing the Continental Divide at nine thousand, six hundred feet and seeing the Grand Tetons, "one of the amazing sights of America. Incredibly they rise just jagged shafts of rock with snow in the crevices. I never saw mountains anything like them!"[18] The Fourth of July at nearby Landor, where he watched Indian dances and representations of different periods in Wyoming history, was "a day—to remember all my life." He danced with Alice Shave Head, an Indian friend, "and we had a marvelous dance, she a fat old hag of a woman in a black dress, a red silk handkerchief tied on her hair, and some sort of boddice [*sic*], on which were sewed at least a hundred elks' teeth. . . . I shall teach you that dance . . . though to get it right one has to have six Indians pounding a single drum in a marvelous rhythm, and wailing a formless chant, now quietly, now in high screams, to the thumping."[19]

For all the drudgery, his experience led him to rethink his values. As he pruned the trees on the mission grounds he imagined himself cutting off his own weaknesses, among them "this great branch my social dependence; this great branch my dependence upon my children; this great branch my academic pride and craving for recognition."[20] During a High Episcopal "Mass" he watched the priest in his bright green vestments consecrating the Host, while through a side window he saw a pair of sparrows outside making love, and, struck by what he saw as the contrast between artificial and natural religion, he concluded, "What is man that thou art mindful of him?"[21] Another time, he wrote, "To be a mountain, completely self contained, growing pines, wearing a snowy miter, warm in the depths, anchored to the earth, but cool and sharply, cuttingly, pinnacled at the top, piercing the blue of the heavens. Beautiful, but indifferent to its own beauty. Conscious only of its strength to cut the sky, and to pour out clear water at its base. That is true living, and God grant I may come somewhere near it."[22]

As the divorce negotiations continued, Goodenough's lawyer insisted that he come to Laramie for the proceedings. Looking back on his stay at the mission, Goodenough exclaimed that his letters could not have adequately expressed "such experiences of sorrow, agony, discouragement, victory, vision, perception, ecstasy, as have been packed into these months."[23] Although dreading the move, he took the bus to Laramie and found a rooming house for $4.00 a week and a week's board for $5.30, at "a pretty crummy joint."[24]

He had kept up his work as editor of *The Journal of Biblical Literature* in Ethete during hours free from grass cutting and piano and algebra lessons. In Laramie he continued the editorial involvement. For, after the half-year absence because of ill health and the divorce, he felt that once back at Yale "I must show them that my divorce has in no sense incapacitated me, and that they need not feel . . . that I am broken and through."[25]

Goodenough's divorce was granted in Laramie on 25 July 1941. Because the bus was ten dollars cheaper than the train, he took a Trailways bus to Pittsburgh, where he arrived pale, unshaven, rumpled, and generally bedraggled from the long, hot trip. When Evelyn met him she was shocked by his appearance. But as she expressed it humorously in a document she dated 30 July 1941: "I, Evelyn Ivy Wiltshire, being of sound mind and body, free, white, and twenty-one, do hereby, for value received and hereby acknowledged, pledge and betroth myself for the bonds of Holy Wedlock, now and evermore, to Erwin Ramsdall Goodenough, of uncertain age and competence."[26] They bought a secondhand Ford with the seventy-five dollars she had saved and drove to Emporium, a small town about 130 miles northeast of Pittsburgh, where they had decided to be married.

Erwin was eager for an immediate secret marriage, to protect Evelyn if their relations should be disclosed. They chose 9 August as the date, and Erwin was ready with a newly cleaned white suit and whitened white shoes. But the Ford broke down the day before, so he had to shake out his old, black suit from his bag and polish his old, black shoes, as more appropriate for the transportation to the court house in the truck of the mechanic from the garage where the Ford languished. Then, with license in hand, on to the justice of the peace, Geo. F. Gallaher, optometrist: "A huge Irishman he was, with a great body, huge head, and small features." When Gallaher admonished his imaginary audience about speaking now or hereafter holding its peace, "he paused but not a single chair or flower in the wall paper protested." There was trouble ahead, however, with Erwin's name.

"Repeat after me, please: 'I, Edwin, . . .'"

"Erwin."

"Ratstail . . ."

"Ramsdell!"

Evelyn's last name was pronounced "Whitshire" by the official rather than Wiltshire, but Erwin let that go "since she was so beautifully abandoning it anyway, and said the words by which I took her for my wife. She took me for her husband; I put on the ring in the name of the Holy Trinity, but we were pronounced married in virtue of the power conferred on one Geo. F. Gallaher by the Commonwealth of Pennsylvania. I was much confused as to what greater power had done it, but it was done—my sweet Evelyn was my wife."[27]

Having described the whole scenario to Johnny and Hally Faulk as hilarious, he concluded more seriously, "Geo. has bound my sweet Evelyn and me together, and if we have to thumb a bit to get through life, she will be beside me as she was today in her lovely white dress, her beautiful spirit, to giggle with me, and bless my heart."[28]

Chapter 10

A New Life and *Jewish Symbols in the Greco-Roman Period*

After the months in Texas and Wyoming, the divorce, and the secret marriage, Goodenough went back to his teaching and research at Yale in September 1941. He arranged to live in a bed-sitting room in the Hall of Graduate Studies and furnished it from the Woodbridge house, which was rented until it could be sold. He was nervous about rumors that there was "another woman" responsible for his divorce, which Helen's friends circulated, but relieved when the administration expressed no such concern.

Helen was deeply distressed, but with the support of her older children and her friends she restructured her life. In 1942 she became the house head of Martha Wilson House at Smith College and remained there until 1953, when she retired because of illness. From Northampton she moved to Rockport. In 1958 she became engaged to a widower, who died suddenly before they were to be married. She lived alone in Rockport until 1979 when, at eighty-eight, crippled with arthritis, she entered a nursing home, where she died at ninety-three.

In the fall of 1941 Evelyn was teaching and living at the Gateway School, and they were very discreet in their meetings. Then the Wiltshires announced their daughter's marriage on 29 January 1942, and there was no need for further secrecy. Erwin and Evelyn went to live in a pleasant apartment at 5 St. Ronan Terrace, on the second floor of the Gateway School, and their two children were born there.

Evelyn had always wanted a husband who would be an ideal father of the children she was eager to have, and she saw Erwin as such a father. Initially, he had no interest in more children and would have enjoyed a life with only Evelyn, but he appreciated her need, and a print of Picasso's *Mother and Child* had a prominent place in their living room. Ursula Wiltshire was born on 16 March 1943, Daniel Adino on 6 July 1944.

(Erwin, always an admirer of physical strength, liked the Goodenough family name Adino because in the King James version of the Old Testament Adino is one of David's "mighty men," who "lift up his spear against eight hundred.")[1]

These children became as special to him as those of his first marriage had been. Ursula was baptized in their home by a Presbyterian minister friend,[2] Evelyn's mother and I "standing up" as godparents. For Daniel's baptism Erwin called upon another friend, this time a Lutheran minister,[3] whom he vested with his scarlet Oxford gown to give the occasion the proper pageantry.

A young woman who lived across the hall at the Gateway School recalled, years later, that she saw the Goodenoughs as an ideal family. Erwin was more lenient than he had been with his first children. But he was just as proud of Ursula's precocity as he had been of Ward's, writing that she, not quite two, "now sings fifteen songs as I play them on the piano, and her talking is similarly interesting."[4] He nicknamed Ursula and Daniel "Sulie" and "Danny" and composed a verse for each, expressing the traditional view of gender differences that reflected a deeply rooted, unconscious sexism. For Ursula it was:

Ursula, Sulie, Sukey, Sue
Call her whatever pleases you
She'll be a lady and cook on a stove
Serve a fine tea and powder her nose.

And for Danny:

Danny Danny dumpling, my son Dan,
He'll grow up to be a great big man.
He'll grow whiskers and drive a truck
And take a helicopter up.[5]

He summed up the early years of his new life in a letter of 1945 to Olga Fröbe-Kaptayn, the founder of the Eranos conferences on Eastern and Western religions and the study of Jungian thought, in Ascona, Switzerland, whom he had met in the United States in 1940. Not having corresponded since then, he now wrote that he had married "a beautiful girl, much younger than I, and since then I have been increasingly happy in spite of the pharisaic censorship which most of my former friends thought it their duty to manifest. I have two beautiful new babies and have carried on through the strain of the war years, teaching summers and winters consistently since the autumn of 1941, yet getting done a great deal of the best writing I have ever produced."[6]

In 1946 he and Evelyn bought a white-clapboard two-family corner house at 264 Fountain Street and lived there until they moved to Cambridge in 1960. The fact that part of the house dated from the eighteenth century delighted Erwin, for it gave him a sense of history, as he wrote in *Toward a Mature Faith,* "The screams of travail, the agony of death, the funerals, the weddings, the generations of young children, the joys of hundreds of birthdays and Christmases, tragedy, drunkenness, happy passion and illicit love—all these, I know, have gone on in this house. Now in living in it I live in the rich echoes of all that life. It is my own, and I am only adding one more life pattern to its continuity."[7]

They chose a two-family house for financial reasons, since the rental of the other half helped to meet the mortgage payments, which were a burden because of the alimony Erwin was paying Helen and the yearly payments of six hundred dollars on an earlier loan from Yale.

In 1947 they opened their home to their friend, the distinguished linguistics scholar Leonard Bloomfield, and his wife, Alice, known as Goodie. The Bloomfields had been living at the Taft Hotel until Leonard had a stroke and was hospitalized. Goodie could not function in the hotel alone because she was mentally unstable. The Goodenoughs therefore took her to stay with them, and after Leonard left the hospital, no nursing home would take them both. So he joined his wife at the Goodenoughs. Erwin was very kind to Leonard, and a dinner guest at the time recalled how Erwin as host made Leonard feel he was an active part of the group, although he was practically helpless and his speech was limited and slurred.[8] The rent was welcome, and Goodie always had a nurse whom Evelyn could rely on to keep an eye on the children when she and Erwin went out in the evening. But the quarters were very crowded, especially since there was only one bathroom for both families. The Bloomfields remained with them until 1949, when Leonard died; after that Goodie stayed on alone there until her death. This hospitality and kindness was characteristic of Erwin's feeling of responsibility for others.

He continued to idealize Evelyn, writing, "I adore you, my sweet, my dear embodiment and vision of loveliness and beauty."[9] When she and the children were visiting her parents and he was alone in New Haven, he lamented, "Oh my dear my darling, you are all so sweet. I move about, and feel as though I was in a dream. I am a ghost haunting the castle . . . ruins."[10] Again, during another absence, "It was as though all tone had gone out of the piano, the color faded from the dress."[11] He wrote, in emulation of Apuleius's "Isis aretalogy" in the *Metamorphoses*, "Some call her Isis, says Apuleius, some Persephone, some Aphrodite, some Astarte, and some, I might add, Mary the Mother of God; but I just call her Evelyn and find infinite love and infinite life, in her sacred lozenge, infinite sustenance in her nipples and lips. Dear, dear goddess, as I become a baby in your arms I come near to being God almighty himself."[12]

Before their marriage Evelyn had written him a light verse, "The Student to Her Love," in which she assured him:

> If I could live with you and be your wife
> Never need you wash every dirty knife
> Or iron or mend your clothes or scrub the floors;
> For I myself would do the menial chores![13]

But in fact he took an active part in the domestic routine, as he had with Helen. And he relished advising her, teaching her to cook, as he had earlier taught her to drive, and counseling her on various aspects of child rearing.

He also advised her in choosing a career. He had earlier discouraged her from continuing as his research assistant, which she had been briefly, and urged her instead to pursue her interest in early-childhood education, which he saw as a promising new profession as well as appropriate for a mother. Evelyn's interest in the subject had begun as an observer of Ursula's and Daniel's classes in the Gesell Institute's nursery school and continued when she was asked to head the nursery school, after Dr. Gesell retired. Since she had no academic training in early-childhood education, on Erwin's advice she enrolled in Yale's graduate program on a part-time basis, receiving her Ph.D. in education in 1956, with a dissertation that led to the publication in 1989 of *Boys and Girls at Play: The Development of Sex Roles in Young Children*.

Apart from the professional opportunities such a new field offered, both the subject and the commitment to only part of the day fitted well with Erwin's view of a woman's role as wife and mother, which he defined in *Toward a Mature Faith*: "She is not truly a mother who does not find in her children's satisfaction and growth the most important part of her own growth, to the point that she has largely forgotten the problem of her own growth. The woman who has personal ambitions, social, financial or other, so that her children and household duties are a frustration to her, is indeed disloyal in her heart, one who seeks satisfaction for herself outside the family. It is not that a woman should have no outside contacts or interests. . . . But when outside appointments, or the desire for them, interfere with her wholeheartedly identifying herself with her husband and children, not only will her family suffer, her own ego will go sour."[14] This view, which, he naively assumed, also represented Evelyn's, was clearly rather a reflection of his own sexist attitude.

Erwin did not fulfill the conventional father role. He didn't take the children to museums or watch Daniel play soccer, and Saturdays he usually went to the library rather than joining them in outdoor activities. But he never took research or writing home, and he spent the evenings with the family, as he had during his first marriage, playing the piano, composing songs, reading poetry, or playing gin rummy with the children. And in spite of what they felt about the priority he placed on his scholarship, he gave the children deep emotional bonding. Daniel remembers that Erwin never failed to climb the stairs to their third-floor bedrooms to kiss them good night and that, when he and his father went to hear a musical performance together and Daniel cried, his father made him feel his tears were validated by saying, "You cry like me."[15] Ursula loved him so passionately that she was jealous of her mother, she later told Evelyn.

Although Erwin lost some former relationships because of the divorce, he had both continuing and new ones. Andy Morehouse of the Romance languages department and his wife, Pokey, were close friends, as were Herman Weigand of the German department and Frank Baumer of the history department and his wife. Yale President Whitney Griswold wrote in 1955 that he could not adequately tell Erwin "what your constant faith and friendship have meant to me. They are among the most cherished rewards of my whole life. I only hope I may continue to deserve them."[16]

Erwin also shared Evelyn's old friends. He wrote to Hazel Barnes, who was then teaching at the University of Colorado, Boulder, "My blessing for your own brave life of searching. Evelyn and I love you."[17] He and Evelyn enjoyed visiting me in New Jersey and, later, in South Glastonbury, Connecticut, where I lived with my husband and children.

He had always delighted in a party, finding conversation with friends more interesting than the theater and enjoying his own parties more than those others gave. He instructed Evelyn in the fine points of entertaining, very different from the required olives, celery, white tablecloth, and maid that Erwin had come to chafe under when Helen had dinner guests. He and Evelyn always created an informal, friendly ambience. Erwin was an expert at mixing cocktails, and he also saw to it that wine

Erwin with Ursula and Dan, 1951.

accompanied the meal to sustain the elevated mood created at the cocktail hour. Guests included scholars, physicians, artists, and singers. Time and again friends expressed their enjoyment of these intellectually stimulating, yet relaxed, occasions, with the chance for old and new encounters. Erwin, interested in art, music, psychology, and literature, relished displaying his knowledge in these different fields. When he hosted a recital featuring Helen Boatwright, a well-known soprano, she included in her repertoire nursery songs he had composed for the children and love songs for Evelyn. His daughter Ursula, who grew up in this environment, when looking back, commented, "My father sort of saw himself as a larger-than-life figure and very much played up to that role. He hosted lots of dinner parties where other faculty were invited, and it was all a very serious affair, with engaging, sometimes outrageous conversation. There was a lot of theater."[18]

At first the family vacationed at Wellfleet, Cape Cod, and at North Hero, a Methodist retreat on Grand Isle, Lake Champlain. Then they bought a cottage on Cedar Island, off Clinton, Connecticut, which could be reached only by boat. Erwin delighted in meeting guests at the Clinton dock and rowing them to the island, although once he made headlines in the New Haven newspaper because his boat sank and he had to be rescued by the Coast Guard. They spent entire summers at Cedar Island, since it was only a half-hour drive if they needed to return to New Haven.

In July and August of 1950 Evelyn, who had never been abroad, spent six weeks in Europe traveling alone and thereby "satisfied a longing of many years."[19] Although Erwin had strongly encouraged her to make the trip, he wrote that "to stand and see you go until you were lost in the mist above the sea was one of the most intense moments of my life. . . . I had a strange feeling that something was attached to the plane and was steadily pulling out of me, like Ariadne's thread, pulled so that I could feel it go out and out in a really physical sensation.[20] But he was delighted that his "darling little Flyaway Girl"[21] could see England, from which her father had emigrated as a young man, with Oxford, which Erwin knew so intimately, and Paris and the other cities on the Continent that he had visited in the early twenties. So he wrote her, "Remember me sweetly at times, but mostly forget us in the experiences of the moment";[22] and again, "I feel about you as I do about a child away at school. The better time you have, the more fun, the more gaiety . . . the better."[23] He bought a typewriter so that he could type the letters she wrote him, because he wanted to share her "great gift of creative writing"[24] and could, obviously, not use his assistant for that purpose. Because he was afraid that the Korean conflict would result in rationing like that of World War II, he stocked up on six pairs of nylon hose for her "at $1.50 each, the best they had."[25]

Although he could look for help from Goodie Bloomfield's attendants, he was himself a skilled caretaker, ironing the children's clothes, mopping the floor, cleaning the cellar, mowing the lawn. He maintained the children's usual schedule, and they said grace at dinner, as they always did as a family. Taking the place of Evelyn in the kitchen, he made cookies with them. He also endured less congenial activities, going with them on picnics to the beach, although he never liked meals where he had to eat without a knife and fork.

Then he welcomed Evelyn back with great fanfare.

When Goodenough settled into the fall 1950 semester at Yale, buoyed by his fulfilling personal life, he engaged in his professional activities with energy and enthusiasm. He was secretary of the history department. He conducted an occasional noonday religious service at Yale's Battell Chapel. He was often a speaker at the Unitarian Society of New Haven. As for the priority he gave to teaching or research, there are sharply differing accounts. His daughter Ursula affirms that his attitude was summed up in his saying: "Teaching is like writing on sand."[26] Samuel Sandmel, his graduate student and later friend, wrote, "I have never known a scholar quite so content with scholarship as Erwin"; [27] but he also described him as "that rare academician who felt that his obligation to his students was greater than his obligation to his own scholarship."[28] And Sandmel stated that Erwin was only half serious when he said, in another version of Ursula's quotation, that "teaching undergraduates was like writing on water," for when Sandmel confronted him with it, he responded, "I guess I feel that way some of the time . . . but after all, if you're a scholar, it's because you have people to teach."[29] Erwin pointed to the satisfaction of teaching as an example of successful living in *Toward a Mature Faith:* "When the struggling mediocre student begins, even at what would be a low level for a bright boy, to grasp a subject; when the boy of brilliant mentality masters and begins to think independently and creatively, so that he nettles the professor by asking questions which throw the professor off base; this is real 'finding himself' for the professor who has properly identified himself with his students."[30]

While *Toward a Mature Faith* states that the teacher finds himself in his students' development, Goodenough gives a rather different view of the satisfaction he found in his work in "The Mystical Value of

Scholarship," his favorite essay.[31] There he speaks of "the call" to study as a spiritual call in which the scholar finds a fulfillment he can not find elsewhere—in which he is not only teaching the young and contributing to knowledge, but "saving his own soul."[32] Goodenough describes scholarship in Platonic terms as the discovery of a form or a pattern within the phenomena of data: the scholar's goal is to discover meaning in the seemingly meaningless. For Goodenough, when constructive research goes beyond the accumulation of information or commenting on the implications of an already established theory, it is pursuing a religious quest. It seeks to develop a new understanding of some small aspect of life, and the scholar's experience of seeing the pattern he has found validated is, for Goodenough, similar to that of the mystic. This essay summarizes Goodenough's conception of scholarship as he came to view it in midlife. In line with his religious upbringing and his early sense of destiny, he views scholarship as a "call," and the pursuit of the form or pattern behind phenomena as a mystical pursuit. It shares with the mystic the search for and discovery of meaning, and at its best it can be "a sacrament."[33]

Goodenough continued his interest in the origins of Christianity as editor of the *Journal of Biblical Literature* from 1934 to 1942, and in 1945 he published an essay, "John, a Primitive Gospel," in the journal. This essay challenges the widespread, although not universal, assumption of biblical scholars that John is later than the synoptic Gospels (Matthew, Mark, Luke) and dependent on them for its material. After refuting the reasons for presuming a late date of John, Goodenough presents his evidence for John's independence of the synoptic tradition, pointing out that John knew nothing of the Virgin Birth and has a different account of the Eucharist's establishment. He then states the thesis he had developed in his studies of Philo—the importance of Hellenistic Judaism at this time—and sees John's portrayal of Jesus as the result of his encounter with Judaism in a Hellenistic synagogue either in Palestine or the Dispersion. Therefore, he concludes, "Jn represents a primitive attempt to explain Jesus' person and work by seeing in him a fulfillment of pre-Christian dreams of the Logos-Life-Light of God made available to men."[34]

Goodenough's thesis met immediate criticism. In the same issue of the *Journal of Biblical Literature* Robert Casey asserted that Goodenough's substitution of oral tradition and lost materials for documents that indicate John's dependence on the synoptics leaves earliest Christianity "in a fog of vain conjecture."[35] To which Goodenough replied, in the same issue, arguing for the greater value of trying to reconstruct the oral traditions and lost records John may have used rather than to limit the interpretation of John to the known documents—the synoptic Gospels.[36]

Extensive commentary on the date and origin of John followed Goodenough's article, much of it prompted by the discovery of the Dead Sea Scrolls and the Coptic Gnostic manuscripts at Nag Hammadi in 1945. New Testament authority C. H. Dodd, in *Historical Tradition in the Fourth Gospel* (1963), saw John, as Goodenough did, to be mostly independent, drawing upon traditional material as the synoptic writers did.[37] In 1985 J. A. T. Robinson's *The Priority of John,* published posthumously, proposed that John is "a primary source."[38] On the other hand, Anthony Hanson, in *The Prophetic Gospel* (1991), supported D. Moody Smith, considered to be the "dean of U.S. Johannine specialists,"[39] in Smith's conclusion in *Johannine Christianity* (1984) that John came after the synoptics.[40]

"John, a Primitive Gospel" was reissued in 1990 by A. T. Kraabel in a collection of essays, *Goodenough on the Beginnings of Christianity,* with an introductory commentary in which Kraabel stated that this essay is "still frequently cited by students of the gospel of John."[41] D. B. Wallace in "John 5:2 and the Date of the Fourth Gospel" in *Biblica* (1990) described it as a "provocative study."[42] In 1993 Craig A. Evans included it in the bibliography of *Word and Glory: On the Exegetical and Theological Background of John's Prologue* (1993).[43] And scholars who do not mention Goodenough for the most part give John a first-century date and see it as a Jewish gospel,[44] one at least concluding, as Goodenough did, that it drew on "the world of Hellenistic Judaism."[45] The discussion continued at the 1994 Society of Biblical Literature meeting's session on "The Gospel of John at the Close of the Twentieth Century." Goodenough would be gratified by such a session, for he was not only an early stimulator of discussion on the subject, but always valued the examination of new evidence by younger scholars.

While he followed various interests in the articles he published during the 1940s, the study of Jewish symbols was Goodenough's main commitment and satisfaction, as he wrote to Joseph Maguire, a former graduate student and friend, "What fun it all is. I only wish I could keep it up just like this for another thirty years—then I could possibly get done what I should like to do."[46] He was convinced that the extent and nature of these symbols would demonstrate the existence of a Jewish art during the Greco-Roman period. Beyond that, as he became increasingly interested in the psychology of religion, he saw these symbols as an expression of basic human hopes and longings and part of a continuum of representations of similar hopes and values in different cultures. In 1939, when he read *Sartor Resartus* on Evelyn's recommendation, he had been impressed by Carlyle's emphasis on the importance and continued need for the renewal of symbols, writing to her, "Its ideas on the necessity of restating symbols, on symbolism in general, are, you will know, very congenial to me, and I was thrilled by the book."[47] Specific to his interest in explaining the development of early Christianity, he was convinced that the early Jewish symbols would testify to the prevalence of a Hellenistic Judaism that was an important strand in this development.

He had been introduced to the probable existence of Jewish art during his Oxford years, when a student suggested to him that some mosaics the student had seen in Santa Maria Maggiore in Rome resembled the Old Testament allegories of Justin Martyr that Goodenough was studying. Goodenough went to Santa Maria Maggiore to examine the mosaics and was convinced that they were Christian borrowings from the art of Hellenistic Judaism, just as he attributed Justin Martyr's allegories to the literature of Hellenistic Judaism. But when he shared his ideas with several Oxford dons, they all said that no such Jewish art existed. So he gave up the notion and did not mention it in his dissertation on Justin. Instead, he turned to Philo, to find out from Philo whether the literature of Hellenized Judaism might explain how Christianity, which began in Palestine, was Hellenized so early and so easily.

In 1928 the likelihood that there was indeed a Jewish art recurred to him when Paul Baur published an article on an early lamp with an Old Testament scene, for Goodenough thought that the lamp might well be Jewish. But again he was told that could not be, because there was no Jewish art, hence the lamp with its scene was clearly a Christian artifact.

Then, in 1932, he was describing his theory about a possible Jewish art and his supporting material to his colleague Professor Rostovtzeff, when Rostovtzeff interrupted him with, "But have you not heard about our cable from Dura?" Yale and the French Academy of Inscriptions and Letters had excavated the ancient trading city of Dura-Europos on the Euphrates River. Their findings included a third-century synagogue that had walls covered with paintings of Biblical scenes, as the cable reported. When Goodenough saw the photographs of these paintings, he was sure he was looking at the Jewish art of his theory. As he proudly stated in *Jewish Symbols,* "I had prophesied the existence of an art and had described its essential features, and now my prophecy had been fulfilled."[48] Still, no one else at that time saw these paintings at Dura as having the mystic meanings of Hellenistic Judaism. So, after writing *By Light, Light* to point out the literary sources of this Judaism, in 1934, with *By Light, Light* in the press, he began the long process of accumulating evidence of Hellenistic Jewish art.

Goodenough's interest in the psychological meaning of symbols was early awakened by his close association with the analyst Thomas French, his sister Dedy's husband, with whom he talked at length about Freud and psychotherapy. His focus on the psychological aspect of the Jewish symbols was encouraged by Carl Jung when Jung was at Yale. Jung gave the Terry lectures on "Psychology and Religion" in 1937,[49] and Goodenough wrote, years later, that in 1938 "he spent many hours in my study, scrutinizing the material I was gathering, and giving highly stimulating suggestions as to its meaning. More and more I came to think in terms of the new world of the unconscious which Freud and Jung had opened up"[50]—as a key to the meaning of the Jewish symbols.

His discussions about undergoing analysis, his talks in Texas with Dr. Knapp about Freud's and Jung's theories, his reading of Menninger's *Man against Himself*—all disposed him to explore further the psychological meanings of the Jewish symbols. The perceptions he gained from Jung's "Concerning the Two Kinds of Thinking" in *Psychology of the Unconscious* and Suzanne Langer's *Philosophy in a New Key,* published in 1942, gave him additional insights into the psychological aspects of religious symbols.[51]

During these years his relationship with Evelyn convinced him that the sexual desires that as an adolescent he had been taught to repress and that he felt had been frustrated in his first marriage were avenues to the spiritual. He therefore gave increased attention to the sexual aspects of religious symbols. By early 1940 he was stressing their phallic meanings in various lectures.[52] As he wrote to Evelyn, he shocked his colleagues in the Department of Religion with his interpretations. Professor Austin Harmon of the classics department vigorously rejected his theories. And a prankster placed cutouts of little rabbits on Goodenough's desk to poke fun at his emphasis on the erotic meaning of symbols like the Easter bunny,[53] which he claimed represented fertility (because of its reproductive rate), thus the source of life, hence the Resurrection.

He was hurt by these rejections of his theories, but unshaken. In a letter to Evelyn he regretted that he must alienate "the people with whose spiritual life I am most akin . . . because of the symbols and ideas in which my religious experience must find expression." Among these he might have had in mind Amos Wilder. They had known each other since they met at Oxford and later when Wilder took his Ph.D. at Yale in 1933 and went on to teach at the Andover Newton Theological School. Wilder admired Goodenough but felt he had taken the wrong direction when he came under the influence of the psychological theories of Jung and members of the Eranos conferences.[54] "Yet," the letter to Evelyn continued, "I am convinced that on the whole, if I can work this all out, I am in a position to present religion to my contemporaries which those people have permanently lost."[55]

In another letter of the same period he gave full credit to Evelyn for what he described as the "house" he was building, saying, "I did have the basic idea—yes—but I did not have the reality. I could write about it, but it was not my warm present experience. Consequently what I am writing about Dionysus is much better, cuts much deeper, and is *so much* more vital than what I wrote about Egypt before I knew you. That is, *you* are in it."[56]

In May 1940 he wrote to Wallace Notestein, a colleague in history, "I have got about fifty thousand words written on my book, and the quality I think is excellent. With a good summer of work ahead of me I should round out the twelve months with a decent bit of accomplishment. The work that I am doing is fascinating beyond description."[57] And later that month to Olga Fröbe-Kaptayn, "The ideology of the symbols is working into a convincing whole with convincing evidence for each step in a way quite beyond my fondest expectations. . . . That there was something in paganism which really could be attractive to Jews and Christians alike . . . is only too obvious from their borrowings. Yet that something has never been reconstructed, and now I am really beginning to hope that I shall make a beginning of reconstructing it."[58]

By 1945 he was able to report to Olga Fröbe-Kaptayn: "My work on the Jewish symbols has grown and grown. I have it now blocked out in four volumes, of which one volume (the second) is finally done, and about three-fourths of the rest in first draft."[59] In 1946 his friend Morton Enslin exclaimed in a letter, "How busy you are with that volume which is to encompass two thousand pages and all the world's knowledge."[60] And two years later Goodenough wrote, when he sent Enslin a section he had been working on, "Naturally I am terribly stage struck at letting you see this. It, whether sound or not, is so novel an approach that for this and all the work I am doing I frequently wake up nights in terror and despair."[61]

After Jung met Goodenough in 1937, he spoke of him to Mrs. Fröbe-Kaptayn, with whom Jung was closely associated. When she met Goodenough during her visits to the United States, she found out that he needed financial assistance for his work on symbols, suggested that he apply to the Bollingen Foundation, which supported scholarship and research in such projects, and wrote to John Barrett, editor of the Bollingen series of publications, "He is one of those scholars who go their own way . . . and, based on what Jung has said of him, I think this is one of the cases suited to the Bollingen fellowships."[62] Goodenough applied for a grant, having written Jung for his endorsement, and eloquently pleaded to Barrett his need to be relieved of the routines preceding publication: "Years spent in such drudgery would seem all the more tragic to me since with the completion of this work I shall at last be ready to begin the work I have all my life been preparing to do, namely to write an equally extensive study of the origins of Christianity in view of all the new material I have presented on its Jewish and symbolic background. I am by no means an old man, only 54, but old enough so that the completion of this whole program will require steady application."[63]

In 1948 the foundation approved a grant-in-aid of four thousand dollars for a research assistant to type Goodenough's manuscript and verify his references and to buy the photographs needed for illustrating his work. He wrote gratefully to Mrs. Fröbe-Kaptayn that they "have come all out in their help to me, and for research assistance have given me $3500 a year until the work is completed. With this I have hired Dr. Beatrice Goff who worked with me a year or two ten years ago, and knows the project very well. Her help is quite incredible in its scope and depth, and the work will not only appear years sooner for her help, but will be tremendously improved throughout by her criticisms. . . . Miss Goff and I are now making splendid progress, and all is rosy."[64]

Dr. Goff's responsibility was not only to transcribe Goodenough's almost illegible handwriting in pencil on yellow typewriter paper, but to read relevant works in various languages and offer constructive suggestions on his interpretations of his materials. She became a part of his personal as well as his professional life, always willing to take the children on outings. At times he found her trying, for it seemed to him that she felt she was not adequately appreciated. He also began to resent some of the corrections she proposed, and when Evelyn was abroad in 1950, he complained to her how difficult "dear Beatrice" could be.[65] Dr. Goff minimized whatever tensions she, in turn, might have felt. For years later she wrote in a festschrift in his memory, "Whatever new avenues I may have followed . . . I am constantly in his debt. Thus I am happy to contribute this article to the volume in memory of Professor Erwin R. Goodenough, pioneering scholar, guide, and friend."[66]

The Bollingen Foundation support continued until the *Symbols* volumes were completed. It also provided Goodenough with a travel grant of nine thousand dollars, so that he and Evelyn could visit the main museums and sites where the Jewish symbols he had identified were located, and he could photograph many of them. In February 1951 they set out for a seven-month trip. From Paris they went to Tunis, Carthage, Tripoli, Benghazi, Cyrene, Cairo, Luxor, Alexandria, Beirut, Damascus, Jerusalem, Nazareth, Cyprus, Istanbul, Athens and Delphi, Rome, Siena, Florence, Alassio, Nice, and back to Paris. Then they proceeded to England and Germany, on to Switzerland and the Eranos Conference at Ascona. The trip ended officially there, but they went down to Lake Maggiore purely for pleasure, before the flight home.

Erwin could rely on Evelyn to take care of all the schedules and travel arrangements, as well as to keep records of the scholars they saw and the objects they viewed and photographed. She learned where in Beirut and Damascus to shop for embroideries, for glassware, and for the Oriental rugs that everyone admired when they covered their floors and tables with them on their return.

In Tripoli the Arabs were overly attentive to Evelyn, much to Erwin's amusement rather than annoyance, and to Evelyn's disgust at his lack of concern. In the desert they stayed at a British army camp named Marble Arch, near where Erwin found good grape, vine, and the goddess Victory symbols. In Benghazi the materials he found in some ruins so excited him that he climbed over these ruins like a goat.

In Cairo they were delighted with the treasures of the Coptic Museum and the Egyptian Museum. The administrators of the Egyptian Museum were so impressed with Erwin's official blue-sealed letter from Yale that they brought out boxes "full of the most magnificent phalli I have ever seen," Evelyn wrote in her diary, adding, "What a way to spend the Sabbath!"[67] In Luxor the egyptologist Alexandre Piankoff guided them through the tombs in the Valley of the Kings and interpreted the symbolic representations. They saw figures with large phalli in dark tombs, and Evelyn was amused to see Erwin flashing his light on the breasts of other figures, "trying to decide if they were full enough to be female, what kind of nipples they had, etc."[68] Her amusement did not interfere with her careful listing of all the tombs' relevant symbols; for she had

Erwin at Lake Maggiore, 1951.

early noted in her diary, "Erwin's work is taking on an immediate interest to me that is most rewarding."[69] Rome had particular associations for Erwin because its Santa Maria Maggiore first gave him the idea that Christian art was borrowed from the art of Hellenized Judaism. Evelyn's sexual appeal gave Erwin unusual privileges in Rome, as it had in the Middle East, for a monk showed them special rooms in the catacombs, where he took advantage of the darkness to kiss Evelyn's hair and pat and caress her.[70]

At Oxford "Erwin was as excited and thrilled as a child to return. . . . He took photographs, pointed out all his favorite places . . . the old library at Merton, with the books chained to the shelves . . . Lincoln, the circular room where Erwin took his degree, the great library."[71] He was especially pleased that a secretary at Lincoln College when he was there recognized him and remembered his D.Phil. subject.

The Eranos Conference at Ascona was their last professional objective. But upon their arrival Erwin developed a lung infection and had to give up his scheduled lecture, "Evaluation of Symbols Recurrent in Time as Illustrated in Judaism." He also missed seeing Jung, whom Evelyn met for the first time and described as "a magnificent looking man, looking the part worthy of his eminent position."[72] Erwin did attend the morning conference meetings and could say goodbye to Frau Fröbe-Kaptayn, the conference administrator, who had played a key role in making the seven-month trip possible.

After their return to New Haven, Goodenough resumed work on *Jewish Symbols,* the first three volumes having been approved for publication. He wrote to his friend Joseph Maguire, "I seem to have become a complete monomaniac. I am trying to finish my work, with only my family as an anchor to reality."[73]

Mrs. Claude Lopez succeeded Dr. Goff as his assistant, after Dr. Goff returned to her own research. Mrs. Lopez deciphered fragments of words on the charms and amulets Goodenough was describing, provided indexes, and made valuable suggestions: "a magnificent help,"[74] which he acknowledged in the prefaces to volumes 1, 4, and 5. As the wife of a distinguished Yale professor, Mrs. Lopez often found Goodenough a trying taskmaster. He wrote in *The Psychology of Religious Experiences,* "In our cruelty to our subordinates and children . . . we avenge the cruelty we suffered from our parents and still suffer from those 'above' us or the more 'successful' ";[75] and this "cruelty to our subordinates" at times applied to Mrs. Lopez. He insisted that she work Saturday mornings, although her family commitments made this inconvenient. When she learned that library regulations specified if they worked in the library there were to be no Saturday hours and informed Goodenough of this, he replied, "So you did find out." When she became pregnant, she occasionally suffered from nausea, and once, in the late afternoon, she vomited while working. Goodenough sympathetically washed her face, helped her clean up, then looked at his watch, and said, "It's only 4:35; we have twenty-five minutes more to work."[76]

Dr. Goff, Mrs. Lopez, and, briefly, Fanny Bonajuto, converted Goodenough's almost illegible handwritten sheets of yellow paper to typescripts that eventually became the handsome volumes of *Jewish Symbols in the Greco-Roman Period.*

The Bollingen support was crucial. Not only did it underwrite the research assistance, but it made possible the published form of the *Symbols,* lavish with illustrations, mostly black and white, but some in color. And it allowed Goodenough to expand the work, as he saw the need, from eight to thirteen volumes.

But he gave primary credit to Evelyn. As he wrote in the preface to volume 1, "She has not only made many practical suggestions. . . . Much more, in giving form to my life she has given form to my thought, and so has essentially created this work."[77]

Volumes 1, 2, and 3 of *Jewish Symbols* were published boxed as a unit, volumes 1 and 2 giving an overview of the archaeological evidence for Jewish symbols, volume 3 providing illustrations. The fourth volume outlines Goodenough's methodology and discusses the meanings of the strictly Jewish symbols. He planned that a fifth volume would consider the three Jewish food symbols: fish, bread, and wine; a sixth would describe symbols borrowed from pagans; and a final volume would interpret the Old Testament illustrations in the synagogue at Dura-Europos and elsewhere. But the material expanded. As published, volumes 5 and 6 deal with the Jewish food symbols, 7 and 8 with the symbols borrowed from pagan religions, 9 through 11 with the Dura-Europos synagogue symbols. And he felt the need for another volume, 12, to give a summary of his main points and his final conclusions. Volume 13 consists of indexes, maps, and corrigenda: Both volume 12 and volume 13 were published after Goodenough's death.

As he reviewed the completed project, he saw it falling into three divisions: volumes 1 to 3, all the designs and figures in known Jewish remains; volumes 4 to 8, a method for interpreting the symbols and an application to those symbols Jews had used; volumes 9 to 11, analysis of the Old Testament scenes and pagan representations in the Dura synagogue paintings. Volume 12 provides a "table-model"[78] of the whole.

The preface to volume 1 states that Goodenough's "immediate purpose . . . is to try to discover the religious attitudes of the Jews in the Greco-Roman world"[79] from their archeological remains. Even this was an ambitious and controversial proposal, since scholars had not generally accepted art as a key to basic religious attitudes, nor the existence of a Jewish art. Then he presents a more sweeping claim: he realizes that in the course of his work he has outlined "a new methodology applicable to the whole spiritual history of the civilizations behind us . . . the spiritual history of . . . a continuous adaptation of certain basic symbols."[80] And he sees his study as a way "to understand the values of these old symbols in terms meaningful to modern man, so that we can begin the basic task of expressing their values to the new age."[81]

The meaning of the first three volumes' dedication "To the Tradition of Academic Individualism as Championed by the Department of History of Yale University" is clear. Goodenough is going beyond the boundaries of any individual academic discipline in using art as an interpreter of religion and in developing a methodology of interpretation that draws upon both art and psychology, areas of knowledge that historians of religion did not generally consider pertinent to their field.

The first chapter focuses on resolving the problem of the rapid Hellenization of Christianity—"the problem . . . which has been before me all my life."[82] He points out the role of his previous work in solving this problem. *The Theology of Justin Martyr* proposed, at its close, that Jews in the Greco-Roman world had incorporated pagan ideas into their Judaism, so when these Jews were converted to Christianity, they took with them the pagan ideas they already knew in their Judaism and assimilated them into their Christianity. "To investigate the possibilities of this hypothesis has been the concern of all my subsequent investigations."[83] Since Philo is the main literary evidence for a Hellenized Judaism, Goodenough examined Philo's writings to describe how Philo combined his Judaism with ideas he took from paganism and to show that Philo was not unique, but representative of other mystic Jews. He intended *By Light, Light,* which identified the literary records and nature of Hellenistic Judaism, to be the first in a series, followed by an examination of Hellenistic Jewish art.

In the *Jewish Symbols* volumes he presents the vast amount of Jewish art in and on synagogues and graves of the Greco-Roman period that he has collected. He interprets these as the artistic evidence of a Hellenized Judaism that provided the materials for the Hellenized Christianity, which borrowed them, as the Jews had borrowed from the pagans.

The first three volumes present the archaeological evidence in the various sites of what was then known as Palestine and the other lands inhabited by Jews, preceded by a brief summary of the existing literary evidence as to the religion of Jews in the Roman world.

Volume 1 describes the symbolic art found in the remains of Jewish tombs in Palestine, in the various types of synagogues, and what Goodenough sees as the third representation of Jewish symbols—their coins. In the synagogues, which contain the most important evidence of Hellenistic Judaism, he describes many symbols: the menorah, the Torah shrine, the lulab and ethrog, the wine jar, vine leaves, bunches of grapes, lions, all of which Goodenough claims were associated with life now and also hereafter. He then draws the controversial conclusion that these synagogues give "the impression of a mystic sort of Judaism":[84] that Jews worshipped in them with the mystical "attempt here and now to partake of the eternal Reality"[85] as well as to have immortality after death.

Volume 2 describes the symbols found in burial places, synagogues, and on small objects of Jews who lived outside Palestine: the menorah, vines with grapes, the lion, the peacock, and palm branches, which he interprets, like those found in Palestine, as Hellenized Judaism's expressions of mystical hope of eternal life now and hereafter. He sees the symbols on Jewish charms and amulets, which he describes as all representing some form of syncretism. He interprets the inclusion of the Egyptian gods Osiris and Anubis and the Greek gods Helios and Aphrodite on the amulets as further examples of a Hellenized Judaism that adapted "pagan details for the glory of the Jewish God."[86] And he concludes: "The picture we have got of this Judaism is that of a group still intensely loyal to Iao Sabaoth [the Jewish name for God] . . . but which accepted the best of paganism (including its most potent charms) as focusing in, finding its meaning in, the supreme Iao Sabaoth"[87]—a Hellenistic, mystical Judaism that he states the rabbis would have found blasphemous.

These volumes prompted many reviews. Most of them gave unqualified praise to the scope of Goodenough's achievement, and several commended his contribution. Salo Baron wrote in the *Journal of Biblical Literature* that "his sustained effort to marshal all available evidence and to set up guideposts for its uniform and consistent interpretation is a major contribution to learning. . . . The forthcoming volumes of this truly *magnum opus* . . . will eagerly be awaited by all scholars in the field."[88] Harry Leon in *Archaeology* stated, "The work is of highest importance in that it has assembled an astonishing amount of scattered and previously unpublished

materials, has organized and classified them, has brought out hitherto un-
noticed details, and has demonstrated that they are not to be taken for
granted as merely decorative elements."[89] Cecil Roth in *Judaism* disagreed with some of Goodenough's conclusions, but described the work
as "the most magnificent, as well as the most important, that has ever appeared in the realm of ancient Jewish art, and perhaps of Jewish art in its
widest sense. . . . The wealth of material that the author has assembled
. . . and the vast scholarship that he has devoted to its discovery, will ren-
der the publication a memorable one in the realm of Jewish studies for
years to come."[90]

Specific criticisms often accompanied this general praise. Baron
pointed out that Goodenough did not acknowledge the work of other
scholars who held his view that Jews could be observant of Jewish law
and still be Hellenized.[91] Leon felt that Goodenough went too far in identifying objects as Jewish and in discovering symbolism everywhere.[92]
Morton Smith had equally strong objections. After praising the volumes
as "a work fundamental for the study of ancient Judaism," he pointed to
serious weaknesses. "It consistently overinterprets and it tries to force all
the evidence into one scheme . . . and . . . this scheme is a drastic over-
simplification"[93] — the scheme that all the decorations Goodenough described were the work of Hellenized Jews. Others were to echo Smith's
criticism that Goodenough forced all his material to prove his point about
Hellenistic Judaism. As Krister Stendahl, his friend in the Harvard Divinity School, phrased it much later, he felt that Goodenough worked
"with blinders on."[94]

Such single-minded focus on Hellenistic Judaism reflected Goodenough's characteristic confidence in the validity and value of his interpretations, however contrary to current views.

Chapter 11

Symbols Continued, and Its Reception

The negative comments in the reviews of the *Symbols'* first three volumes led Goodenough to discuss the problem with his friend Samuel Sandmel. Sandmel suggested that Goodenough had not been explicit about his intentions and the reasons for his method of procedure. He reported that Goodenough agreed, after looking over the three volumes and the reviews, and decided that he should open volume 4 with a chapter explaining his objectives and his methodology.[1]

This he does, preceding his discussion of the specific symbols he will interpret with what he describes as "the most important single chapter of the entire study."[2] This chapter develops both his theory of the nature and function of symbols, especially religious symbols, and what he sees as the appropriate method for interpreting the motivation of those who chose the symbols and the values they represented.

Goodenough sees two steps as essential for understanding these motives and their significance. First, one must assemble and describe all the available evidence of symbolic materials. Then, instead of trying to explain them by referring to the literature of the period, one must determine the meaning of the symbols as art forms. For he insists that the archaeological evidence of its art is the primary source for understanding the popular Judaism of the Greco-Roman world, because the rabbis barely tolerated the religious views of this Judaism and the rabbinic evidence is therefore minimal. He sees the symbols in the Jewish art as "a picture book without text"[3] that provides the clues to the motives that led Jews to borrow pagan art motifs and adapt them into their Judaism. Hence we need a methodology to interpret these clues—a methodology that combines "historical with psychological techniques."[4]

He defines a symbol as "an object or a pattern which, whatever the reason may be, operates upon men, and causes effect in them, beyond mere recognition of what is literally presented in the given form."[5] The religious symbol he defines as "not only a direct purveyor of meaning in itself, but also a thing of power, or value, operating upon us to inspire, to release tensions, to arouse guilt, or to bring a sense of forgiveness and reconciliation."[6] The historian of symbols must let this nonverbal language speak to him, as the language of Bach's fugues speaks to the musician.

He also asserts the need for a psychology of religion to interpret these symbols, and claims that the one he draws upon is his own. He sees himself as neither a Freudian nor a Jungian. For he states that "the systems of these schools have grown out of interpretation of the phenomena that analysts have observed in their disturbed patients,"[7] apparently unaware that this was the very criticism Jung had made of Freud when he wrote, "Freud's teaching is one-sided in that it generalizes from facts that are relevant only to neurotic states of mind; its validity is really confined to these states."[8] Rather than drawing upon Freud or Jung, Goodenough cites the concepts of Thomas French, who sent him his *Integration of Behavior* shortly after it came out in 1952. He also states how "congenial"[9] he finds the language of the philosopher Suzanne Langer in *Philosophy in a New Key,* and he both quotes and paraphrases her, although he challenges her view that religion is "a young and provisional form of thought" that scientific thinking must supplant.[10]

Goodenough's psychology of religion stresses the basic human drive for life. He sees this conception as similar to French's "concept of the craving of all healthy organisms for stimulation and functional activity."[11] But it also echoes William James's approving quotation of Leuba in *The Varieties of Religious Experience* that "the love of life, at any and every level of development, is the religious impulse."[12]

He sees the life urge for self-fulfillment as manifested in either the yearning for mystic union with the mother–father, or for security by obeying the father's laws. And he claims to have been "amazed"[13] to find that the symbols for these desires are all basically erotic: that this is "the major element all the symbols had in common."[14] This leads him to consider the central role of the erotic in religion as a whole and to explain in terms of his psychology why the symbols of mystical experience are so generally the symbols of sex. According to his interpretation, the quest for the perpetuation of life in the Great Mother, which is central to the mystical experience, is expressed in the symbols of sexual union, because phallic symbols or rites were originally the instrument of bringing fertility to crops, then were used to obtain a richer life, and finally as a means of obtaining union with deity.

He then proposes that the sexual symbols found in the synagogues and on graves of Jews in the Roman Empire suggest a Judaism in which legalism was fused with the "mystery" that promised the experience of living in God now and hereafter. It freely adopted pagan symbols to represent this experience. And he concludes his "method chapter" triumphantly: "There can be no dispute . . . that these Jews were so hellenized that they could borrow for their amulets, charms, graves, and synagogues the mystic symbols of paganism. . . . For no error of induction or fancy in my own thinking can obscure the fact that Jews did borrow this art, not sporadically, but systematically and for their most sacred and official associations. This is a fact I have not invented, and now no historian of the field may ignore or slight it."[15]

By his explanation of his methods, his psychology of religion, and the conclusions he will draw, Goodenough prepares the reader for the detailed examination of the symbols he had identified in the sites and objects described in volumes 1 and 2.

Volume 4 discusses symbols that were associated with worship in the Temple in Jerusalem: the menorah, the Torah shrine and scroll, the lulab and ethrog, the shofar, and the incense shovel, interpreting their meaning in the settings of the synagogues and graves where they appear.

The menorah, the candelabrum used in Jewish worship, which is a paramount symbol of Judaism, was originally a tree, according to Goodenough, and he hypothesizes that the menorah became "a symbol of God and his rule," because "its light is the Light from God"[16] holding out the mystical hope of present union and immortality. The representation of the Torah shrine facade symbolized that God had come to man and that through its doorway man could go to God, meet Him in a mystical union, and have the hope of immortality. The scroll, an abbreviation of the Torah shrine, was a symbol of the divine presence. The lulab (a bundle of twigs made up of a palm branch, three shoots of myrtle, and two of willow) and the ethrog (a special kind of citrus fruit) were both carried in ceremonial procession during the Feast of Tabernacles, a harvest festival with associations of water and light. Thus, Goodenough proposes, they came to have the connotation of the immaterial light, representing new life now and immortality hereafter.

He comes to similar conclusions about the mystic meanings of other Jewish symbols. Because God substituted a ram for the sacrifice of his son, Isaac, that he had demanded of Abraham, the shofar, a ram's horn, became a symbol of God's mercy. As he did with the other symbols, Goodenough points out supporting allusions in the Talmud, the Midrash, and Philo to confirm that the shofar also became a symbol of the mystic hope of new life and immortality.

Goodenough affirms that the Jews used these symbols of cult objects as equivalents of the pagan symbols used to promise immortality, expressing the same assurances in Jewish terms. But in order to answer adequately the central question of his study, "the question as to what sort of Judaism produced all this art,"[17] he must also analyze the pagan symbols that the Jews used and their meaning both for the pagans and for the Jews who borrowed them. This he does in the four volumes that follow.

Volumes 5 and 6, completed in 1954 and published in 1956, are transitional in the series. While volume 4 studies the symbols taken from Jewish worship, and 7 and 8 examine those definitely taken from other civilizations, volumes 5 and 6 analyze food symbols that borrow the pagan forms of representation but that portray objects of eating and drinking common to all cultures. Since Goodenough's discussion of these symbols includes their use by pagans and Christians as well as Jews, these volumes have a broader scope than the descriptions of the strictly Jewish symbols of the earlier volumes. But the question they propose to answer is that of his study as a whole: what meanings the symbols—in this case of fish, bread, and wine—had for the Jews who put them on their graves and synagogues.

In volume 5 Goodenough identifies the meanings of fish symbols: the great fish as an image of the coming Messiah, the fish as a symbol of hope of immortality. He proposes that the fish meal, represented as a heavenly banquet in paganism and Christianity as well as Judaism, probably came to Judaism from the Greeks and, for the Jews, symbolized a mystic sharing here and now in the divine power that would be fully revealed in the messianic age.

Symbolic representations of bread in the form of "round objects" suggest to Goodenough that bread, like fish, had sacred associations for Jews of that time and that the round objects symbolized for Judaism and Christianity alike both bread and the eating of bread, which brought life here and hereafter.

When he discusses wine, he states that in Jewish art symbolic representations of it, both the vine and wine drinking, confirm his "strong presumptions of a genuinely mystic sacrament among the Jews."[18] The many examples of wine symbols on coins, tombs, and ossuaries that he describes lead him to the hypothesis that "a wine-drinking ritual was at that time of great importance in a mystic hope for the experience of God and for immortality."[19] Then, after taking the reader on a "journey into paganism"[20] to see the symbols of "the divine fluid" in Babylonia, Assyria, and ancient Egypt and Greece, he asserts, "It was the vine and its wine which were the god and which have been valid as such from earliest times to the present. Wine could be anthropomorphized as the hope of man and given arbitrarily the name of Dionysus, or that of Davidic Messiah; or Jesus Christ could be the true vine, ostensibly in contrast to but really a continuation of his predecessors. This vine is still the god of our civilization."[21] As he had expressed it earlier to Evelyn, writing to her in 1941 after attending a service at the Presbyterian Church in Kerrville, "It was communion Sunday, and I ate the flesh and drank the blood of Dionysus with profound comfort."[22]

Relating the wine symbols specifically to phallicism and pointing to their common religious meaning, he affirms, "The phallicism and the vine and wine are all symbols of the divine. Phallicism and the vine or wine are one. It is eroticism which makes the vital juice of the god available. . . . The giving of the juice by the vine is an act of love."[23] He points out that for both the Greeks and Christians the symbols of vine and the trampling of grapes "stood for the god in whose dismemberment and shed blood the believer had hope of immortality."[24] In accordance with his thesis that the lingua franca of symbols is constant from religion to religion, he proposes that the Jews' representation of vintage scenes in the synagogues and on sarcophagi expressed their hope that the loving mercy of God would give them immortality.

The last chapter of these volumes, on the ritual use of wine in Jewish observance, was Goodenough's response to the request for such a survey by Louis Finkelstein, chancellor of Jewish Theological Seminary, who saw it as having special interest for Jews. Goodenough describes this ritual use of wine on the occasions of birth, circumcision, marriage, death, the Sabbath meal, and again at the Saturday evening meal, providing a detailed account of its function and meanings on each occasion.

In summary, he comes to the conclusions to be expected from the developing theses of the volumes: that fish, bread, and wine rites were borrowed from pagans and adapted by Jews in the Hellenistic period, and that, as observed in home and synagogue, they expressed the Jewish hope of immortality, possibly also of mystic union with God here and now. For, Goodenough affirms, "it is the mysticism, the craving for a sacramental access to Life, which lies beneath the whole body of phenomena we have here studied and does so, I am convinced, because it was the basic and original meaning of the rites in paganism and Judaism alike."[25] He also asserts that his methodology for studying the movement of symbols from religion to

religion has enabled him to demonstrate the constancy of the basic meaning behind the use of bread and fluid symbols in the different civilizations.
And he closes with the sermonlike flourish, though not the message, of a
Methodist preacher: "The roots of the symbols of form and language which
we have been discussing go so deep that food, drink, nature, the fertility of
the earth, the paths of the stars, birth, death, water, wine, sex . . . all come
to mean the greater security we seek now and in the future, a security which
can be found only in greater life. . . . In this all religious symbols have
blended and always will blend: the very movement of the air comes to be
the movement of the Spirit through which we may be reborn."[26]

Volumes 7 and 8, published in 1958, complete Goodenough's study
of pagan symbols borrowed by the Jews in the Greco-Roman period, except for those in the recently discovered Dura-Europos synagogue.
(These he could not discuss until Carl Kraeling, professor of New Testament and curator of Gerasa Antiquities, whom Yale had given the right
to the first official account of the synagogue, published his book *Synagogue*.) Goodenough's purpose is to show the symbolic meanings of various figures and objects that the Jews took from the pagans.

The bull, the lion, the tree, the goddess Victory with her crown, and
miscellaneous symbols are the subject of volume 7, and Goodenough
demonstrates that, regardless of their different origins and associations,
all of them expressed for the Jews who used them the hope of a greater
life here and now, or of immortality, or both.

He asserts that representations of the bull in all civilizations signified
its life-giving powers. The lion symbols Goodenough identifies as representing the hunter, the power of the deity, and in Egypt as also associated
with the Nile, the phallic source of life, giving fertility to the crops and
the hope of resurrection. He discusses in detail the harnessed lion, which
symbolized the taming of savagery by love and kindness. According to
Goodenough, "The taming of the lion, whether in God or in ourselves, is
the essence of mystic salvation and . . . of the hope of immortality."[27] And
he hypothesizes that the Jews had in mind these various values when they
placed the lion figure in their synagogues and graves.

He affirms that the tree symbol always had the basic meaning of deity, and the date palm, specifically, was the tree of life, as it was the
source of wine. He then concludes that by the Christian era the Jews who
used the date palm and other tree symbols in their art were mystical,
rather than law-oriented, Jews who were expressing by these symbols either the hope of future immortality or the mystical hope of greater life on
earth, or both.

Goodenough sees the goddess Victory and her crown, like the other symbols that the Jews of the Greco-Roman period borrowed, as representing immortality for these Jews, rather than the usual military meanings. He concludes that, as the symbol was taken over by Hellenized Jews, it expressed their belief that by following their Judaism they would be met at death by Victory, God's messenger, and would receive the crown of immortal life.

He regards the other pagan symbols—rosettes, wheels, "round objects," masks, and the Gorgon head—as having similar mystic meanings for the Jews who borrowed them. He proposes that, because the mask had symbolic importance in Greece, Rome, and syncretic religions, and putting on a mask in the mysteries meant putting on deity, for some Jews the mask may have symbolized the hope of a present mystical union with God. He also finds a mystic intention in the use of the Medusa or Gorgon head in Greco-Roman Jewish art. He points out that scholars have demonstrated the transition of the Medusa figure from horror to beauty, that in mysticism the terrible is at the same time the lovely, and that therefore the Jews who put the Medusa head in a grave hoped that it would both ward off evil and provide eternal life.

Volume 8 discusses the erotic symbols and the psychopomps and astronomical symbols the Jews borrowed. Goodenough finds in the symbols of cupids, birds, sheep, the hare, and the shell that the Jews used a long history of erotic associations; he asserts, "With mystic Jews eroticism—that is, the necessity of union with God in love—and fertility—that is, the hope of new life and immortality from such a union—played a conspicuous and basic part."[28] He concludes, "The erotic urge always finds its deepest meaning not in physical sensation but in spiritual union, and it drives sensitive souls beyond the 'merely physical' to seek a spiritual union ultimately with the deity."[29] Herein, he argues, lies the appropriateness of these erotic symbols for the mystic Jews, who, from the archaeological evidence he has assembled, clearly used them. For their hope of immortality and of a present new life so clearly resembled pagan hopes that they put the pagan erotic symbols of these hopes on their graves and in their synagogues as a natural expression of their expectations.

Goodenough affirms that, from the earlier identification of cupids with lust, then with the idea that "it is love which makes the world go round," cupids came to symbolize that God's love makes his saving power available and makes men immortal. He points out that since eroticism figured prominently throughout Jewish mysticism, one can suppose that the Hellenistic Jews used cupids with the symbolic meaning that their hope of salvation lay in God's love. He also proposes that, as pagans came to identify the symbols of various birds with divine love and the hope of immortality assured by a loving God, so one can assume that the Jews used these symbols on their graves to express the same hope.

Other symbols he classifies as erotic—the sheep, the hare, the shell, the cornucopia, the centaur—he identifies as originally fertility symbols that later came to represent the expectation of eternal life.

He suggests that the Jews, like the Egyptians, Greeks, and later the Christians, used figures of the sheep and the sheep–savior who was killed in Isaac's place as symbols of the medium for obtaining God's mercy: hence of the hope of immortality and the present availability of the divine. He sees the hare as another symbol of immortality in Egyptian, Greek, and Roman art, stemming from its identification with Dionysus and other fertility deities who personified love, and he assumes that the Jews who portrayed it were expressing a similar mystical belief in immortality. He concludes with its contemporary meanings, as he often does, noting that the Easter bunny retains its erotic value as the egg giver, the source of life: "Even today, therefore, the hare is a living and beloved symbol of Resurrection, with no explanation at all for this value."[30]

The shell was originally a symbol of sexuality, according to Goodenough, then was associated with the birth of Aphrodite from a shell, and with the sea. He suggests that, because of these psychological associations with the Great Mother's womb and the sea, for the Jews who used the shell symbol it meant "the saving power and love of God which the Torah brings to men."[31] The cornucopia he interprets as a symbol of the female principle, an abbreviation of the fertility goddess with her fruits, and proposes that the cornucopia on Jewish graves came to symbolize life giving or immortality. The centaur figure on Jewish synagogues he sees as also a symbol of immortality. For the centaur Cheiron, Achilles' tutor, was immortal, and the centaur offering fish and the centaur among the heaven-associated palm trees on the tiles in Dura, Goodenough assumes, represent immortality.

The symbols of the psychopomp—the guide to the other world— which the Jews borrowed, Goodenough sees as all related, whether they are symbols of the figure who led to the next world or the means of transportation to it. In Goodenough's interpretation, the eagle represented the power to take men to immortal life; the griffin and winged Pegasus assured a safe passage of the soul after death and the hope of immortality; boats drawn on Jewish graves symbolized the homeward journey after death to the harbor of immortality. They further suggest to him that their representations on the synagogues spoke to many Jews of a mystic journey here and now, of a guided means of transportation to God. And he concludes with a strong statement of his controversial thesis that there was a Judaism in which Jews observed the Law and worshipped in their own buildings, but at the same time "covered these buildings and graves with mystic symbols from paganism because their Judaism included in addition to legalism a mystic aim and satisfaction which the pagan symbols expressed for them."[32]

He comes to a similar conclusion after reviewing the Jewish use of astronomical symbols. Their adoption of Greco-Roman astral and cosmic symbols suggests to him that the Jews used these symbols to promise an enhanced life and immortality, while at the same time they combined them with the menorah, pointing to the Jewish God as the guarantor of their hopes.

Goodenough ends by reviewing his contribution in these volumes. His demonstration of the religious reasons for the Jews' borrowing of pagan symbols has made it highly inprobable to assume that their intentions were only decorative. He has pointed out that the Hellenistic Jews' use of the menorah and other cultic symbols showed that these Jews were distinctly Jewish, but that they also borrowed symbols from the pagans because they felt their hope of immortality and of present participation in divine reality could be expressed in Greek and other pagan artistic forms. And he states repeatedly that his purpose is more comprehensive than a purely historical one. He has tried "to bring the reader to perceive or feel (I see little difference here between intellectual and emotional perception) the power and beauty of the symbolic vocabulary Jews borrowed."[33] Beyond that, "I have tried to . . . bring the reader to feel, as I have felt, that through these great symbols it is possible to get away from the transient and temporal and to come into some of the deepest and highest universal ranges of human life."[34]

Goodenough was clearly convinced of his work's importance. In 1940 he had written to Wallace Notestein, "I am either crazy or I am doing something revolutionary in the study of ancient religions and Christianity. Time will tell which is true."[35] Now he believed that he had indeed done something revolutionary as a historian of religion and had also enriched the contemporary understanding of one of religion's most meaningful expressions—its symbols.

The eight volumes as a whole evoked a wide spectrum of responses.

Nahman Avigad of the Hebrew University in Jerusalem, whom Goodenough had met there in 1957, wrote appreciatively, "I shall draw heavily on your fundamental work which will leave far behind any work
which might be written in future on the subject."[36] Professor Chadwick
of Christ Church College, Oxford, editor of the *Journal of Theological
Studies,* voiced similar praise: "I should take this opportunity of expressing my enthusiasm and gratitude for the outstanding contribution to
knowledge which your book is making,"[37] leading Goodenough to comment, "Kind of sets me up!"[38]

Samuel Sandmel reviewed volumes 4, 5, and 6 in the *Journal of Biblical Literature.* Although he had many "quibbles," as he called them,
with individual interpretations, he wrote, "I am persuaded that Goodenough is right in his fundamental principal contentions," and concluded, "Goodenough's series, whether one agrees or disagrees, represents religious scholarship at its best and most admirable dimensions.
Moreover, its focus is not on comparatively remote matters, but on the
central problems of early Christianity and the Judaism of its time."[39]

Ralph Marcus wrote in *Classical Philology,* "This series . . . I do not
hesitate to describe as one of the most valuable works to have been produced in the field of Judaism and early Christianity in the past fifty years.
Whether the author's general theory is right or wrong can only be determined by further study. But at the present time it is beyond question that
he has given a work of extraordinary value both for its factual material
and for its bold hypotheses."[40]

The chief criticisms came from Morton Smith, a longtime friend, who
was in the history department of Columbia University, and from Arthur
Darby Nock of Harvard, who had in the past challenged Goodenough's
interpretations of Philo. Jacob Neusner considered these criticisms important enough to summarize and comment on in the foreword to his
1988 one-volume abridgment of *Jewish Symbols.*[41]

Smith, like Marcus, commended Goodenough's effort in producing a
copious collection of generally unavailable material that was very useful for the student of religion.[42] He praised him for raising the question
of the relationship between the rabbinic literature and the archaeological
evidence of Judaism that he assembled. But Smith charged that, in finding one symbolic meaning for all these ancient representations, Goodenough described it in vague, overgeneralized terms like "life" and
"divine power." He claimed that Goodenough's psychoanalytic interpretations were inappropriate when discussing ancient symbols. And he

held that Goodenough insisted on attributing symbolic significance to objects that were clearly decorative conventions.[43]

Of Goodenough's important reviewers, Nock was the most critical. He argued that there was insufficient evidence for an esoteric mystery worship in the synagogue or for a mystic eucharistic meal anticipating the Christian eucharistic sacrament, stating flatly, "The words of Jesus over Bread and Cup represent the transformation of filial piety to a wholly new end in what was deemed to be a wholly new situation."[44] He complained that "the rediscovery of the subconscious and nonrational threatens us with a new crop of overconfident rationalization,"[45] like some of Goodenough's psychoanalytic theories. While agreeing with Smith as to the value of the work as data for scholarship, he concluded, patronizingly, that its "abiding importance . . . is as a Materialsammlung."[46]

Nock's evaluation was faint praise to Goodenough, as he made clear in the preface to volume 12, in 1963, stating, "I have not spent thirty years as a mere collector: I was trying to make a point."[47] But there was the compensation of those who, even if they challenged it, recognized the importance of his point: the existence of a Hellenized Judaism, as revealed by the archaeological evidence of the period.

Chapter 12

Toward a Mature Faith: Goodenough Presents His Own Position

In 1954 Goodenough had a severe, almost fatal attack of the same illness from which he had made a "miraculous" recovery as a baby. It had recurred less seriously every eight or nine years since, but the attack of 1954 lasted six months and kept him in bed most of six weeks. Then, when he and Evelyn were at a cocktail party on an evening when he felt able to go out, they met Dr. Rachel Burgess, a pediatrician, and Erwin, always eager to discuss his health, described the history and symptoms of his illness. She diagnosed it as celiac disease, the damaging effect of gluten on the intestines, and recommended what she prescribed for infant celiac sufferers—to avoid all wheat, rye, and barley products. Erwin experienced another "miraculous" recovery. From then on he followed the diet as much as possible, at first even carrying bananas with him when he was a dinner guest, uncertain whether he could eat what was served. He had no recurrence and carried on his scholarly projects with new confidence that ill health would not interrupt them.

"Vol. IV [of *Symbols*] is far enough along so that it does not need me at all,"[1] he wrote Karl Lehmann in 1954, and he could work on something quite different. *Toward a Mature Faith,* written that year, developed from a course he offered on types of religious experience, in which he outlined religious attitudes and experiences that he considered essential for his contemporaries.

Goodenough had made earlier, brief formulations of his religious position. His regard for his friend and colleague Andrew Morehouse, who was a devout Christian, had led him to explain his own situation in 1940:

> The great difficulty with me is that I am trying to examine scientifically something which I am trying to keep alive, and in myself. . . . I am trying to dissect religion as a scientist without killing it, for all that I read in the

histories of religion is a report of anatomy, not of the living organism. And
it is not the anatomy of religion, but its organism, which I want to understand. . . . And always I must be at once the surgeon and the patient. . . .
    To the man who begins his thinking with "Of course, God!" great
philosophies are possible. But I must begin my thinking with "Of course,
experience!"[2]

In the article "Scientific Living," in a 1942 issue of *The Humanist,* he
criticized the then fashionable neoorthodox position for its lack of scientific objectivity. He accused it of totalitarianism, which he described
as "no more attractive wearing the iron gray beard of piety than with the
Hitlerian mustache,"[3] and insisted that in matters of religion one must
cultivate the "*tentative* loyalty"[4] learned from science, being willing to
test a religious hypothesis as one would a scientific, but also to live with
it while testing it, as the scientist uses his hypotheses as he tests them. In
this way he resolved the difficulty he had complained of to Morehouse,
and also to Paul Minear, when commenting on an article by Minear, "*We
cannot worship what we analyze: the very process of analysis assumes
the potential superiority and actual detachment of the analyst.*"[5] As in
Religious Tradition and Myth he had pointed out the need "to reconcile
a religious temper with an agnostic mind,"[6] "Scientific Living" advocated "to live for an hypothesis while testing it. . . . That is the only scientific living, and, for society, the only hopeful life."[7]

This position led a reader of *The Humanist* to write to him, "The program you place before us is the program for aspiring realistic humane
men and women in these extraordinary times."[8] But by 1945 it was clear
to him that few in the Conference on Science, Philosophy, and Religion,
of which he was a founding member, shared his views. So he resigned
from it, expressing his reasons to the chairman, Rabbi Louis Finkelstein,
in his typical vivid imagery, "The Conference is a magnificent opium
party at which we escape from the realities of our ignorance into a Utopia
where we know the answers. . . . The problems of this age are not to be
solved at a Conference or at a series of Conferences. We have yet to dig
up, painfully, laboriously, the facts of the nature of man. . . . If you will
turn the Conference into a group trying to start real research into the
problems of life I'll be with you like a shot."[9]

He had earlier in 1945 proposed such a study of religion to Frank Aydelotte, director of the Institute for Advanced Studies at Princeton University. Since he assumed he would be chosen to head such a project, he
had high hopes that it would be a way out of the increasing tensions he

was having with the Yale Divinity School faculty. But, although he was optimistic when he returned from the Princeton interview, after some months Aydelotte wrote that he had regretfully decided against the project.[10]

William F. Buckley Jr., class of 1950, published *God and Man at Yale* in 1951, with a chapter on "Religion at Yale" in which he quoted Goodenough as claiming to be 80 percent atheist and 20 percent agnostic and concluded, "No wonder that the preponderant influence of a scholar of his persuasion is to drive his students *away* from religion, the subject he 'teaches.'"[11] But one former student recalled, "You once told us in class that you have students come into your course as strong Catholics, and leave as great doubters, and that you have great doubters come into your class, and finish the course by going into the ministry."[12] So Goodenough obviously had a different view from Buckley's of his effect on the undergraduates.

Another former student, Bill Tewkes, who had gone to New Guinea during World War II, wrote Goodenough from his station there, thanking him for his help when he was a student and asking him if there were books expressing Goodenough's religious views, for "I am about to arrive at the same concepts as your own."[13] This kind of response to his views no doubt encouraged him to put into book form the ideas developed in the course on types of religious experience.

Goodenough describes *Toward a Mature Faith* as his "report on a long spiritual search" that has brought him to a "thoroughly realistic solution . . . in which spiritual values still seem to be the most important element in human life."[14] He is convinced that "the dreams, the poetic fancies, the symbols of all kinds, which have gone into making up what men have called religion . . . unquestionably have the most important place of anything in human life."[15] In attempting to understand these, he has adopted an empirical approach and has drawn heavily for his interpretations on the theories of depth psychology.

He wrote in a relaxed mood in a serene setting, on the porch of the Cedar Island cottage. The arguments develop in an easy flow, with quotable aphorisms like "Married happiness does not come from having the right code so much as from believing that the code one has is Right."[16]

The book opens with Goodenough's account of the key experiences that contributed to his early "Faiths," his loss of these, and the steps that led him to new, acceptable beliefs or hypotheses. He selects the personal factors that have contributed to his present religious values, stressing the psychological implications of the major influences upon him. He has less to say about the impact public events during the times in which he lived. *Toward a Mature Faith* provides a wealth of reliable factual details, but Goodenough's perception of his earlier self or his wish to highlight certain aspects of his life results in a very selective portrayal. To stress the limitations of his paternal and religious upbringing and what he had to overcome, he describes himself as a prig, a prude, and a misfit during his youth. Yet we have seen from the few letters of his Hamilton years and his contributions to its literary magazine that he was a young man who could at least *write* about girls and "good grub" and was conversant with the literary and political currents of the time. In his portrayal of his parents and the independence from them he won at Oxford, he does not mention the continued financial support during those years, or the weekly letters to them in which he shared his opinions of people and national customs, as well as accounts of the rich cultural experiences their generosity made possible.

Following what he had learned from Freud about the key role of parents, Goodenough gives central importance to the influence of what he describes as the cold, severe, work-addicted, passionate, but repressed, father and of his warm, loving mother. He points out that for him God became the stern, severe Father; Jesus was like his warm mother; and his early identification of the two helped him understand the role of the mother goddess in the religions he later studied. He shows how both the Methodists' Calvinist ethic, with its insistence on the rightness of its way of life, regardless of society's opinions, and the emotional response to God and Christ that he also learned from Methodism as a child, remained influential throughout his life.

He claims that the Methodist emphasis on living life as it should be lived, indifferent to generally accepted bounds, led him to be involved in six departments at Yale. For he came there in 1923 as instructor in history; but by 1937 he was also listed with the faculty of the classics, Oriental studies, philosophy, and religion departments, offering courses in Greek philosophy, Hellenisim, Hellenistic Judaism, and early Christianity in these departments, while professor of the history of religion and director of graduate studies in history. Thus, in a day when departmental boundaries and specializations were respected, Goodenough pioneered in the interdisciplinary commitment that marks many current university programs and faculty appointments.

Goodenough sees his early encounter with the emotional outpouring in Methodist worship, which he terms "only slightly veiled eroticism,"[17] as responsible for his understanding of the importance that sexual symbols and ritual have in civilizations less repressive than ours. And he claims that this understanding is lacking in his fellow historians of religion.

He identifies the other key influence of his boyhood as Uncle Charlie, his father's brother, who introduced him to mysticism, the experience of being "sanctified" and absorbed into the world of spiritual reality. The feeling of rapture this produced gave him, he asserts, a sympathy with the Dionysiac ecstasies that he studied. Uncle Charlie's commitment to spiritual reality helped him, when he encountered Platonism, to understand its distinction between the social world of opinions and the ideal world of true knowledge. Because of his experience Goodenough regards himself as unlike most historians of religion in that he can sympathize with the mystics' craving to participate in the divine, which he sees as an element in all religions.

The last formative influence he stresses was his encounter with the empirical approach to Biblical and other early Christian documents in the classes of G. F. Moore, Kirsopp Lake, and others at the Harvard Divinity School. These men introduced him to a new kind of thinking, teaching him to distinguish verifiable facts from statements of faith, and to call the latter hypotheses. He italicizes hypotheses, which became a key word in the historian Goodenough's vocabulary, as it had been earlier for William James in *The Varieties of Religious Experience*.[18]

Goodenough in the next chapters traces his encounters with other new concepts. He describes his introduction to depth psychology and its importance for the understanding of religion, although "at first sight, but only, I believe, at first sight, it seems so devastatingly opposed to religious traditions and attitudes"[19] and "is now the greatest problem in religious adjustment for intelligent people."[20] He stresses the role of his friend from boyhood, psychoanalyst Thomas French, who introduced him to the theories of depth psychology. The other personal influence he mentions is that of Jung. When Jung was at Yale, he impressed Goodenough with the importance of psychology for understanding the symbols he was studying.

He recounts that from depth psychology he came to perceive the key role that wish projection plays in religion and to conclude that all religious teaching—about gods, God, Jesus, the supernatural—is wish projection. But he argues that religion is not alone in this: that scientific theories are also projections—"Nature knows nothing of the laws of physics as we formulate them; they are convenient projections of our own . . . ."[21] This was a revolutionary position in the science-worshipping fifties, although it is now more widely held by scientists, one of whom recently stated: "Physicists do not discover *the* physical world. They invent *a* physical world."[22]

Goodenough also makes a radical departure from the intellectually fashionable acceptance of Freud's atheism. He disagrees sharply with Freud's view that religious wish projections are merely "illusions" and that religion is a childhood neurosis mankind must overcome. As Goodenough summarizes his position: "God is no illusion. He is a marvelous form of projection by which we perceive the truth, as is the law of gravity";[23] for, according to Goodenough, people's belief in the existence of God is no less true or more debatable than the law of gravity.

Goodenough claims that depth psychology's view of religion as wish projection did not disturb him any more than had his earlier introduction to historical Biblical criticism. He describes his gradual realization that all his childhood beliefs were wish projections, a part of the necessary process of projecting a meaning upon life. He sees the problem of his contemporaries to be their sense of superiority to such projections, preferring to dismiss them as "illusions," rather than testing their value by psychological and other techniques. In contrast to their attitude, he concludes: "Depth psychology gives us our great imperative: we must cultivate our projections or dreams, and live by them, even while we admit to ourselves that they are projections."[24] Such a position directly challenged that of Goodenough's Divinity School colleagues, as represented by Halford Luccock's statement in *Marching off the Map,* "If a life is to stand under the pressures that play upon it, it needs more than a subjective feeling; it needs the objective moral and spiritual reality of God."[25] This interpretation of religion as wish projection remained one of Goodenough's most controversial positions.

The chapter on symbols, as it describes what depth psychology contributes to the understanding of religious symbols, draws upon Jung and, more specifically, Suzanne Langer. Langer, in *Philosophy in a New Key,* stated that recognizing the power of symbolism was the "new keynote" that affected the course not only of philosophy, but also of modern psychology, psychiatry, and logic. She affirmed, "In the fundamental notion of symbolization . . . we have the keynote of all humanistic problems,"[26] as we recognize that the human mind can use "symbols to attain, as well as to organize, belief. . . . It is the power of using symbols . . . that makes him [mankind] lord of the earth."[27] Goodenough, following Langer, insists on the need of his contemporaries for "symbols in which we can again have faith . . . simple symbols which put the mystery of life into workable terms for us."[28] He then develops the essentials of a mature faith by describing the symbols he lives by, using an innovative procedure; for "I believe deeply in my method for anchoring my symbols in the new world of scientific, historical, and psychological thinking."[29] This, of course, was the method in the *Symbols* volumes.

His examination of the symbols that he considers of value in his own time focuses on what he terms the old symbols—for faith, hope, love, salvation—and culminates in "the great symbol,"[30] Jesus, who incorporates them all, according to Goodenough. He radically redefines each of the Pauline values of faith, hope, and love, in order to provide "new meaning from the new world for the old symbols."[31]

In place of reliance on our traditional belief in divine revelation, which, Goodenough states, science and psychology have led his generation to discredit, he urges his readers to embrace a new faith—in doubt, as a means to greater understanding, and in myths that make life meaningful. In place of accepting the stories of Jesus' birth and his resurrection, he commends the observance of seasonal festivities like Christmas and Easter because they have symbolic value and give our life richness that we can't explain logically. He also urges that we have faith in the moral and legal traditions of our society, because they have continued power in our lives as they prescribe kindness, honesty, and respect for others. Finally, he asserts, we must have faith that, although we do not know the meaning of life, our imaginations can give it meaning.

Goodenough sees hope, like faith, as a basic element of Christianity that he still lives by and finds essential to human life. He points out that hope, based on belief in God and themselves, motivated the founders of America. And he affirms that at the time of his writing, in spite of domestic and international problems, the same grounds for hope exist. "One basis of hope is in the very character of the universe itself. The other ground of hope is in ourselves . . . man's proved ability to muddle through in the long run."[32]

In discussing love, Goodenough argues against denying the value of self-love, as the recent neoorthodox interpretations of the New Testament Greek word *agape* do. For he insists that a key Christian contribution to Western civilization has been its emphasis upon self-love as the basis for love of others: its double insistence on the value of every individual as a child of God and also on a person's social responsibility. Goodenough, who knew Paul Tillich, no doubt heard Tillich's Terry lectures of 1951, published as "The Courage to Be," in 1952. In these lectures

Tillich described the experience of knowing God as a way to transcend the diverse claims of the self as oneself and the self as social participant, by becoming a part of a church in which, without losing oneself, one also embraces the world.[33] Goodenough, perhaps deliberately, presents the very different view that Christianity's strength lies in its stress on the tension of the dual obligation to the self and to society rather than on its resolution.

When he considers the doctrine of salvation, Goodenough points out the parallel positions of psychotherapy. He notes the Christian doctrine's emphasis both on mankind's natural perversity and on the possibility of its redemption or renewal—by "grace" provided by Christ's life and death—and states that psychiatry, when dealing with guilt, seeks the same renewal. Therefore, he asserts, "salvation is a term we need not fear at all—it means radical psychotherapy. . . . The best religious teachers of all ages have meant . . . an elevation above the ordinary human condition. . . . This elevation, the mastering of the problems and impulses which fill us with guilt, can be indifferently called salvation or psychotherapy."[34]

After describing the perennial struggle between social demands or ideals and individual desires as a problem common to Christianity and psychiatry, he concludes that both agree that the person as a whole must be enabled to accept what his or her mind or conscience believes to be right. In summarizing the answers of early religions as to how to achieve this, he focuses on the idea that salvation comes through personal identification with a suffering, saving god, and he shows how Christianity gave concrete form to this hope. For it affirmed that a divine person, born of God and a human mother, had lived on earth as a man, been killed by wicked men, but rose from the dead, triumphing over the evil forces in the world and offering a new, higher life to those who identified with him. And Goodenough asserts, "Nothing has ever brought a solution of the problem of guilt to so many people, or given to so many power actually to live by their ideals rather than by their immediate desires and impulses."[35]

Yet Goodenough himself holds to the myth of human self-sufficiency, as promoted by Nietzsche and by Freud, although some younger intellectuals have found it unsatisfactory for their needs. For he states that it is the basis of American democracy. Moreover, "it seems to me that through his myths and projections and symbols man has always been his own savior."[36]

His reconciliation of these two seemingly contradictory beliefs in the power of a saving God and in ourselves comes with Goodenough's final suggestion. He concludes that, just as we need a social myth that democracy and science will produce new truths, we also need a personal myth of someone who loves us, forgives our failings, and can and will help us. He affirms that we can make such an ideal person "to order," project onto him the perfection we seek, and "we can get the strength of the ages, and the comfort of the ages, by calling that person Jesus."[37] He then states, in a radical interpretation of Christianity's history, "In doing so we shall only be doing what men through the ages have done with the figure of Jesus."[38]

Goodenough presents Jesus, so conceived, as the final element, "the great symbol,"[39]for a mature faith. He asserts that there are too few facts to reconstruct a life of the historical Jesus, echoing Albert Schweitzer's earlier conclusion in *The Quest of The Historical Jesus*. He points out that each age has found a new aspect of Jesus' personality on which individuals could pattern themselves, from medieval monks to the modern Bruce Barton, who characterized Jesus as the great salesman. He affirms that the meaning and new sense of direction that each generation has found in Jesus is "still the best psychotherapy for the mass of men."[40] Furthermore, for Goodenough, the doctrine of Incarnation "meant that the ideal woman could, and did, conceive and bear the divine child,"[41] thus giving mankind faith in human possibilities.

Jesus has been the ground of faith, hope, love, and salvation for both the churches and the individual, Goodenough states. Although insisting that Jesus as savior is a myth, lacking historical or scientific proof, he also affirms that this myth has reassured and inspired people, offering them a vision of divinity. And Goodenough wants his readers to experience such visions: "Salvation will come to us as we too once again can see visions."[42]

In a final, personal chapter Goodenough characterizes the path he has outlined as "a way of courage and profound faith."[43] He reaffirms that most people want to have their assurance of meaning and value in life embodied in an ideal person. He also reaffirms the value of self-acceptance, but states that at times people still need the comfort of prayer. Therefore, he states, "I still pray devoutly, and have the consolation of the old 'Presence' with which I lived in my youth"[44]—a position like the one he adopted in the conclusion of *Religious Tradition and Myth,* in which he recommended reaching out in prayer to the "Power-Not-Ourselves."[45] But pray to what name? he asks, and answers: to the symbolic name of Jesus for Christians and the God of their fathers for Jews.

Even a mature faith, he states, must have a tie with what we came to know as children, and we pray to those symbols of our childhood. "So I forget my qualifications and quibbles and call upon Jesus—and he comes to me."[46] When we pray, not to get something, but to be made whole—"More like thee, my God"—he concludes, "the Person does come to us, touches us, quiets us, and makes us whole again."[47]

Goodenough closes by repeating the point he has developed throughout. We are limited to our projections and cannot know the nature of reality. "So the great thing in religion is not to understand the nature of objective spiritual reality, but to find it and use it. For so long as men are men, spiritual reality will always remain the most important factor in human life."[48]

As early as in *Religious Tradition and Myth* Goodenough had deplored the inadequacy of the intellectual's religious life and proposed that the answer was to "become again intelligently religious."[49] In that work he focused on the myths and traditions that constitute Christianity and affirmed the continued relevance of many of these when they are viewed as "mythical accounts of an experience . . . in which we escape from the littleness of ourselves into a larger personal and social life."[50] *Toward a Mature Faith* shares the earlier volume's emphasis on the need to reinterpret the basic components of the Christian tradition, while at the same time recognizing their enduring value when so reinterpreted. But it expresses more skepticism as to the truth of Christian dogmas and draws more upon depth psychology for understanding religious experience and the symbols he was studying. Also, in this later work there is an emphasis on self-acceptance.

After going over the manuscript, Goodenough concluded that there was "no emotional drive to draw others to my position."[51] Yet, although he did not hear from any actual converts, he received several enthusiastic responses. The historian Arnold Toynbee wrote him that, when reading the page proofs, "one felt the excitement of traveling with a pioneer."[52] Monroe Stearns, the Trade Book Division editor of Prentice-Hall, informed him, "*Toward a Mature Faith* is one of the very few books I have felt proud to have published."[53]

The comments on the book jacket, while admittedly chosen to commend the work, give a spectrum of favorable responses, though some include respectful criticisms. Ashley Montagu, anthropologist and writer, described it as a blessing for the spiritually confused.[54] Robert Pfeiffer, a Harvard professor of Hebrew and Oriental languages, would place it on the bookshelf beside St. Augustine's *Confessions*, stating that because of its contemporary relevance "perplexed Christians have here a safe guide in their search for the faith that need not fear the challenge of modern science and modern philosophy."[55]

James Pike, then dean of the Episcopal Cathedral of St. John the Divine in New York City, saw in it a very different contribution to religious thought: "The book is a good statement of a position, and there will be much of value in it for those of us who hold another position. . . . It is a worthy statement of what has been a widespread point of view"[56]—a distinct contrast to Toynbee's description of Goodenough as a pioneer.

Goodenough's friend Morton Smith perceptively identified the sometimes contradictory directions of Goodenough's positions: "As the analyses are sometimes extremely radical, so the conclusions are sometimes surprisingly conservative."[57] Another friend, a psychiatrist, scornfully identified this conservatism as the determinant factor in the work, saying, "At the end Erwin is still just a little Jesus boy."[58]

The commercial reception of *Toward a Mature Faith* disappointed Goodenough; he complained that it was remaindered after two years, having sold only four thousand, five hundred copies, "in spite of the fact that it was received with tremendous excitement by readers from Harvard professors to very simple people."[59] But the Yale University Press reissued it as a Yale paperback in 1961. And the University Press of America reprinted it in 1988 as one of the Brown Classics in Judaica Series. According to Jacob Neusner, who was representing the editors of the series, those interested in Goodenough's work on Philo and the symbols in early synagogue art should know how his own religious views contributed to his interpretations. Beyond that, for Neusner, in Goodenough's religious quest, "he forms a model of what one can do, what one can become."[60]

Goodenough followed *Toward a Mature Faith* with statements concerning the appropriate role of a historian of religion and also further developments of his own religious position.

In April 1959 the American Council of Learned Societies' Committee on the History of Religion organized a Conference on the State of Studies, Research, and Teaching in the History of Religions in the United States and Canada, and Means for Their Improvement. It asked Goodenough, as chairman of the committee, to give a paper providing the rationale for organizing a national society to advance the scholarly study of the history of religion. He did this in "Religionswissenschaft," a term of the German theologian Rudolph Otto, which Goodenough translated as "the scientific study of religion," with the German word's meaning of "critical, ordered, analytical study."[61]

"Religionswissenschaft" develops the major premises of his own research. He stresses the importance of the scholarly study of religion,
since it examines the basic, universal human efforts to adjust to the unknown, which Goodenough calls the *tremendum,* Otto's word in *The
Idea of the Holy.* Such a study must be scientific, proceeding from empirical data to hypothesis and back to data, always correcting hypotheses with the new data. And this method must be applied to our own as
well as to other religions, for "we cannot let our own or our Church's
ideas or preferences interfere consciously or unconsciously with our de-
cisions as to what Jesus did or did not teach."[62]

He asserts that the study of the history of religions will use data from
psychology, sociology, anthropology, law, and linguistics in analyzing
"the sacred literatures and ethics, as well as the myths and rituals, of people of the world from earliest times to the present."[63] Historians of religion must devise their own methods for evaluating their data, be aware
that these methods provide only hypotheses, yet always have in mind
their "true objective, total understanding."[64] He concludes, *"Religionswissenschaft* in the mid-twentieth century can take us . . . to somewhat
greater comprehension of man in his religious problem. It can do so only
as we combine science and religion in our very marrow, combine them
into a dedication to learning about religion by the slow, dogged approach
of science. . . . For if we still have to kill the old dream that religion is a
matter of revelation, through *Religionswissenschaft* we may discover
that the scalpel itself has become a sacramental instrument."[65]

Willard Oxtoby of Yale forcefully expressed his view of the paper's
importance in "Religionswissenschaft Revisited," an essay he contributed to the Goodenough festschrift *Religions in Antiquity* (1968). Oxtoby wrote, " 'Religionswissenschaft' stands . . . as a very personal credo,
even a spiritual autobiography, coming in the fullness of Goodenough's
career. We see him . . . as an unorthodox but profoundly religious man.
Looking back at his essay from the perspective of the present, we see it
also as one of the important statements in the history of the discipline. It
. . . enshrines points with which any discussion of scientific attitude in
the study of religion must come to terms. It is, as it were, an oracle which
we shall do well to visit now and again."[66]

"Honest Doubt," another work of 1959, was an address given to various undergraduate organizations and published in the *Yale Alumni Magazine.* It is a shorter development of Goodenough's personal religious
position than *Toward a Mature Faith.* In it he deplores the common assumption of many intellectuals that they are irreligious when instead, he

asserts, they are, like him, agnostics or "honest doubters." Having read *In Memoriam: The Way of a Soul,*[67] a study of Tennyson's journey from his early, unexamined faith through doubt and questioning, Goodenough quotes Tennyson's words:

There lives more faith in honest doubt,
Believe me, than in half the creeds,

and commends him for recognizing the faith of those who live in such "honest doubt."

Goodenough affirms that, being among those who have many "honest doubts," he terms himself an agnostic, whom he defines as "a humble person who would not dream of denying, with the atheist, the existence of a personal God or revelation . . . but who does not see such evidence for these that he must, or can, build his life upon them."[68] Agnostics, for Goodenough, recognize the need to adjust themselves to a mysterious world outside and within themselves by having a myth or screen to explain and protect themselves against the unexplainable *tremendum.* He also states that the agnostic must live by certain ethical myths while recognizing them as myths, namely, "that honesty . . . is better than dishonesty; justice than injustice; love than hate; kindness than cruelty."[69]

Goodenough, then, regards the life of questioning by the agnostic as more truly a life of faith than the unquestioning acceptance of traditional beliefs and moral codes. The result, as he describes it, is "a genuine and beautiful type of religious life which has no loyalty to any creed or tradition as such. It demands the same strong faith in the value of life when lived right as do all the higher formulations of religion, and seems to me no less valuable a religion for its questing and open mindedness."[70] And he concludes: "The agnostic, finally, has an access to the Unknown which is uniquely his own. For the very asking of questions . . . when rewarded by even so small a bit of new insight, gives the questioner a sense of relating to the *tremendum* quite comparable to the ecstasy of a devout Christian communicant."[71]

In 1959 Goodenough negotiated with Harper to prepare for its Religious Perspectives Series a manuscript that he tentatively titled *Religion and Reality,* in which "I propose to state my agnostic approach to reality."[72] But, in spite of the enthusiastic endorsement of the series editor, Ruth Nanda Anshen, Harper decided not to include what was now entitled

Agnostic Religion.[7] Later, the publisher of the Credo Series of Pocket Books also would not accept it. The Yale University Press judged it "off-beat" and too much of an overlap with *Toward a Mature Faith,*[74] which it had reprinted as a Yale paperback. So *Agnostic Religion* never appeared, and Goodenough had to settle for incorporating much of its material when he wrote *The Psychology of Religious Experiences.*[75]

Chapter 13

Travel in the Late 1950s and the Completion of *Jewish Symbols*

Although Goodenough could not find a publisher for *Agnostic Religion,* the years following the appearance of *Toward a Mature Faith* brought other satisfactions, culminating in his completion of *Jewish Symbols.* Evelyn received her Ph.D. in education from Yale in 1956, and she became codirector of the Gesell Institute. What Erwin looked back on as the "agony" of Ursula's adolescence[1] abated, if only because of distance, when she enrolled in the Rocky Mountain School in Carbondale, Colorado, and enjoyed the experience thoroughly. Daniel was accepted at Groton, the school that Erwin had earlier chosen for Ward and John because he considered it the best preparation for future academic and social success.

His life with Evelyn continued to be Erwin's greatest joy. He wrote, when they were apart, "Of one thing you may be sure, darling, and that is the utter reliability of my love. . . . You have all of me";[2] and, again, "You have taken me over completely to be your own."[3] Evelyn, in turn, wrote, "I love you very deeply and more and more in each new place my love. No delight compares with the delight of my love for you, indeed I only *recognize* rather than *experience* all delights when I cannot share them with you."[4] And in another expression of the effect their separation had on her, "I am sure part of me is suspended in living, only waiting for you, to resume full function. I love you."[5]

The companionship of women his own age depressed Erwin, he claimed, and he contrasted their interests with those he shared with Evelyn, reporting his reaction when he played bridge with some of them in a crossing to England, "We are quite right in planning lives where bridge is not necessary."[6]

When the Hebrew University in Jerusalem invited Erwin to present a paper in the summer of 1957, Evelyn decided to lead a Brownell tour of

Europe during that time. Erwin would travel with Ursula and Daniel, enroll them for six weeks in the summer program of the Institute la Villan near Geneva, proceed by way of Rome to Jerusalem, meet the faculty at the Hebrew University, present his paper, and then go back to the Institute la Villan, pick up the children, and return home with them by way of Paris.

Every aspect of the trip proved highly satisfactory. At Rome Goodenough made a pilgrimage to Santa Maria Maggiore, "where all my scholarly dreams began."[7] He fell asleep by a statue of the Virgin Mary, which led him to comment to Evelyn, "I never slept with the Virgin before, but feel it was my final acceptance by her."[8] Hebrew University gave him a royal reception. "From the President of the University down they are all so 'deeply honored that I have come,' "[9] he wrote Evelyn with characteristic delight in recognition.

When he traveled back from the Institute la Villan with Ursula and Dan, he thoroughly enjoyed the time he spent with them. As he wrote Evelyn, "My stay with the children has been most successful. I dreaded this time all summer. . . . But tonight I am really completely proud of the success. The kids are marvelous—so incredibly mature in so many ways—so dearly childish in others. Actually, I have loved every minute with them."[10] Not only had he become a father for the second time, in his fifties, but in his sixties he could appreciate and feel intimate with these children.

The next summer he made another trip, this time around the world. The American Council of Learned Societies asked him to represent it at the International Congress of the History of Religions in Tokyo and Kyoto from 27 August to 9 September 1958 and to attend a UNESCO symposium on East-West relationships to be held immediately after the congress. He decided to "see as much of the inner life of Asian religion as possible, and . . . get help such as would have been available in no other way."[11]

Evelyn's prompt reaction was, "Just try to go without me."[12] For she was as eager as Erwin to see that part of the world. They arranged for Ursula to spend the summer at the Rocky Mountain School, while Dan stayed at Cedar Island with Erwin's sister Dedy, to whom Erwin could always turn for help. So he and Evelyn could have a ten-week trip, traveling from Europe to the Middle East, India, Bangkok, Hong Kong, Taipei, Tokyo, Kyoto, and home.

During their stay in Baghdad some disaffected Iraqi factions started a revolution, which led to the execution of all the royal family there. The United States provided planes to evacuate its women and children. But at the last minute Evelyn decided to stay with Erwin. She unpacked the suitcase she had prepared for her departure, which brought him to a state of "utterly and properly adoring her."[13]

In India they met with the faculty of Benares Hindu University, exploring the philosophy of Buddhism and Hinduism. They saw the practices of worship in Benares and in Calcutta, visiting Buddhist and Hindu shrines and temples. In Bangkok Erwin learned about Buddhist images and symbols and attended worship at various Buddhist temples.

Goodenough's paper for the congress, titled "The Evaluation of Symbols in History,"[14] made a case for the key role of the historian of religion studying symbols. Refuting Mircea Eliade's claim that symbols are outside the province of history and inaccessible to scientific criticism, Goodenough developed the thesis that history provides the most valid method for understanding religious symbols and the various meanings people find in them. He demonstrated how the historian traces the uses of a symbol through successive civilizations in order to identify an unchanging value behind the different explanations in each age and culture. The historian's method, which was, obviously, the method used in *Jewish Symbols,* should be to examine each symbol in its historical context and both identify the various interpretations of its respective devotees and point out its constant value in different civilizations. "For," he concluded, "history is written only with an eye to both."[15]

His personal happiness and professional satisfactions contributed to the enthusiasm he brought to continuing the *Symbols* volumes. Much to Goodenough's resentment, Yale had assigned the right of the first published account of the Dura synagogue to Carl Kraeling. But Kraeling's *Synagogue* finally appeared in 1956, and now Goodenough could present his own version of the building's symbols.

Volumes 9 through 11 of *Jewish Symbols* develop his interpretation of the synagogue's wall paintings, which confirmed his early hypothesis that there was a Hellenized Jewish style of art that presented allegorized versions of Old Testament events. He had had to wait twenty-four years after the Dura discoveries to offer his own analysis. Now, with the generous support of the Bollingen Foundation, he was able to enrich his work with a volume of illustrations that provided new photographs, mostly color plates, of the synagogue paintings, which had been removed to the Damascus Museum. For the Bollingen Foundation backing enabled him to commission Fred Anderegg, supervisor of photographic services at the University of Michigan, to visit Damascus for this purpose.[16]

Kraeling's *Synagogue* provided the archaeological data and identified the importance of the wall paintings for the history of art. So Goodenough could limit himself to explaining their meaning as expressions of Hellenistic Judaism—an interpretation that differs radically from Kraeling's.

Kraeling affirmed that the frescoes at Dura were commissioned by "normative" rabbinic Jews who had an intense, well-informed devotion to the established traditions of Judaism, that they were attempting to remind the Jews of their history and its associated religious symbols, and that the biblical scenes represented in the frescoes drew directly and exclusively upon biblical sources. Goodenough cannot imagine "a less apt description of what we have seen in the synagogue."[17] He insists, rather, that the artists were not providing simple illustrations of Biblical narratives and their Midrashic interpretations. Instead, he affirms, a master symbolist chose specific scenes and motifs from the Bible and borrowed conventions of pagan art to set forth his own concept of Judaism.

Goodenough's purpose is to examine the Dura synagogue paintings in order to characterize this type of Judaism, which he claims to be Hellenistic. He asserts that the Old Testament scenes depicted at Dura "show a sensitivity to, and acceptance of, Jewish mystic ideas which the symbolic vocabulary of Jews elsewhere had repeatedly suggested to us,"[18] citing examples described in his earlier volumes. He recognizes that the gouging out of the eyes of various figures in the paintings on levels within reach suggests the dissatisfaction of some Jews with these figures because they violated the scriptural injunction against graven images. But he denies that these feelings were representative. Instead, he concludes, "Here men worshiped as loyal Jews, loyal to their People, to their Torah as the supreme revelation of human hopes and metaphysical reality. But while that reality was revealed in Judaism, it was not confined within Judaism, so that whatever from paganism helped make it vivid could freely be used in presenting it."[19] He surmises that a religious thinker, whom he terms a "philosopher," one who knew the meaning of symbols, planned the wall paintings and specified the details of the Old Testament scenes, drawing upon an already established art tradition that included Iranian and Greek elements. The resulting interpretation of Judaism he presented was, according to Goodenough, essentially Hellenistic Judaism, offering a promise of "material and messianic triumph, mystical association with the universe in its worship of God."[20] It was a vision strikingly similar to what Goodenough had already identified in the symbolic materials of his preceding volumes.

Volumes 9 and 10 provide a detailed, systematic description of the synagogue's key elements, always showing their relationship to Goodenough's thesis. He sees in the building's structure a combination of Hellenistic, Roman, and Jewish architectural concepts and a resemblance to the pagan temples of Dura, indicating that the Jews of Dura were cosmopolitan, rather than isolated, and congenial to borrowing ideas from their neighbors, even their neighbors' religion. His examination of the ceiling tiles finds in their designs "a single symbolic value, that of immortality."[21] He describes the painting of a great tree vine on the reredos, with Jacob at the bottom, Orpheus across the middle, and a group of figures representing Moses at the top, which he interprets as an expression of the Dura Jews' aspiration to leave fleshly desires and follow the guidance of their great religious leaders to God.

He explains the biblical scenes on the walls of the synagogue in detail. Throughout he points out specific analogies with Philo's allegorizing of Moses' vision of the burning bush, the migration from Egypt, and the ark. He also affirms an overall similarity of the Dura art to Philo's view of the Torah as the revelation of a metaphysical reality not limited to Judaism.

The west wall, illustrated by a two-page foldout in volume 11, is the only one with complete, undamaged paintings and is the principal focus of Goodenough's analysis and hypotheses. He discerns in the west wall paintings an overall contrast between the material rulership of Israel and its higher, immaterial rulership, as depicted in parallel scenes on the left and right sides of the central Torah shrine. He reads Mordecai's and Esther's triumph over the Persian king Ahasuerus on the left side as a representation of material rulership, which is balanced on the right side by the anointing of David by Samuel, denoting a nonmaterial, metaphysical kingship. Similarly, the paintings of the temple of Aaron on the left side, with Aaron in priestly robes, bulls and a ram ready for sacrifice, and a menorah on the altar, represent for Goodenough a Judaism that led the worshiper through Law and cultic observances—material worship—to God. He contrasts this with the right side's portrayal of what he calls the closed temple, with its abstract symbols that suggest, as he interprets them, a mystic type of Judaism. And he interprets the portrayal of the Ark of the Covenant, with broken pagan idols strewn before it, as another symbol of immaterial Judaism, showing God's victory over paganism. As a final example of his thesis that the west wall contrasts temporal and immaterial values, Goodenough sees the depiction of Moses leading the Israelites out of Egypt, on the right side, as the artist's affirmation that "Moses leads the people out to true spiritual Victory."[22]

Goodenough surmises that the artist also used symbolic language in the mostly mutilated paintings on the south wall. The fragmentary state of the east wall's paintings limits him to only tentative interpretation of their meanings. But he is certain that the north wall, with its cycle of episodes in the life of Ezekiel, clearly portrays the contrast between true, mystical Judaism, represented by Ezekiel, and the hostile, legalistic Judaism of the Jewish leaders, represented by Ezekiel's executioner.

He insists that the visual representations in the Dura synagogue must be read independently of Jewish literature and sees them, so read, as giving a whole new perspective on Jewish history. "The synagogue had quite as radical implications for our knowledge of Judaism as the Dead Sea Scrolls, if not far deeper." Yet, he continues, "whereas hundreds of people were prepared to read the Scrolls, no one alive knew how to read the language of the murals."[23] The way to do this, he points out, is the method he has used in his previous volumes: to study the history of the pagan symbols that the Jews borrowed and the meaning and value these pagan symbols had for the Jews who borrowed them.

The Dura artist, he affirms, used pagan symbols in his biblical scenes to express for Jews the same values the symbols expressed for pagans. As he reads the artist's purpose, the Dura Jews believed that their Torah was the ultimate revelation of reality, and "Greek and Iranian notions are adopted, only to show that Judaism, when properly understood, presents all religious values, even the pagan values, better than the pagans themselves."[24]

Goodenough's conclusion, after examining detail after detail, is that the artist used pagan symbols to express, for a body of Jews, the Torah's promise of "material and messianic triumph, mystical association with the universe in its worship of God, and a leaving of Egypt to be purged of material dross and to come into . . . metaphysical reality."[25] And he closes by affirming: "We cannot understand their Judaism or their paintings unless at least in sympathy we share in this sort of devotion to reality ourselves."[26]

Goodenough's analyses of the figures and incidents in each scene of the synagogue paintings often seem superabundant, and his method of development, giving detailed analogies with figures and incidents in other regions and periods, with relevant literary references, may seem to labor his points. For scholars, however, who constituted the majority of his readers, the wealth of material was impressive. General readers especially appreciated the new photographs and colored plates.[27]

A wide-ranging criticism of specific interpretations came from Elias

Bickerman's "Symbolism in the Dura Synagogue," in the *Harvard Theological Review*. Bickerman pointed out that Goodenough's assumption of a radical contrast between rabbinic and Hellenized Judaism was based on a dichotomy invented by nineteenth-century German theologians. He charged that, while Goodenough insisted on the importance of letting the art speak for itself, he actually turned to Philo for supporting evidence, while dismissing rabbinic literature. He criticized Goodenough's practice of drawing conclusions from inadequate evidence, as when he identified the rescuer of the infant Moses from the Nile in the Dura painting as the goddess Anahita merely because she is naked and wears a necklace like that on representations of Anahita. And he commented that Goodenough "reads into the popular art [of Dura] a system of mystic theology which would have pleased a cabbalistic mind."[28]

Sister Charles Murray, writing in 1981 of Goodenough's treatment of the Dura synagogue, complained of his selective use of material, expressing what was a frequent criticism of *Symbols* as a whole: "The difficulty in relying on Goodenough is that in the treatment of any subject with which he deals, the evidence is always meant be [sic] support the whole overriding thesis of his work, namely, that the symbolic value of any image, ornament or decoration of any kind, is as the expression of an alleged mystical Judaism. . . . In accord with this he has the habit of giving only selective access to his sources of information; references are made to scholars who support his thesis, but rarely to those who do not. . . . This tendency to draw acceptable conclusions from selected pieces of evidence, and his disregard for inconvenient treatment of facts, make the use of his indispensable work always a hazardous business."[29]

Jacob Neusner, who edited a one-volume abridgment of *Jewish Symbols* in 1988, pointed out in his foreword that the strength of Goodenough's work lies in his portrayal of Dura as a cosmopolitan town with its Jews living amicably beside diverse groups, and of the artist of the synagogue as a man who used symbols from the religions around him. Neusner sees this portrayal, rather than Goodenough's emphasis on the mystical aspects of the paintings, as the major value of the work, concluding, "The power of Goodenough's reading of Dura derives from the simple fact that the premise is sound: there was no ghetto, and Judaism lived out its life in the affairs of a Jewish community at one with the world."[30]

Goodenough did not complete *Jewish Symbols* with a volume of summary until 1963, after his retirement, but while he was still working on the Dura materials, he felt the need for a final volume "in which I try to pull the whole job together rather than become involved in fresh data and research,"[31] as he wrote his friend Nahum Avigad in 1958. In 1961 he reported to Morton Smith that he was still "painfully trying to pull myself together for Vol. XI [actually volume 12], summary and conclusions, but the first stage of pregnancy, is the one most given to vomiting and miscarriage."[32] He asked Smith rhetorically, "Why do we do it, anyway?" Then he gave the answer when he explained to Paul Friedman, " 'I have written myself out of all but a very few readers, and my work will be used as a quarry as the medieval people used the Greek temples unless I do this last [referring to Volume 12, which is a summary and review of the preceding volumes]. I have no objection to its use as a quarry, so long as its thesis is not forgotten.' "[33]

He advises even a scholarly beginner to read volume 12 first, with the other volumes beside him so that he can turn to the illustrations.[34] This volume follows the plan of the earlier ones. Goodenough first recapitulates the literary evidence for a Hellenized Judaism, drawing heavily upon his own writings on the subject. He then reviews the archaeological material from Palestine and the Diaspora. He restates his method for interpreting the symbols. Then he describes the cult symbols found in the Jewish graves and synagogues, reviews the Jewish uses of fish and bread, the Jewish use of wine symbols, and their relation to the appearance of these symbols in paganism and Christianity. He discusses the presence in early Judaic art of pagan symbols, such as the bull, the lion, and Victory, and the primarily erotic symbols of cupid, the shell, the centaur, and others. A chapter on the Dura synagogue reviews its structure and paintings and their meanings. At the end he draws what he now regards as the probable conclusion from the material he has amassed and interpreted: that many Jews were Hellenized, "influenced by paganism, to the point not only that, like Philo, they expressed their religious aspirations in the language of Greek mystery and metaphysics, but also that they found the symbolic vocabulary of later Greco-Roman art equally suitable to their thinking."[35]

Since volume 12 reviewed points that Goodenough had already made in the earlier volumes, critics did not have much to say about it specifically. But *Jewish Symbols* as a whole won much praise and also drew significant criticism.

Frederick Grant, professor emeritus of Union Theological Seminary, commended it enthusiastically in the *Journal of Biblical Literature*: "Nothing has yet appeared to match the magnificent volumes in the Bollingen Series by Dr. Goodenough."[36] And he supported "Goodenough's main contention in his 'mystery religion hypothesis,' provided one does not go the length of transforming Judaism into a mystery cult."[37]

Paul Friedman, a psychoanalyst, paid tribute to it in the article he wrote for Goodenough's festschrift: "Goodenough's monumental contribution to our understanding of symbolism will endure as a source of inspiration for many years to come, primarily for the psychological researcher. . . . Goodenough's belief that the motifs and pictorial representations gleaned from paganistic cultures were not intended to serve merely as a decorative appeal but had an active symbolic meaning finds ready acceptance by modern psychology."[38]

Harry J. Leon in *Archaeology* acknowledged, "The work is . . . deserving of the greatest admiration as a notably rich contribution to our knowledge of Jewish ideas and of Jewish art in the period covered." But he was unconvinced that Goodenough "has revealed to us the true meaning of the symbols for those who used them."[39]

Jacob Neusner, in his abridgment of *Jewish Symbols,* summarized the comments of Arthur Darby Nock of Harvard and Morton Smith of Columbia, whom he considered Goodenough's key critics, and offered his own.

Neusner gave a brief digest of Nock's main objections to both specific points of detail and Goodenough's thesis that mystery worship was widespread in Judaism. Then he pointed out Nock's agreement that Judaism was diverse rather than uniform and concluded that the attention Nock gave Goodenough's work reinforced Goodenough's insistence that the symbols are important.

Morton Smith, as Neusner presented his arguments, challenged Goodenough's claim that a symbol always has basically the same value. He affirmed that Goodenough failed to prove a widespread Jewish belief in "sacramental salvation." He criticized Goodenough for drawing too heavily upon his own religious background and beliefs for his interpretations. Yet he concluded that, although Goodenough failed to prove the existence of a single, mystical Judaism, "Columbus failed too. But his failure revealed a new world, and so did Goodenough."[40] And he expanded this comment in his final words, which Neusner did not quote, "Informed opinions of ancient Judaism can never, henceforth, be the same as they were before he published. So long as a subject is studied and the history of the study is preserved, his work will mark an epoch."[41]

In his "final judgment" in the foreword to the abridged *Symbols,* Neusner, who had been Goodenough's research assistant, concluded, "He was the greatest historian of religion of his generation, and, as a premier scholar, he cared not so much for conclusions as for process, not so much for scoring points as for the reasoned conduct of argument and inquiry."[42] Such a judgment counterbalances the view of some fellow scholars that Goodenough was overcombative in his disagreements with Wolfson, Kraeling, Nock, and others whose ideas he challenged or dismissed. It also describes the ideal scholarship that, in spite of his lapses, Goodenough sought to exemplify in *Jewish Symbols*.

Chapter 14

Retirement, Divorce Again, and Third Marriage

Goodenough might have expected his retirement to be uneventful. Instead, after the satisfaction of establishing a connection with Harvard, he faced the traumas of Evelyn's divorcing him to marry a younger man, the excruciating adjustment to life without her, his experience of another love, and remarriage.

Knowing he would retire in 1962, Goodenough, in anticipation, encouraged Evelyn to seek a position in Cambridge before that time. He did not want to stay on in the Yale community as a retired professor, and he wanted to associate himself with Harvard. So when in 1959 Evelyn had an offer to be the director of the Eliot-Pearson School for Nursery School and Kindergarten Teaching, which was affiliated with Tufts University in Medford, Massachusetts, she accepted, although she hated to move.

Evelyn began her work in September 1959, living in Cambridge at the home of Mathilde Pfeiffer, the widow of a Boston University professor. Erwin and she rented out their New Haven home, planning to sell it, and Erwin had a room in the home of Florence Frank, widow of the lawyer Jerome Frank, on Everett Street. He arranged a Thursday-Friday teaching schedule at Yale and planned to spend the rest of the week in Cambridge, except for Evelyn's occasional weekends in New Haven.

The drive to and from Cambridge was strenuous, and the emotional strain of separation was great. He and Evelyn corresponded regularly, as they always did when apart, and Evelyn wrote, "I almost feel as if I am transplanted back to our old courtship days when I was so lovesick, so aching all the time";[1] but she consoled herself with the thought that, "then you'll come back and I think we'll start still another chapter in our fascinating story of the dear little girl and the naughty boy and how their lives open on to more and even lovelier vistas."[2] Erwin, in his turn, exclaimed, "What a lovely experience our brief weekend was!"[3] and from Marburg, where he was attending a conference, "How I wish I could spend the rest of this day with you . . . because I love you so dearly, dearly."[4]

Evelyn welcomed the opportunity to use her talents fully. When she assumed the leadership of Eliot-Pearson School, Abigail Eliot, the former director, enthusiastically approved Evelyn's proposed curricular changes and other plans, and in the spring of 1960 Evelyn had the honor of being invited to the White House Conference on Children and Youth.

Erwin had become the John A. Hoober Professor of Religion in 1959, a notable honor, though with no raise in salary. He would have preferred the Sterling professorship, which he felt he had earned, but he learned that the university reserved this plum to hold promising young scholars or to attract "big shots."

In September 1960 he went to Marburg to the meeting of the International Association for the History of Religion to serve on the governing committee and to give a paper that would do the United States credit. There he met as equals "all the really great ones in the field";[5] his lecture went very well, he reported with his usual pride in successes.

Erwin and Evelyn had bought a large house at 89 Irving Street in Cambridge, with a fine study for Erwin, just like the one in New Haven, which was later enhanced, he proudly reported, with the gift, by William James's grandson, of the desk on which James wrote. The Irving Street location was especially desirable because he could walk to the Widener Library, where he had the use of an office as well as its rich resources for research. Harvard was always Mecca to Goodenough, and he happily discovered that its faculty welcomed "the Yale barbarian" warmly.[6] They made him a member of the Harvard Faculty Club, where he enjoyed having lunch, occasionally at the special table reserved for Harry Wolfson, although he continued to have negative feelings about Wolfson because of their disagreements regarding Philo.

After Arthur Darby Nock, his other Harvard adversary, died, the Harvard History of Religions Club no longer had a problem in inviting Goodenough to join.[7] The club met once a month for dinner at a member's house to hear a paper. Goodenough was initiated into the Secret Knowledge of the Harvard Divinity School Community at the club's meeting in Lexington, where Helmut Koester, then associate professor of New Testament, was the host. Koester has a vivid memory of his embarrassment when he asked the newcomer to name his preferred drink and Goodenough replied, "I'm a gin man"—the one liquor Koester didn't have.[8]

Erwin and Evelyn jointly taught a course at Tufts on religious education for children. They also collaborated on an article for *Religious*

Education, "Myths and Symbols for Children," in which they explained the role of symbols in the religious experience of little children.

Erwin had written to Evelyn in 1960 that her not loving him anymore, although possible, was "not especially likely."[9] But he was overconfident. Lucile Pitcher, president of the board of managers of the Eliot-Pearson Corporation, who worked closely with Evelyn, had a brain hemorrhage and died suddenly in May 1961. At the family's request, Erwin arranged and led the funeral service, and Robert, Lucile's widower, wrote him, "You conducted the service in a manner that I have never heard equalled. . . . You and Evelyn are true friends."[10] Robert, the general agent in Boston for the John Hancock Insurance Company and a financial adviser and generous supporter of Eliot-Pearson, succeeded Lucile as president of the board. As a result, he and Evelyn had close professional and, later, personal relations as well.

Robert had been in a class of Erwin's in the summer of 1929, when Erwin had been lecturer on Greek religion and Roman history at the Harvard summer school, and Robert, a sophomore at Amherst College, took the course to make up credits that he had lost. When they met again and became friends, Erwin treated Robert like a son and continued to do so for some time.

Goodenough had an unusual attitude toward the women he loved. He said that he had no interest in a woman whom other men didn't desire and welcomed the attention men paid his successive wives: Ed Mason's close relationship with Helen at Oxford; his Yale colleagues' overtures to Evelyn; and the attempts of their Middle Eastern guides to fondle her. When Robert became an admirer of Evelyn, this only enhanced her value in Erwin's eyes.

He also took full practical advantage of men's attraction to Evelyn. He had encouraged the attentions paid her by the curator of the Egyptian Antiquities Museum in Cairo, who thereby made special artifacts and manuscripts available to Erwin. So, now, he saw the benefits of Robert Pitcher's interest, saying it was like knowing the mayor of Boston, because Robert had so many influential associations. After Lucile's death, he insisted that he and Evelyn accept Robert's invitation to spend a weekend at the Pitcher farm in Vermont, pointing out that the friendship would be professionally useful to Evelyn. He did not object when Robert gave Evelyn a car. He allowed Robert to be their host for a week's holiday at Caneel Bay, a luxurious vacation spot on St. John's in the Virgin Islands. He did not regard even this *ménage à trois* situation as a threat to their marriage. But he was wrong.

Evelyn, in her mid-forties, was beautiful and was irresistibly attractive to Robert, who was grieving and lonely in his large Belmont home. On her part she felt the contrast of Robert with Erwin, who at sixty-nine, gaunt and with scant gray hair, seemed old. She also thought he was likely to die in a few years, leaving her alone, which she dreaded. Robert, in his early fifties, was extremely tall, with thick, brown, slightly wavy hair, an engaging smile, courtly manners, and great vigor. His obvious need of Evelyn also moved her. They fell in love, in spite of Robert's religious scruples and Evelyn's mixed emotions. She felt that if only Erwin would struggle to keep her, she might be induced to stay with him, but he did not. Instead, when Robert pressed her and she decided to marry him, Erwin responded, "It's a free country."[11]

Much bitterness and mutual recrimination preceded and followed Evelyn's decision. Erwin insisted that the divorce settlement include Evelyn's making over the house, the insurance policy, and her salary to him, so that he would not suffer financially. She agreed, went to Sun Valley for the divorce, and married Robert there on 6 August 1962.[12]

Erwin's reactions were very mixed. On the one hand he had said to Evelyn, "I expected this," and wrote his friend Henri Peyre that for Evelyn "this was, as she called it, the next step." But he went on to express "the horror of having one so loved reject me."[13] Earlier he had voiced his despair in a letter to "Dear Little Lord Jesus," written while he was in Damascus in the spring of 1962. He described himself as "still incredulous that she would reject me for one so obviously (and admittedly by her) my inferior spiritually, sexually, and intellectually." And he begged for "strength to take this rejection, this dissolution of my whole life's structure."[14]

He asked Jesus, "Has Evelyn too, like all else, been only a stepping stone, with the reality of true loveliness something that could not become flesh? . . . Are you, Lord Jesus, going to whip me up Philo's ladder of love by taking the flesh from me?" but he refused to accept this, answering, "No! No! I want loveliness in the flesh!"[15]

He thought he had found this loveliness in a young woman with whom he had a brief, intense relationship when they met in New York, England, and France. But he confided to Henri Peyre that "she turned out to be moody and unreliable. . . . She would reject me as tartly some times as she would receive me lovingly at others."[16]

Then he found Cynthia Galligan, at the 1962 August conference of the Institute on Religion in an Age of Science at Star Island, off Portsmouth, New Hampshire. As one of the institute's founders, Goodenough had participated in earlier conferences, and in 1962 he co-led, with Kirtley Mather, the Conference on The Purpose of Life. Cynthia Galligan, an attractive, blue-eyed, thirty-two-year-old married woman, had, like Goodenough, been at previous conferences and knew him. Unhappy in her marriage, she and Goodenough developed a close relationship. She divorced Gerard Galligan in January 1963, and at that time Goodenough wrote to Peyre, "With her I now find life is becoming beautiful again." They were married on 11 May, in a service performed by a Unitarian minister.

They lived in the Irving Street house, now Erwin's by the settlement with Evelyn. Daniel, who was a student at Harvard, enjoyed bringing his friends to the home, where Cynthia welcomed them warmly, Erwin opened the liquor cabinet for them, and they played their guitars.[18]

Goodenough completed his 1962–1963 appointment as professor of Mediterranean studies at Brandeis University and was visiting professor of Hellenistic studies there in 1964–1965. For the Radcliffe seminars he gave a seminar on Plato, Plutarch, Philo, symbols, and the New Testament. He continued the strenuous lecture schedule he had maintained since his retirement in 1962, speaking at Trinity College, Hartford, the Bnai Brith Hillel Forum at the University of Toronto, and numerous Jewish Temples and Unitarian churches.

More important, however, was "writing, writing, writing."[19] He had complained to his friend Earl Hansen in 1961, before retiring, "There is so much to do in so little time. All right, talk about another twenty years. Even so, it is not enough." He summed up his ideal for future years by including a doggerel he had composed and recited at his last class at Yale:

When a scholar's last lecture has ended
He returns to his study alone.
But there the immortals await him
With the best man ever has known.

The fire of our longing and questing
Burns hot, with his heart as its coal;
If the young no longer demand him
The world still engages his soul.

He struggles to finish his writing,
Though he dreams of far more than he can.
For the scholar properly aged
Has assumed the ageless in man.[20]

Chapter 15

The Psychology
of Religious Experiences

Goodenough completed *The Psychology of Religious Experiences* in 1964, only months before his death, and dedicated it to Cynthia, but he had worked on it since the late fifties. Several motivations, besides his increasing interest in psychology, lay behind the project. After the favorable reception of *Toward a Mature Faith,* he again sought both the general public's recognition and the financial returns from a popular book. Just as he had wanted to assure Yale of his undiminished effectiveness after his divorce from Helen, so he determined after Evelyn left him: "My spiritual potency must continue."[1] Perhaps he also wished to offer a telling challenge to "the people in religious ascendency today [who] *hate* me and my work."[2] He was no longer concerned to reinterpret Christian concepts like faith, hope, love, and salvation to show their contemporary value, as he did in *Toward a Mature Faith.* He now wanted to apply a psychological perspective to a wide range of religious experiences that would lead to a new view of religion for the present age.

Early in 1956 he corresponded with Monroe Stearns, editor of the trade division of Prentice-Hall, about writing for the general religious market another book like *Toward a Mature Faith,* which it had published. He sent Stearns the chapter headings of a partially finished manuscript with the tentative title *Paths to God: A Study of the Psychological Aspects of Religion.*[3] When Stearns later read the early chapters of the manuscript he "thought the first three rather dull, liked Supraorthodoxy—told me to keep working on it & revising it."[4] Goodenough did so. Then, having entitled it *The Psychology of Religious Experiences,* he chanced to meet an editor of Basic Books who said he would take it in its present state.[5] So Basic Books, not Prentice-Hall, published *The Psychology of Religious Experiences.*

Yale University Press had issued Jung's *Psychology and Religion,* his

Terry lectures of 1937, and also Erich Fromm's 1950 Terry lectures, *Psychoanalysis and Religion,* which included a chapter titled "An Analysis of Some Types of Religious Experience." Disregarding these works, Goodenough stated in 1959, "I know no really important book on the psychology of religion published in the last thirty-five years."[6] In *The Psychology of Religious Experiences,* he deplores what he views as this current neglect of the psychology of religion, since he sees religion as a basic element of human life and its psychology as a key aspect of any study of mankind. Goodenough believes that his training in the history of religion and his knowledge of psychology qualify him to give a psychological interpretation of religious experiences from the perspective of a historian of religion. And he believes that William James, who wrote what Goodenough describes as the "magnificent *Varieties of Religious Experience,*"[7] but focused only on Protestant and some Catholic experiences, would have supported him in his broader attempt.

His informal style has apt turns of phrase like "my supraorthodox friends would rather be proved wrong than trite."[8] Although he disclaims any evaluation of what he describes, he freely expresses his views on Jesus' teachings, on Marxism, Nazism, and Tillich's characterization of God as "ground of being." He dismisses opinions different from his own more arrogantly than he did in *Toward a Mature Faith,* stating contemptuously: "The Catholic Church has the answer if we want order and control at any intellectual price,"[9] and, "Relatively few of our contemporaries are modern in their thinking at all."[10] His agnosticism is also more dogmatic.

The opening chapter titled "What Is Religion?" develops Goodenough's definition, which is much like that in "Religionswissenschaft." He states "that religion lies in the act of acceptance, compliance, belief . . . it is the attitude of trust, not the object trusted, which constitutes religion. . . . The common element is that of a devotion to something on which the people committed seem to themselves to depend, or in which they hope for security, or in which they actually find it."[11] He explains that it arises from terror in the face of the external and inner threats we experience—the "tremendum"[12]—a term used by Rudolph Otto that Goodenough had adopted as a key word in his religious vocabulary. According to Goodenough, humans cannot bear to know nothing about their origin and destiny or to have no control over their lives, so they provide themselves with religious beliefs and practices. "Man throws curtains between himself and the tremendum, and on them he projects accounts of how the world came into existence, pictures of divine or superhuman forces or beings that control the universe and us, as well as codes of ethics, behavior, and ritual which will bring him favor instead of catastrophe."[13] Religion involves the sense of right and wrong as much as it is concerned with myths and rites, and in every society it includes the belief that we know what is right.

He also points out the essential role religion has played in enabling one to cope with the *tremendum* within oneself. Although, for many, depth psychology and psychiatry have replaced religion, he asserts that "the many-thousand-dollar couch" offers no better results than "the mourners' bench" did in the past.[14] Emphasizing the failure of scientific knowledge to explain the key aspects of our existence, Goodenough concludes, "Man must live by religious trust in the patterns he projects on his curtains, which means, so far as I can see, that he will always have to live by religious faith . . . . for, if we recognize the inadequacy of our old faiths, it still remains that only by faith, by belief in curtains and their designs, can we come into a stability which gives life any value."[15]

In the chapter "The Divided Self in Greco-Roman Religion," he describes the Greek idea that one's personality is made up of multiple, separate parts, often in tension with each other, and that the basic problem is one of bringing the parts into harmony. He summarizes Plato's, Aristotle's, and the Stoics' answers to this problem. Then he outlines the thinking of Philo on the subject: that God's spirit, or Logos, was incarnated in the Hebrew patriarchs, with whom humans can readily identify and thus attain oneness with the divine mind. According to Goodenough, Paul preached a similar solution, namely, that God sent Jesus to earth so that people could identify with his life and resurrection, be no longer ruled by the "deeds of the body" and the "mind of the flesh,"[16] and achieve inner harmony. As Goodenough views Paul's contribution, "Paul transferred to Christ the psychological ideas that thoughtful hellenized Jews used in explaining religious experience." And, while Paul's and the various Greco-Roman mythological solutions are projections of what they could live by, Goodenough concludes, "We can still feel a kinship with them . . . as we see how they tried to explain man's religious experience by the best their generations knew."[17]

Goodenough points to the parallels with these early ideas as he develops the assumptions of modern psychology: that the personality is more than a person's conscious mind and that it is made up of independent emotional compulsions that conflict with each other. He affirms that both ancients and moderns have the same goal of inner harmony and social adjustment in order to live fully. To achieve this, he concludes, people of his day need to find means of fulfillment between the extremes of the Freudian path of individual assertiveness and what Nietzsche saw as the Jewish-Christian one of unquestioning submission. And he asserts that one can do this only by a deeper understanding of both religion and psychology.

He then discusses the various types of religious experience, which he identifies as legalism, supralegalism, orthodoxy, supraorthodoxy, aestheticism, symbolism and sacramentalism, the church (which he terms "a corporate body"), conversion, and mysticism. Much of his description covers familiar ground, but he makes several arresting contributions to the subject. He gives a vivid account of Cardinal Newman's pursuit of orthodoxy, as his craving for certainty of beliefs led him to Roman Catholicism. In discussing what Goodenough characterizes as supraorthodoxy—the making of an individual metaphysical system—he chooses the interestingly dissimilar examples of Spinoza and Kierkegaard to illustrate the supraorthodox's insistence on his own formulations.

Defining the religious experience of aestheticism as "the quest for beauty . . . in the sense of perfection of form in shape and in motion,"[18] in addition to athletics, dance, the arts, literature, and music, he includes sexual intercourse. Elaborating on the religious aspect of sex, he asserts, "The simultaneous reconciliation of the urges to dominate and to be dominated, to come into a higher life through the fusion of personalities, especially with one we regard as a beautiful personality and who responds to us beautifully—these are not only the experiences of religion at its highest, but are both represented and achieved in beautiful intercourse as in nothing else man does."[19]

When he describes mysticism, unlike the eloquent account of mysticism's appeal in *Toward a Mature Faith,* Goodenough's interpretation is analytic. He uses Jung's distinction between the horizontal and vertical religious paths, the horizontal being legalism or orthodoxy, which follows designated rules or beliefs, and the vertical being mysticism, which seeks to move up to the divine. He characterizes the usual vertical path as the continuation of a child's relation with the mother, in which the adult looks up to the Great Mother, called "Jesus." But he also outlines a more abstract, metaphysical approach to union with impersonal Being. Recognizing that few seek either of these mystic states, he affirms that many, like him, at times experience moments when they "sense the 'something far more deeply interfused' "[20] and find that it affords them both insights and the strength to rise above the stress of day-to-day matters.

Goodenough closes with an account of his own approach to religion. He asks the rhetorical question whether his contemporaries can be comfortable with the old types of religious experience. The obvious answer for him is no. They need a new one, to incorporate the scientific concepts of universal evolution and infinite mutation, concepts that preclude the idea of a Creator with a purpose and of a personal God who directs everything with loving care. As they accept the world of change, people today must now live, not by "truths," but by hypotheses. Goodenough therefore proposes that the appropriate religious position in the contemporary world is agnosticism, "one's acceptance of the fact that we do not know the reality in which we live."[21] Such agnosticism involves questioning the doctrine that humans are the culmination of creation, for the scientific evidence suggests that they are a late form of mutation and will eventually be extinct. Goodenough's modern agnostic also sees no more reason to believe in immortality and eternal life for humans than for the mosquito or the pig. He sees his agnosticism supported by historians, who have shown there is no evidence for Jesus' divine birth or for the authority of the Bible as the source of ultimate truth. Furthermore, he asserts, the agnostic must accept the findings of sociology and anthropology that ideas of right and wrong are regulations that have proven useful for individual civilizations rather than absolute norms. He affirms that depth psychology has shown us to be determined by our childhood experiences and that the meaning of these experiences is submerged in the unconscious, beyond our understanding. He points out that the concept of individuals as a product of their genes further challenges the idea of moral responsibility.

Yet, Goodenough asserts, people can still be religious, if they recognize their religion as a quest. The scholar has the religious experience of elucidating some fact or proposing some hypothesis. The scientist has faith in his contribution to further understanding of the natural world and in his methods. Others have faith in the new perspectives on the *tremendum* offered by the hypotheses of the creative thinkers. "I adjust in humility and reverence and joy at new learning—all of them religious attitudes."[22]

Finally, moving beyond his position in "Honest Doubt" that the agnostic can still pray, Goodenough now states, "Prayer for modern man is replaced by eager search, which is a form of prayer itself."[23] He admits that such a search will never become the religion of most people, who require the assurance of dogmas and rituals. But he asserts confidently in closing that "increasingly the quest will become the way millions of trained minds continue in religion."[24]

The Psychology of Religious Experiences offers Goodenough's final answer to the need to accommodate religion to current scientific thinking that he had felt as early as his graduate school days. The empiricism of Harvard Divinity School had first shown him the way for a historian of religion to employ the scientific method. One reason Philo appealed to him was that he saw in Philo's philosophy "a possible answer to the demand of human hearts that we square science in some way with human experience and hope."[25] Agnosticism was the solution he advocated as early as *Religious Tradition and Myth,* in which he asserted, "Christianity can never appeal to the modern world so long as it poses as having ultimate truth. . . . We must hold ourselves in steady agnosticism."[26] In *Toward a Mature Faith* he stated, "The skeptical and critical attitude is . . . our approach to truth, our mystic exercise. . . . The attitude of the new age . . . is *Dubito ut intelligam,* I doubt in order to understand."[27] *The Psychology of Religious Experiences* defines "religion as search" and recommends this type of religious experience as the meaningful one for his thoughtful readers.

In this definition of religion Goodenough ennobles the life of scholarship he had chosen and the direction and form it had taken, as he had earlier described scholarship as "a sacrament."[28] As we have seen, when Evelyn left him he prayed to "Dear Little Lord Jesus . . . the rudder of my life."[29] But when at the end of *The Psychology of Religious Experiences* he replaces prayer with "eager search,"[30] he is close to what Thomas Kraabel (his research assistant for his last work) recorded as Goodenough's final position. For he said to Kraabel shortly before he died, "I still pray, but I no longer live on prayer as I used to. . . . Religion is searching. That's what scientists live on. We have no right to expect peace; there is none."[31]

The Psychology of Religious Experiences evoked mixed responses, as could be expected. The *Library Journal* recommended it for general religion and psychology collections,[32] and the Mental Health Association of Westchester County, New York, endorsed it highly for its Mental Health Library.[33] Josephine Leamer wrote in *The Iliff Review,* "This book should be an oasis to any liberal religious thinker who is finding himself caught in a desert of orthodox interpretations and sixteenth-century techniques."[34]

Others questioned the value of Goodenough's position. Jacob Neusner, reviewing it in *The Connecticut Jewish Ledger,* wondered whether people can believe something when they do not know if it is true, but only that it meets their needs.[35] George Meyer in *The Journal of Religion* doubted that "modern man as blue-collar or white-collar worker, will feel much personal relevancy"[36] in Goodenough's recommendation of religion as search.

Goodenough's scholarship also provoked criticism. Meyer faulted him for closing with a statement of his personal religion rather than with conclusions drawn from earlier chapters. Meyer, with several other reviewers, also criticized Goodenough for ignoring contemporary work in psychological research and in theological schools. Arthur Vogel in *The Living Church* found fault with "his insensitivity to basic philosophic issues in his attempt to be modern" and concluded, "Professor Goodenough lets his name down when dealing with many of the complicated issues he raises."[37]

When the Brown Classics in Judaica Series reissued *The Psychology of Religious Experiences* [38] in 1985, it clearly saw it as a part of Goodenough's "rich spiritual legacy," as Neusner termed it. It was not a powerful personal statement like *Toward a Mature Faith,* nor an important scholarly contribution like *Jewish Symbols* but it represented Goodenough's endeavor to provide a historian of religion's perspective on the psychology of religion, which he considered to be a neglected, yet "crucial part of the study of man."[39]

Chapter 16

"Last Rites"

With Cynthia's companionship, at home and in their travels, and her encouragement of his ideas, Goodenough thoroughly enjoyed his life and his work. Writing in 1964 about talking with her, he commented, "She drew me out as she has such a wonderful knack of doing. This is one of her special gifts which she so little recognizes herself, that she can listen in a way to make me say things that I never formulated before."[1] Thus he found in Cynthia the same role of inspiring listener that Evelyn had played.

In 1962 he met Jacob Neusner, a research associate at Brandeis University, through a letter of introduction from Goodenough's friend Morton Smith, who had been Neusner's doctorate adviser at Columbia University. Neusner lived on Harvard Street, only a few blocks from Goodenough. Their relationship grew when Neusner drove Goodenough to Dartmouth to give a lecture, and a warm friendship, with shared intellectual interests, developed.[2] Neusner gave a favorable and thoughtful review of volumes 1 to 8 of *Jewish Symbols* for *Conservative Judaism* in 1963. The same year, in the preface to *Jewish Symbols,* volume 12, Goodenough expressed his appreciation for the "critical aid that a recent acquaintance, a brilliant young scholar, has given during the last two years, Jacob Neusner."[3] Later he chose Neusner as his literary executor.[4]

In *The Psychology of Religious Experiences* Goodenough had followed his Harvard teacher Kirsopp Lake's advice that "to understand the history of religion one must understand the psychology of religious men."[5] He had also made a final statement of his own religious position. Now, with the last volume of *Jewish Symbols* in the publisher's hands, he could concentrate on "the studies I have all along been preparing for, studies of the hellenization of early Christianity."[6]

As he explained in his article "The Inspiration of New Testament

Research," he at first shared the motivation of much early twentieth-century New Testament scholarship: "the hope that man would know better how to live in the present if he could understand the secret of early Christianity, because a man would have a base of certainty for his judgments and hopes."[7] He gave a more pragmatic explanation of his focus on Christianity's Hellenistic Jewish background when he wrote to Paul Minear of Garrett Biblical Institute that as a historian he could find "pay dirt"[8] in that subject that he could not find in the synoptic Gospels.

Goodenough, in his early research on Justin Martyr's writings, had become convinced of Hellenistic Judaism's importance as a strand in early Christianity. For he found such a Hellenism as part of the tradition Justin drew upon in presenting his beliefs. Justin also led Goodenough to Philo Judaeus, whom Justin quoted as an authoritative expression of Jewish Hellenism. Philo, in turn, was a stepping stone to Goodenough's larger purpose, as he stated in 1940, in the *Introduction to Philo Judaeus:* "I have for many years been convinced that hellenistic Christianity must have arisen out of a hellenized Judaism such as Philo shows existed. What Christianity took from this Judaism, and what it added to make the new religion . . . is a subject toward which most of my study has all along been pointing, but I am not ready for it yet."[9]

In a letter of 1946 to John Barrett, director of the Bollingen Foundation, requesting funds for research assistance to relieve him of the routines involved in the publication of *Jewish Symbols,* Goodenough gave as a reason for needing this assistance: "Years spent in such drudgery would seem all the more tragic to me since with the completion of this work I shall at last be ready to begin the work I have all my life been preparing to do, namely to write an equally extensive study of the origin of Christianity in view of all the new material I shall have presented on its Jewish and symbolic background."[10] In "The Bible as Product of the Ancient World," a paper read to the American Council of Learned Societies in 1960, he stated that he would "describe for the first time the point of view I have myself reached, and which I propose . . . to spend my remaining years in elucidating . . . the problem of the origin of the New Testament and with it the origin of the Christian Church."[11]

The summary volume of *Jewish Symbols,* completed in 1963, opened by describing his future project: "If the reader of this series of volumes is to recognize at all what its author is trying to do, he must understand that the study of Jewish symbols is itself part of a larger investigation. For many years the author has been trying to answer the question how Christianity, starting with the teaching of a Galilean carpenter, could so quickly have become a religion of salvation from the world and the flesh, of a Savior who in his person brought divinity to lost humanity, a religion of sacraments, organized priesthood, and theological formulation— that is, a Greco-Roman religion even though it called itself the Verus Israel?"[12] And in the "Conclusions" to that volume he stated that a later study would show how early Christianity can be understood only when seen as a "Christian reworking" of Hellenistic Judaism.[13]

Although during much of 1964 he still expected to write at least one volume on this Hellenization of early Christianity, when he became terminally ill, he had to settle, first, for a "book about St. Paul,"[14] then for only an essay, "Paul and the Hellenization of Early Christianity." To accomplish even this he asked the Bollingen Foundation's financial support for a research assistant, Thomas Kraabel.[15]

Kraabel's introduction to this essay on Paul in his collection of Goodenough's articles, *Goodenough on the Beginnings of Christianity,* speculates that Paul attracted Goodenough because they both resisted the letting go of Judaism as a part of Christianity and both were moving from an old, traditional faith to a new one.[16] Goodenough also saw Paul as his prime example of a man who viewed himself not as having attained, but as "reaching forth unto those things which are before,"[17] representing the "religion as search" Goodenough commended to his readers. But a more obvious reason for focusing on Paul in his study of early Christianity's Hellenization was that, from the time of his work on Justin Martyr, Goodenough saw Paul as a key figure in opening the doors through which "a hellenistic Judaistic tradition . . . had been running in."[18] The introduction to volume 1 of *Jewish Symbols* explicitly describes the letters of Paul as "completely oriented to Hellenism."[19] Goodenough felt that he had the requisite qualifications for interpreting the letters of Paul, because he believed they must be read with "an adequate understanding of Hellenism, hellenized Judaism, and rabbinic Judaism,"[20] which he had.

"Paul and the Hellenization of Christianity" opens by pointing out the discrepancy between the Paul whom Luke portrayed in Acts and the writer of the Pauline letter. Then Goodenough focuses on the letter to the Romans.

He chose Romans because in his mind it contains "the essential message of Paul," is Paul's most systematic exposition of Christ's gospel, and so is the "single critical text" for interpreting Paul's meaning.[21] In this judgment he agrees with Karl Barth, but there is little agreement with the approach or conclusions of Barth's neoorthodox interpretation, *Christ and Adam: Man and Humanity in Romans 5,* published in 1952.

Erwin in his Irving Street home in Cambridge, 1964.

The essay comments on each chapter of *Romans* in the accepted method of Biblical exegesis. Goodenough's purpose seems threefold: an interpretation of Paul's often obscure statements; a development of Paul's answer to the psychological question: "What is he, Paul?";[22] and, most important, an emphasis on the Hellenistic, especially the "philonic," character of Paul's thought. He accomplishes the latter two objectives by drawing on his earlier studies. But he moves beyond them in what he considers the only new, original interpretation of Paul's thought—what Paul meant by faith.[23] In accordance with his other "philonic" readings of Romans, he asserts that in chapter 3 "faith" is not faith *in* Jesus Christ, namely, the obedient accepting of Christ—for that would be legalism—but "the faith *of* Jesus Christ," because we receive the free gift of his faith when we "become one with him."[24] This appropriation of the faith of Christ parallels, Goodenough affirms, Philo's view of the patriarchs' saving power to bring mankind to oneness with God.

He ends by coupling Paul and Philo, affirming that Paul shared with Philo essentially Hellenistic Jewish beliefs—Goodenough's major thesis in the essay. For he concludes, "It is clear that both of them are trying to lead man into a life in which the higher part, the part engulfed by God, takes over and the fleshly impulses are no longer in control."[25]

Because of his chronic intestinal problems, Goodenough often worried about the likelihood of cancer. When he saw blood in his stool in December 1964, he consulted his doctor, who examined him and told him he had inoperable colon and liver cancer and had about three months to live. Evelyn recalls that he received the diagnosis calmly, called her at her Tufts office to tell her, quoted, "Brave men die but once, cowards many times," and said he was going to the Boston Symphony that afternoon.[26] But his daughter Hester has a different recollection. She remembers the anger he felt at not having longer to live: "He felt 'gypped,' deprived, cut off too soon. He had not found the answer he was looking for."[27]

His plan for completing even the limited project of the essay on Paul took a new form. He had to dictate the material, which Kraabel then transcribed, and which Goodenough directed him to rewrite and edit. As he wrote to his son Ward, "I am . . . just pushing to get my main ideas down. . . . If I can only keep going until I get this work down, however rough it is!"[28] And he had depressing doubts about his contribution as a whole. One afternoon near the end, when Evelyn went to see him while Cynthia was out, he said, in the course of a long talk, "People tell me I am so great. But I am nothing, nothing, just a little boy."[29]

He had become closer to his children after Evelyn left him. One Thanksgiving he invited all of them, with their families, to celebrate the occasion at the Irving Street home and had a professional photographer take a picture of them, with him sitting at the center, surrounded by his descendants.[30] Now satisfaction in his family continued to sustain him. As he became weaker and confined to bed, John, who was married and teaching at MIT and living in Cambridge, visited him regularly. Dan, at Harvard, spent time with him during the week to relieve Cynthia in keeping him company and nursing him. Ursula, who was married and a graduate student at Columbia University, upon hearing of her father's illness, cried out to herself, "Oh no, oh my God, he won't be able to play Bach anymore."[31] She came up from New York every weekend to be with him and take her turn in relieving Cynthia. During his last weeks Ward, Ruth, and their children were in Truk in the Caroline Islands of Micronesia, where Ward was engaged in an anthropological project, and his father wrote him how much he relished Ward's accounts of his family's activities there, "and then the encouraging reports about the work." The letter continued, "John is a great comfort. The youngsters are living very rich lives. Dan is one of the most wonderful young men I ever knew. Ursula got her acceptance at the Harvard Graduate School of Biology the other day by telegram! So happy news keeps tickling me."[32]

But he also wrote Ward, "I run a temperature every day & am losing about a pound a week, and am steadily more feeble."[33] Toward the end, when he played back what he had dictated, he was shocked by the periods of silence between thoughts or even in the middle of a thought and realized that his ability to develop his ideas was slipping away. In addition to having less and less strength for his work, he also suffered increasing nausea and pain, with fewer and fewer periods of relief.

He had often discussed with his sister Dedy the rationale for ending one's life in the event of a terminal cancer and the method for doing so, and they agreed that she, as a doctor, could undertake it for him, if necessary. Erwin, Cynthia, and Dedy now decided that the time had come to hasten the end.

Erwin had received the unbound proofs of *The Psychology of Religious Experiences* from the printer. Ward, on his brother John's advice, had flown from Truk to be with his father. Erwin had seen his other children that week. Dedy was prepared. She, Cynthia, and Ward sat by Erwin's bed after supper on 20 March, and Ward, twenty-three years later, wrote a sonnet that poignantly portrays what followed.

LAST RITES

"Now is the time," you said, as we three sat
Around your bed, the supper dishes done,
Your young, new wife, your sister, and your son,
Just settled down for quiet, evening chat.
"Now is the time," you said, making your great,
Last choice—ours to abet, yours to command—
The means beside you just as you had planned,
Resolved to die still managing your fate,
Mindful of Socrates you took the draught,
The glass in your own hand. "Why now so sad?"
You asked. "Sit close and let us all be glad
Together in our love." And so we laughed,
Or tried to, holding hands until you slept.
Then we three went to separate rooms and wept.[34]

Goodenough's friend Krister Stendahl of the Harvard Divinity School conducted a memorial service at First Parish Unitarian Church in Cambridge, with Goodenough's three wives, former and present, and all his family attending. Stendahl's text was Matthew 21:28–32, the Parable of the Two Sons,[35] and he used the parable eloquently to show that, although Goodenough had chosen not to be a part of the church, yet he was definitely there in spirit: "He was one of us."

Because he had willed his body to Massachusetts General Hospital, there was no committal. But a stone was placed in the Woodbridge east side burying ground, describing him as professor of history of religion at Yale, with the inscription he had requested: "The scholar is dead but scholarship lives on."[36]

Postscript

After Goodenough's death Cynthia planned to write a book about him. Before she abandoned the idea, she asked his friends for their impressions and reminiscences. Responses came from men as different as Norman O. Brown, interpreter of Freud; Walter Harrelson, theologian of Vanderbilt Divinity School; Johnny Faulk, folklorist and CBS radio personality; and Allen Ludwig of the Yale fine arts faculty. They all emphasized his importance in their lives, with the same keen feeling that former student McGeorge Bundy, at the time he was President Johnson's special assistant, had written to Goodenough after learning of his serious illness, "There are things I think & do all the time that would be different if I had not worked with you."[1] Ludwig wrote Cynthia that Goodenough was "certainly the major influence of my life,"[2] and he dedicated *Graven Images: New England Stonecarving and Its Symbols* to Goodenough's memory.[3]

Tributes to Goodenough's contributions in his scholarly field were brought together by Jacob Neusner in *Religions in Antiquity: Essays in Memory of Erwin Ramsdell Goodenough,* originally planned as a festschrift to be given to him on his seventy-fifth birthday in 1968, but published after his death. The volume was subsidized by Yale University, the National Foundation for Jewish Culture, the American Council of Learned Societies, and the Dartmouth College Comparative Studies Center, for which he had worked on shaping its seminar during his final illness.

The volume included "In Memoriam" by Morton Smith of Columbia University, a longtime friend, who commended Goodenough's concern "to determine the valid and enduring elements of religion and to redefine the religious life in the light of scientific discoveries."[4] In "An Appreciation" Samuel Sandmel, his former student and later friend, wrote that

Goodenough's commitment to scholarship was for him "a religious experience."[5] Alan Mendelson, who had been his student at Brandeis University, described him in "Memoir" as one who had "the heart of a mystic" and was also remarkable for his "passionate pursuit of something which has substance—wisdom."[6]

Contributors represented a range of countries: Carten Colpé of Göttingen University; Geo Widengre of Uppsala University; Peder Borgen of the University of Bergen, Norway; Gilles Quispel of Utrecht University; Michael Avi-Yonah of Hebrew University, Jerusalem; as well as those from the major universities of the United States.

The essays paid tribute to Goodenough's contributions in specific areas. Some pointed out his role in showing Hellenistic Judaism's significance in Roman Palestine and in the development of early Christianity. Frederick Grant of Union Theological Seminary characterized Goodenough's psychological interpretation of the Bible as "a new kind of biblical criticism,"[7] and the psychoanalyst Paul Friedman wrote of the value for the psychological researcher of his "contribution to our understanding of symbolism."[8] Baruch A. Levine of Brandeis University acknowledged his debt to Goodenough's "intellectual leadership and to the methodology which he developed."[9] Wayne A. Meeks of Indiana University identified the special features of this methodology: "first with rigorous care to describe 'what one sees,' then with boldness and imagination to propose what may have been happening in the ancient circle that produced what one now sees from afar."[10]

The relevance of Goodenough's writings for the 1980s and 1990s was recognized by the editors of the Brown Classics in Judaica, who reissued *The Psychology of Religious Experiences* and *An Introduction to Philo Judaeus* in 1986, and *Toward a Mature Faith* in 1988.

William Scott Green's introduction to *The Psychology of Religious Experiences* asserts that Goodenough, by including legalism, orthodoxy, and sacramentalism as forms of religious experience, moved beyond the earlier theological categories and expanded the scope of the academic study of religion. Green also commends Goodenough for using Judaism as a representative example of religion and in so doing "set a standard for the academic study of Judaism that, since his death, has been rarely met."[11] In his introduction to *An Introduction to Philo Judaeus,* Jacob Neusner gives a similar reason why "Goodenough deserves a fresh reading," asserting that "no other single work has so decisively defined the problem of how to study religion in general, and, by way of example, Judaism in particular."[12]

In introducing *Toward a Mature Faith* Neusner justifies giving this work "a life for the twenty-first century,"[13] because Goodenough's story of his religious quest offers an example of how a scholar's personal experience and exploration influence his interpretation of religions. Neusner also states that Goodenough's interest in ancient Jewish symbolic art is meaningful for religious seekers other than those interested in Judaism.

Brown Judaic Studies published two volumes of Goodenough's essays during this period: in 1986 *Goodenough on the History of Religion and on Judaism,* edited by Ernest Frerichs and Jacob Neusner, and in 1990 *Goodenough on the Beginnings of Christianity,* edited by A. T. Kraabel.

Goodenough on the History of Religion and on Judaism contains the relevant articles that Goodenough identified as his "more important":[14] from his early treatments of Hellenistic Judaism and Philo to his late statement, in "Religionswissenschaft," of the interdependence of religion and science. Neusner in a preface identifies Goodenough's importance as twofold. He sees his work as providing essential material and original ideas; beyond that, Neusner regards him as "a model for a new generation of scholars"[15] at a time when the history of religion is receiving new attention because scholars are viewing religion from a nontheological perspective.

Goodenough on the Beginnings of Christianity brings together articles from as early as 1925 to the posthumously published "Paul and the Hellenization of Christianity." A. T. Kraabel's preface points out the value of his interpretation of the differences in New Testament Christianity as the product of the variant religious backgrounds of the early Christians. Kraabel concludes by paying tribute to Goodenough's embodiment of his ideal that there be a "parallel . . . between personal religion and the life of the scholar."[16]

Jewish Symbols received some critical attention in the mid-1980s. Paul Figueras of Ben Gurion University of the Negev in an article on Jewish ossuaries in 1984 faulted it for its "absence of systematization, chronological rigor and attention to the archaeological context"[17] and for "a high degree of subjectivity."[18] Dieter Georgi, on the other hand, a member of the Harvard Divinity School faculty, who was "strongly influenced"[19] by Goodenough, in a 1986 book on Second Corinthians expressed surprise that "Erwin Goodenough's monumental work, especially his volumes on *Jewish Symbols in the Greco-Roman Period* are treated as if they had made no difference." For, he asserts, "the basic theses of Goodenough appear to be vindicated more and more, not the least by the finds at Nag Hammadi."[20]

Then, in 1988, the Bollingen Series sponsored a one-volume abridgement of *Jewish Symbols,* edited by Jacob Neusner and published by the Princeton University Press. For this volume Neusner selected the chapters of the *Symbols* that he saw as most representative of Goodenough's methods and his contribution, and he provided a comprehensive foreword. In it he pointed out that Goodenough's review of the evidence gave new weight to the argument that ancient Jewish decorative art was meaningful rather than merely ornamental. But beyond that, for Neusner, "the importance of Goodenough's work lies in his power to make the particular into something exemplary and suggestive, to show that, in a detail, we confront the whole of human experience in some critical aspects. . . . That is why, twenty years after the conclusion of his research, a new generation will find fresh and important the research and reflection of this extraordinary man."[21]

This view was to be echoed by Kraabel's conclusion to his introductory comment on "Paul and the Hellenization of Christianity" in the *Goodenough on the Beginnings of Christianity* volume: "The republishing of much of his work, initiated by Jacob Neusner, will allow our greatest native-born historian of religions to influence a new generation of readers."[22]

The new generation of scholars has paid attention to Goodenough's work. At the 1989 annual meeting of the Society of Biblical Literature, the Hellenistic Judaism Section consisted of a panel "Erwin Goodenough and His Legacy" presided over by Shaye J. D. Cohen of Jewish Theological Seminary. John Wesley Cook of Yale Divinity School; David Jordan of the University of California, Los Angeles; Richard S. Sarason of Hebrew Union College–Jewish Institute of Religion, Cincinnati; and others presented papers critiquing various aspects of Goodenough's writings. As Cohen summarized their conclusions, together with those of the discussions that followed: Goodenough put real questions on the scholarly agenda, although his interpretations were often partially flawed and required reservations.[23] More recently, Paul Finney, in *The Invisible God: the Earliest Christians in Art* (1994), drew upon Goodenough's *Jewish Symbols* for several of his examples, although his references to Goodenough's hypotheses were often disparaging.[24]

In addition to this scholarly attention, one sees a wider contemporary echo of Goodenough's often pioneering views. His involvement in several departments at Yale was a precursor of the current interdisciplinary makeup of many university programs. In *Religious Tradition and Myth* he affirmed "the value of 'myth' for moderns" as a means by which, in a world of intellectual and political uncertainty, "we . . . can clarify our experiences to ourselves and convey them to each other in a way otherwise impossible."[25] This value has been reaffirmed by Bill Moyers's television talks about myths with Joseph Campbell, who claimed, "Myths are clues to the spiritual potentialities of the human life."[26] And in 1991 the psychoanalyst Rollo May wrote *The Cry for Myth,* deploring the loss of myth by Western society because "myths are narrative patterns that give significance to our existence. . . . Myths are . . . the structure which holds the house together so people can live in it."[27] Goodenough's conviction that the sexual symbols he studied had religious significance and that sexual intercourse is "one of the most universal of religious acts"[28] is echoed in the title *Sacrament of Sexuality* by the popular religious writers Morton and Barbara Kelsy.[29]

Yet beyond the critiques of Goodenough's scholarly contributions and the contemporary echoes of his theories, it is ultimately acquaintance with his life that sheds most light on the work, by introducing us to the man behind it. We see how relations with his father, his mother, and Uncle Charlie introduced him to the ethical–legalistic, the emotional, and the mystical aspects of religion. The letters to his parents from Oxford and the Continent make it clear how he developed the breadth of interests that made him the Renaissance man who taught in several departments. We learn how both meeting Jung and Goodenough's marital problems led him to an interest in psychology that influenced his focus on the psychological meaning of symbols. We read how his love for Evelyn Wiltshire led him to believe that the flesh is "the road to the spirit,"[30] reinforcing his conviction that the sexual symbols he was examining had religious significance. We note his insensitive assumptions about the children's acceptance of his divorce from their mother. But we admire the determination that made him willing to undertake menial employment at an Episcopal mission in Wyoming, even to clean toilets, in order to marry Evelyn. We wince at his condescending portrayal of Justin Martyr as "a philosophic dilettante" with an "inferior mind" and his arrogant assertion that few of his contemporaries were modern in their thinking. At the same time we enjoy his sense of humor when he jokes about falling asleep by a statue of the Virgin Mary and interpreting that as her acceptance of him. We are impressed by his lifelong pursuit of spiritual reality as supremely important and his growing conviction that "true religion lies in the search for the end, not in its attainment."[31]

As Goodenough wanted readers to understand Philo the man, so we have come to understand Goodenough.

Bibliographical Note

T. A. Kraabel contributed "A Bibliography of the Writings of Erwin Ramsdell Goodenough" to *Religions in Antiquity: Essays in Memory of Erwin Ramsdell Goodenough,* ed. Jacob Neusner (Leiden, Netherlands: E. J. Brill, 1968), 621–32, which was reproduced as an appendix in Robert E. Eccles's *Erwin Ramsdell Goodenough: A Personal Pilgrimage* (Chico, CA.: Scholars Press, 1985), 177–85. In *Goodenough on the Beginnings of Christianity* (Atlanta, GA: Scholars Press, 1990), xii–xiii, Kraabel supplemented this bibliography by listing posthumous publications and reprints of Goodenough's writings and Jacob Neusner's one-volume abridgment of *Jewish Symbols in the Greco-Roman Period.* In *Goodenough on the Beginnings of Christianity,* p. 71, he also listed the bibliographical data concerning the printing of Goodenough's annual reports as editor of the *Journal of Biblical Literature.* These listings by Kraabel constitute a complete bibliography of Goodenough's published writings.

Notes

Preface

1. Morton T. Kelsey and Barbara Kelsey, *Sacrament of Sexuality: The Spirituality and Psychology of Sex* (Rockport, MA: Element, 1991).
2. Erwin R. Goodenough, *Religious Tradition and Myth* (New Haven, CT: Yale University Press, 1937), p. 93. Mrs. Erwin R. Goodenough holds the copyright.
3. Erwin R. Goodenough, *Toward a Mature Faith* (Lanham, MD: University Press of America, 1988) p. 180; reprint of Yale University Press paperback edition, 1961, which was a reprint of the Prentice-Hall hard-cover edition, 1955.

Chapter 1

1. Erwin R. Goodenough, *The Church in the Roman Empire* (New York: Henry Holt, 1931), p. 4.
2. One of two undated, unpublished memoirs of Goodenough in a file titled "Notes for E.R.G.'s Autobiography" in Erwin Ramsdell Goodenough Papers, Manuscripts, and Archives, Yale University Library. I designate one, which opens "As a young man," A. The other, opening "My life has been planned by another," I designate B. This reference is from A, p. 4. Future references to the Goodenough Papers at Yale will be abbreviated YUL.
3. "The Academy," with a handwritten note by E.R.G.: "Written by my mother, Mary Ramsdell Goodenough. I don't know when she wrote it." "The Academy" is in the possession of Evelyn Goodenough Pitcher.
4. Interview with Ward Goodenough by the author, 12 June 1988.

5. Erwin R. Goodenough, "A Historian of Religion Tries to Define Religion," *Zygon* 2, no. 1 (1967): 15.

6. Goodenough, *Toward a Mature Faith,* p. 8.

7. B, p. 3, YUL.

8. Julian Ralph, "The City of Brooklyn," in *A Treasury of Brooklyn,* ed. M. E. Murphy, Mark Murphy, and R. F. Weld (New York: William Sloane, 1949), p. 54. First published in *Harper's New Monthly Magazine,* April 1893.

9. Ward Goodenough Sr.'s letter to his mother-in-law, Mrs. E. Ramsdell, 13 December 1891; in possession of Ursula Goodenough.

10. B, p. 1, YUL.

11. B, p. 3, YUL.

12. Ibid.

13. Interview with Ward Goodenough by the author, 12 June 1988.

14. In *Toward a Mature Faith,* p. 6, Goodenough stated that his father liked the bitter taste of quinine.

15. Interview with Ward Goodenough by the author, 13 June 1988.

16. Letter to Evelyn Wiltshire, 17 July 1941. All letters from Goodenough to Evelyn and from her to him are in the Evelyn Wiltshire Goodenough Pitcher Papers in the Schlesinger Library, Radcliffe College. Future references to this collection will be abbreviated SL.

17. Undated letters of Ursula Goodenough to her Ramsdell grandparents, in possession of their great-granddaughter Ursula Goodenough.

18. Letter to Evelyn Wiltshire, 20 February 1941, SL.

19. Letter to Evelyn Wiltshire, 18 March 1941, SL.

20. Erwin R. Goodenough, *The Psychology of Religious Experiences.* Brown Classics in Judaica (Lanham, MD: University Press of America, 1986), p. 94.

21. Letter to Evelyn Wiltshire, 20 February 1941, SL.

22. Goodenough, *Toward a Mature Faith,* p. 12.

23. Ibid., p. 8.

24. Poem in possession of Ursula Goodenough.

25. Goodenough, *Toward a Mature Faith,* p. 15.

26. As described by Mary Ludlum Davis, a schoolmate, in interviews of May 1988 by the author.

27. A, p. 1, YUL.

28. Mary Ludlum Davis provided me with this information in the May 1988 interviews.

29. Letter to Evelyn Wiltshire, 27 February 1941, SL.

30. B, p. 1, YUL.
31. Mary Ludlum Davis provided me with this information in the May 1988 interviews.
32. B, p. 1, YUL.
33. Goodenough, *Toward a Mature Faith*, p. 19.
34. Ibid., p. 17.
35. Ibid., pp. 21–22.
36. Information provided by Frank K. Lorenz, curator of Special Collections, Hamilton College, in a letter to the author, 19 April 1991.
37. Letter to Wally Peck, 4 August 1912. Hamilton College, Library Special Collections.
38. Letter to Evelyn Wiltshire, 18 March 1941, SL.
39. Walter Pilkington, *Hamilton College, 1812–1962* (Clinton, NY: Hamilton College, 1962), p. 248.
40. "Notes made by Erwin Ramsdell Goodenough for an autobiography, begun in Oxford, England, Summer 1964," p. 9, YUL.
41. Goodenough, *Toward a Mature Faith*, p. 23.
42. English literature section of the 1914–1915 Hamilton College Catalogue, pp. 44–45, Hamilton College Library Special Collections.
43. Goodenough, *Toward a Mature Faith*, p. 24.
44. Erwin R. Goodenough, "David Livingstone," *Hamilton Literary Magazine* 47 (May 1913): 389.
45. Goodenough, *Toward a Mature Faith*, p. 24.
46. He wrote in B, p. 1: "The slightest enjoyment of even a touch of the hand to my penis, brought agonies of guilt." YUL.
47. Letter to Mr. F. W. Putnam, 18 February 1921, Hamilton College Library Special Collections. A later letter addressed to Dr. F. W. Putnam suggests the spelling "Puntam" was an error.
48. B, p.2, YUL, and conversation with the author.
49. B, p. 2, YUL.
50. Interview with Evelyn Goodenough Pitcher by the author, 28 June 1992.
51. B, p. 2, YUL.
52. Letter to his parents, 17 October 1922; in the possession of his son Ward Goodenough. All the Oxford years' letters to Goodenough's parents that I quote were given to Ward Goodenough by his mother and are used with his permission.
53. Letter of Dr. Paul S. Minear, formerly student, then professor, at Garrett Biblical Institute, to the author, 21 October 1990.

54. A, p. 1, YUL.
55. Goodenough, *Toward a Mature Faith*, p. 25.
56. Ibid., pp. 25–26.
57. Erwin R. Goodenough, "The Inspiration of New Testament Research," *Journal of Biblical Literature* 71 (1952): 4.
58. Goodenough's spelling in A, p. 1, is *Wesen des Kristentums*.
59. Harnack's spelling is *Das Wesen des Christentums*.
60. Goodenough, *Church in the Roman Empire*, p. xi.
61. Erwin R. Goodenough, *Jewish Symbols in the Greco-Roman Period*, vol. 1 (New York: Pantheon Books [for the Bollingen Foundation], 1953), p. 21. (All quotations from this book are Copyright © 1955, 1964 Princeton University Press. Reprint by permission of Princeton University Press.)
62. Erwin R. Goodenough, "Religionswissenschaft," *ACLS Newsletter* 10, no. 6 (June 1959): 7.
63. Kirsopp Lake, *The Earlier Epistles of St. Paul* (London: Rivington's, 1911), pp. viii–ix.
64. Beatrice Goff, in the essay she contributed to the festschrift *Religions in Antiquity,* wrote: "He brought me to Yale to assist in his work on *Jewish Symbols in the Greco-Roman World.*" Beatrice L. Goff, "The 'Significance' of Symbols," in *Religions in Antiquity: Essays in Memory of Erwin Ramsdell Goodenough,* ed. Jacob Neusner (Leiden, Netherlands: E. J. Brill, 1968), p. 476.
65. Goodenough, *Symbols,* 12:112.
66. Erwin R. Goodenough, "The Mystical Value of Scholarship," *Crozer Quarterly* 22, no. 3 (July 1945): 224.
67. Erwin R. Goodenough, "The Inspiration of New Testament Research," *Journal of Biblical Literature* 71 (1952): 3.
68. F. C. Conybeare, *Myth, Magic and Morals: A Study of Christian Origins* (London: Watts & Co., 1909), p. xxx.
69. Goodenough, *Toward a Mature Faith*, p. 26.
70. Ibid., p. 27.
71. Letter to his parents, 11 September 1921.
72. Erwin R. Goodenough, "The Liber Pontificalis John VIII–Honorius II" (paper for Church History 3), Manuscript Collection of Harvard Divinity School Archives.
73. Goodenough, *Toward a Mature Faith*, p. 30.
74. Catalogue of Graduate School of Theology, Garrett Biblical Institute, 1920–1921, Evanston, Illinois, pp. 50–51.
75. Letter of 10 February 1959, YUL.

Chapter 2

1. Vera Brittain, *Testament of Youth* (New York: Macmillan, 1933), pp. 497–98, 506–9.
2. Vivian Green, *The Commonwealth of Lincoln College, 1427–1927* (Oxford: Oxford University Press, 1979), p. 6. By permission of Oxford University Press.
3. Letter to his parents, 30 January 1921.
4. Letter to Dr. F. W. Putnam, 19 February 1921, Hamilton College Library Special Collections.
5. Letter to his parents, 23 October 1921.
6. B, p. 3, YUL.
7. Letter to his parents, 23 October 1921.
8. Letter to his parents, 22 January 1922.
9. Letter to his parents, 22 January 1922.
10. Letter to his parents, 17 September 1922.
11. Letter to his parents, 9 May 1922.
12. Letter to his parents, 19 June 1922.
13. Letter to his parents, 17 September 1922.
14. Letter to his parents, 8 October 1922.
15. Letter to his parents, 21 January 1923.
16. Letter to his parents, 21 January 1923.
17. Letter to his parents, 30 January 1921.
18. Letter to his parents, 11 September 1921.
19. Letter to his parents, 11 September 1921.
20. Letter to his parents, 2 October 1921.
21. Letter to his parents, 6 November 1921.
22. Letter to his parents, 6 November 1921.
23. Letter to his parents, 12 February 1922.
24. Letter to his parents, 12 February 1922.
25. Letter to his parents, 17 September 1922.
26. Letter to his parents, 5 November 1922.
27. Letter to his parents, 25 November 1922.
28. Letter to his parents, 22 January 1922.
29. Letter to his parents, 26 April 1922.
30. Letter to his parents, 30 January 1921.
31. Letter to his parents, 30 January 1921.
32. Letter to his parents, 9 July 1922.
33. Letter to his parents, 20 August 1922.
34. Letter to his parents, 20 August 1922.

35. Letter to Dr. Putnam, 19 February 1921, Hamilton College Library Special Collections.
36. Letter to his parents, 6 November 1921.
37. Letter to his parents, 5 March 1922.
38. Letter to his parents, 9 July 1922.
39. Letter to his parents, 26 April 1922.
40. Letter to his parents, 9 July 1922.
41. Letter to his parents, 2 July 1922.
42. Letter to his parents, 6 November 1921.
43. Letter to his parents, 26 April 1922.
44. Letter to his parents, 28 September 1921.
45. Letter to his parents, 26 April 1922.
46. Letter to his parents, 22 January 1922.
47. Letter to his parents, 12 February 1922.
48. Letter to his parents, 14 May 1922.
49. Letter to his parents, 22 January 1922.
50. Letter to his parents, 22 January 1922.
51. Letter to his parents, 22 January 1922.
52. Goodenough, *Toward a Mature Faith,* p. 31.
53. Ibid., pp. 104–5.
54. Letter to his parents, 22 January 1922.
55. Letter to his parents, 6 November 1921. F. L. Cross, *Darwell Stone* (Westminster, England: Dacre Press, 1926), p. 203, terms it "the Oxford Society for Historical Theology."
56. Letter to his parents, 26 April 1922.
57. Letter to his parents, 26 April 1922.
58. Letter to his parents, 11 September 1921.
59. Letter to his parents, 6 November 1921.
60. Letter to his parents, 11 September 1921.
61. Letter to his parents, 26 February 1922.
62. Letter to his parents, 23 October 1921.
63. Letter to his parents, 12 February 1923 (misdated 12 February 1922).
64. Conversation with the author.
65. Letter to his parents, 12 February 1923 (misdated 12 February 1922).
66. Letter to his parents, 19 February 1923.
67. Letter to his parents, 11 March 1923.
68. Letter to his parents, 25 February 1923.
69. Letter to Professor Paul S. Minear, 15 August 1941, SL.

70. Erwin R. Goodenough, *The Theology of Justin Martyr* (Amsterdam: APA-Philo Press, 1968), p. 56.
71. Goodenough, *Justin Martyr,* p. vii.
72. Ibid., p. 294.
73. Ibid., p. 73.
74. Ibid., p. 130.
75. Ibid., p. 291.
76. Ibid., p. 292.
77. Letter to President Douglas of American University, 3 November 1943, YUL.
78. J. C. M. Van Winden, *An Early Christian Philosopher* (Leiden, Netherlands: E. J. Brill, 1971), p. 76.
79. L. W. Barnard, *Justin Martyr: His Life and Thought* (London: Cambridge University Press, 1967), p. 83.
80. Robert Joly, *Christianisme et philosophie* (Brussels: Université de Bruxelles, 1973), p. 121. I translated the French "faible" as "feeble."
81. Barnard, *Justin Martyr,* p. 168.
82. Van Winden, *Early Christian Philosopher,* p. 3.
83. Daniel Bourgeois, *La sagesse des anciens dans le mystère du Verbe Évangile et philosophie chez Saint Justin philosophe et martyr* (Paris: Téqui, 1981), p. 131n.6. My translation.
84. Kirsopp Lake, *The Stewardship of Faith* (New York: Putnam's, 1915), p. 127. The Putnam Publishing Group holds the copyright. 85 Kirsopp Lake, *Landmarks in the History of Early Christianity* New York: Putnam's, 1922), p. 96. The Putnam Publishing Group holds the copyright.
86. Lake, *Landmarks,* p. 97.
87. Letter to his parents, 9 July 1922.
88. Letter to his parents, 20 August 1922.
89. Letter to his parents, 26 April 1922.
90. Letter to his parents, 23 October 1921.

Chapter 3

1. Goodenough, *Toward a Mature Faith,* p. 31.
2. A, p. 3, YUL.
3. A, p. 6, YUL.
4. Ibid.
5. Ibid.
6. A, p. 2, YUL.

7. Upton Sinclair, *The Goose Step: A Study of American Education* (Pasadena, CA: [self-published], 1923), pp. 121–22.
8. Henry T. Rowell, *Fifty Years of Yale News* (New Haven, CT: Yale Daily News, 1928), p. 36.
9. George Wilson Pierson, *Yale: the University College 1921–1937* (New Haven, CT: Yale University Press, 1955), p. 143. Yale University Press holds the copyright.
10. Pierson, *Yale,* p. 258.
11. Rowell, *Yale News,* p. 31.
12. Pierson, *Yale,* pp. 99 and 563n46.
13. Ibid., p. 27.
14. Ibid., p. 177.
15. Letter to Evelyn Wiltshire, 5 April 1940, SL.
16. Information provided by Gladys (Mrs. Paul) Minear, 26 May 1993.
17. Letter of 19 November 1940, SL.
18. Letter to Evelyn Wiltshire, 7 May 1940, SL.
19. Letter of 2 October 1958, YUL.
20. The White House, Washington, DC, 19 February 1965, YUL.
21. Quoted in Samuel Sandmel, "An Appreciation," in *Religions in Antiquity,* p. 16.
22. Interview with Harry Buck, professor of religion emeritus, Wilson College, 13 October 1990.
23. Erwin R. Goodenough, *An Introduction to Philo Judaeus* (New Haven, CT: Yale University Press, 1940), p. 33. Mrs. Erwin R. Goodenough holds the copyright.
24. Goodenough, "The Mystical Value of Scholarship," p. 225. This affirmation resembles William James' statement: "Our scientific temper is devout," in *Pragmatism* (Cambridge, MA, and London: Harvard University Press, 1975), p. 14, which Goodenough knew.
25. Erwin R. Goodenough, dedication and preface, to *The Jurisprudence of the Jewish Courts in Egypt* (reprint, Amsterdam: APA-Philo Press, 1968), p. vii.
26. B, p. 6, YUL.
27. A, p. 6, YUL.
28. A, p. 7, YUL.
29. Ibid.
30. Ibid.
31. Ibid.
32. Letter of 15 August 1941, p. 3, SL.
33. Goodenough wrote this in "For Yale Library Gazette." YUL.

34. A. T. Kraabel stated: "G once mentioned that it was the first edition of this book which caused him to begin his study of Philo." Kraabel's footnote in "Paul and the Hellenization of Christianity," in *Goodenough on the Beginnings of Christianity,* ed. A. T. Kraabel (Atlanta, GA: Scholars Press, 1990), p. 171 n. 90.

35. A, p. 4, YUL.

36. A, p. 2, YUL.

37. Goodenough, *Justin Martyr,* p. 45.

38. Erwin R. Goodenough, *By Light, Light* (New Haven, CT: Yale University Press, 1935), p. 46. Mrs. Erwin R. Goodenough holds the copyright.

39. Goodenough, *Introduction,* p. 143.

40. Marian C. Schlesinger, *Snatched from Oblivion* (Cambridge, MA: Gale Hill Books, 1979), p. 222.

41. Letter to Evelyn Wiltshire, 23 March 1941, SL.

42. Erwin R. Goodenough, "The Pseudo-Justinian 'Oratio ad Graecos,'" *Harvard Theological Review* 18 (1925): 187–200.

43. Erwin R. Goodenough, "The Political Philosophy of Hellenistic Kingship," *Yale Classical Studies* 1 (1928): 55–102.

44. Erwin R. Goodenough, "Kingship in Early Israel," *Journal of Biblical Literature* 48 (1929): 169–205.

45. Ibid., p. 205.

46. Goodenough, *Jurisprudence,* p. 255.

47. Ibid., p. 3.

48. Ibid., p. 31.

49. Ibid., p. 30.

50. Ibid., p. 31.

51. Ibid., p. 98.

52. Ibid., pp. 39–40.

53. William Renwick Riddell, review of *The Juris prudence of the Jewish Courts in Egypt,* by Erwin R. Goodenough, *American Bar Association Journal* 16 (1930): 813; reprinted by permission of the *ABA Journal.* The Philo Press reprinted *The Jurisprudence of the Jewish Courts in Egypt* in 1968.

54. Ralph Marcus, "Recent Literature on Philo (1924–1934)," in *Jewish Studies in Memory of George A. Kohut* (New York: Alexander Kohut Memorial Foundation, 1935), pp. 471–72.

55. Reprinted by permission of the publishers and the Loeb Classical Library from F. H. Colson, preface to *Philo,* transl. by F. H. Colson, vol. 7 (Cambridge, MA: Harvard University Press, 1968), viii.

56. Colson, preface to *Philo,* 7:xii–xiii.

57. Samuel Sandmel, *Philo of Alexandria* (New York: Oxford University Press, 1979), p. 173 n. 18. Oxford University Press holds the copyright.

Chapter 4

1. Letter of Hester Goodenough Caldwell (Mrs. John Caldwell) to the author, 4 July 1989.
2. Letter of Caldwell to the author, 4 July 1989.
3. Letter of James Goodenough to the author, 20 July 1989.
4. Letter of Ward Goodenough to the author, 3 April 1991.
5. Letter to Evelyn Wiltshire, 22 March 1941, SL.
6. Letter to President Douglas of American University, 3 November 1943, YUL.
7. Letter of 4 March 1937, YUL.
8. Stewart Means: *Faith: An Historical Study,* with an introduction by Erwin R. Goodenough (New York: Macmillan, 1935), p. x.
9. Goodenough, introduction to *Faith,* p. xiii.
10. Letter to Evelyn Wiltshire, 20 September 1939, SL.
11. Letter of Paul S. Minear to the author, 21 October 1990.
12. Conversation with the author in 1939.
13. Goodenough, *Church in the Roman Empire* , p. 21.
14. Ibid., p. 24.
15. Ibid., p. 64.
16. Ibid., p. 63.
17. Ibid., p. ix.
18. Ibid., p. 87.
19. Ibid., p. 18.
20. Ibid., p. 54.
21. Ibid., p. 95.
22. *Yale News,* 10 October 1931.
23. Quoted in Ralph Henry Gabriel, *Religion and Learning at Yale* (New Haven, CT: Yale University Press, 1958), pp. 242–43. Yale University Press holds the copyright.

Chapter 5

1. Letter of 17 November 1933, YUL.
2. A, p. 8, YUL.
3. A, p. 7, YUL.
4. A, p. 8, YUL.

5. Goodenough, *By Light, Light*, p. 167. Goodenough cites the Greek original in 167n.102.
6. Goodenough, *By Light, Light*, p. 5.
7. Goodenough, *By Light, Light*, p. 6.
8. Goodenough, *By Light, Light*, p. 7.
9. Goodenough, *By Light, Light*, p. 46.
10. Goodenough, *By Light, Ligh*t, p. 46.
11. Goodenough, *Introduction* , pp. 30, 32–33.
12. Goodenough, *By Light, Light*, p. 7.
13. Goodenough, *By Light, Light*, p. 7.
14. Goodenough, *By Light, Light*, p. 7.
15. Goodenough, *By Light, Light*, p. 7.
16. Goodenough, *By Light, Light*, p. 8.
17. Goodenough, *By Light, Light*, p. 8.
18. Goodenough, *By Light, Light*, p. 10.
19. Goodenough, *By Light, Light*, p. 94.
20. Goodenough, *By Light, Light*, p. 154.
21. Goodenough, *By Light, Light*, p. 179.
22. Goodenough, *By Light, Light*, p. 177.
23. Goodenough, *By Light, Light*, p. 179.
24. Goodenough, *By Light, Light*, p. 211.
25. Goodenough, *By Light, Light*, p. 232
26. Goodenough, *By Light, Light*, p. 233.
27. Goodenough, *By Light, Light*, p. 235.
28. Goodenough, *By Light, Light*, p. 237.
29. Goodenough, *By Light, Light*, p. 244.
30. Goodenough, *By Light, Light*, p. 255.
31. Goodenough, *By Light, Light*, pp. 263–64.
32. Goodenough, *By Light, Light*, p. 358.
33. Goodenough, *By Light, Light*, p. 358.
34. Noted by Goodenough, YUL.
35. E. F. Scott, review of *By Light, Light,* by Erwin R. Goodenough, *Church History* 4 (1935): 229.
36. E. F. Scott, review of *By Light, Light,* by Erwin R. Goodenough, *American Historical Review* 41, no. 2 (January 1936): 321.
37. Abram Simon, review of *By Light, Light,* by Erwin R. Goodenough, *Catholic Historical Review* 21, no. 4 (January 1936): 451.
38. Ralph Marcus, review of *By Light, Light,* by Erwin R. Goodenough, *American Journal of Philology* 57, no. 226 (April 1936): 204.

39. Kirsopp Lake, review of *By Light, Light,* by Erwin R. Goodenough, *Journal of Biblical Literature* 55 (1936): 90.

40. Shirley Jackson Case, review of *By Light, Light,* by Erwin R. Goodenough, *The Journal of Religion* 15 (1935): 484.

41. Arthur Darby Nock, review of *By Light, Light,* by Erwin Goodenough, *Gnomon* 13, no. 3 (March 1937): 157, 159–61.

42. Wilfred S. Knox, *St. Paul and the Church of the Gentiles* (Cambridge: Cambridge University Press, 1939), p. ix.

43. Letter to Evelyn Wiltshire, 21 October 1939, SL.

44. Erwin R. Goodenough, *The Politics of Philo Judaeus, with a General Bibliography of Philo* by Howard L. Goodhart and Erwin R. Goodenough (New Haven: Yale University Press, 1938), p. xi. Yale University Press holds the copyright.

45. Phyllis Goodhart Gordan, *Of What Use Are Old Books?* (talk given on 4 April 1972 at Bryn Mawr College Library), privately printed by her friends, April 1973, pp. 7–11.

46. Letter to Evelyn Wiltshire, 30 December 1939, SL.

47. "Goodhart Gift," *Yale Library Gazette,* Autumn 1939, YUL.

48. Goodenough, *Politics,* p. 18.

49. Ibid., p. 20.

50. Goodenough, "Politics in Code" is the title of chapter 2.

51. Goodenough, *Politics,* p. 85.

52. Ibid., p. 120.

53. Ibid., p. 119.

54. Arthur Darby Nock, review of *The Politics of Philo Judaeus,* by Erwin R. Goodenough, *Classical Review* 54, no. 3 (September 1940): 147. By permission of Oxford University Press.

55. Nock, review, *Classical Review* 54, no. 3 (September 1940): 148.

56. "Books of the Day," *The Living Church,* 28 December 1938.

57. Letter of 31 May 1938, YUL.

58. In a letter of 31 March 1941 to the author, who was studying at Union Theological Seminary, Goodenough also identified, as his readers, seminarians who had not been introduced to Philo. "I wrote it largely for just such people as you, the more intelligent theological students who have largely gone through our seminaries with no sense that Philo might be really important for their purposes."

59. Goodenough, *Introduction,* p. 61.

60. Ibid., p. 61.

61. Ibid., p. 110.

62. Ibid., p. 117. Goodenough always spelled "hellenistic," "hellenized," and "hellenization" in lower case.

63. Ibid., p. 117.

64. Ibid., p. 143.

65. Ibid., p. 180.

66. Ibid., p. 180.

67. Ibid., p. 205.

68. Letter to Evelyn Wiltshire, 10 February 1941, SL.

69. Ralph Marcus, review of *Introduction to Philo Judaeus,* by Erwin R. Goodenough, *Review of Religion* 1, no. 2 (January 1941): 179.

70. Samuel Belkin, review of *Introduction to Philo Judaeus,* by Erwin R. Goodenough, *Journal of Biblical Literature* 60 (1941): 61.

71. Letter of Evelyn Wiltshire, 1 January 1941, SL.

72. Harry Austryn Wolfson, *Philo Foundations of Religious Philosophy in Judaism, Christianity, and Islam,* vol. 1 (Cambridge, MA: Harvard University Press, 1947), p. 45.

73. Erwin R. Goodenough, "Wolfson's *Philo," Journal of Biblical Literature* 67 (1948): 89, 91.

74. Ibid., p. 109.

75. Leo W. Schwarz, *Wolfson of Harvard* (Philadelphia: The Jewish Publication Society of America, 1978), p. 156. Schwarz completed the biography in 1965 and died in 1967; but Wolfson, who died in 1974, did not wish to have it published while he lived.

76. Schwarz, *Wolfson,* p. 156.

77. Ibid., p. 146.

78. Ralph Marcus, "Wolfson's Reevaluation of Philo: A Review Article," *Review of Religion* 13, no. 4 (May 1949): 371.

79. Samuel Sandmel, *Philo of Alexandria: An Introduction* (New York and Oxford: Oxford University Press, 1979), p. 147.

80. David Winston, *Logos and Mystical Theology in Philo of Alexandria* (Cincinnati, OH: Hebrew Union College Press, 1985), p. 11.

81. Erwin R. Goodenough, *An Introduction to Philo Judaeus,* ed. Jacob Neusner, 2d ed., Brown Classics in Judaica (Lanham, MD: University Press of America, 1986), p. xiii.

82. Letter to the author, 13 December 1994.

83. Neusner, introduction to Goodenough, *Introduction,* p. xiv.

84. Ibid., p. xxi.

85. Ibid., p. xxi.

86. Ibid., p. xiv.

87. Neusner, "Brown Classics in Judaica," Goodenough, *Introduction*, "In behalf of the board of editors," p. x.

Chapter 6

1. Catalogue (Colorado Springs, CO: Colorado College Publications, February 1935), p. 6.
2. Letter to President Thurston Davies, 10 April 1935, YUL.
3. Interview by the author with Dorothy Mierow, daughter of Charles Mierow, 23 July 1994.
4. Peter Kurth, *American Cassandra: The Life of Dorothy Thompson* (Boston: Little, Brown, 1990), p. 33.
5. Kirsopp Lake, *The Religion of Yesterday and Tomorrow* (Boston and New York: Houghton Mifflin, 1925), p. 117.
6. Goodenough, *Religious Tradition*, p. 11.
7. Goodenough, *Religious Tradition*, p. 11.
8. Goodenough, *Religious Tradition*, p. 96.
9. Goodenough, *Religious Tradition*, p. 1.
10. Goodenough, *Religious Tradition*, p. 2.
11. Goodenough, *Religious Tradition*, p. 3.
12. Goodenough, *Religious Tradition*, p. 3.
13. Goodenough, *Religious Tradition*, p. 4.
14. Goodenough, *Religious Tradition*, p. 4.
15. Goodenough, *Religious Tradition*, p. 5.
16. Goodenough, *Religious Tradition*, p. 10.
17. Goodenough, *Religious Tradition*, p. 11.
18. Goodenough, *Religious Tradition*, p. 11.
19. Goodenough, *Religious Tradition*, p. 19.
20. Goodenough, *Religious Tradition*, p. 31.
21. Goodenough, *Religious Tradition*, p. 48.
22. Goodenough, *Religious Tradition*, pp. 48–49.
23. Goodenough, *Religious Tradition*, p. 49.
24. Goodenough, *Religious Tradition*, pp. 49–50.
25. Goodenough, *Religious Tradition*, p. 71.
26. Goodenough, *Religious Tradition*, p. 72.
27. Goodenough, *Religious Tradition*, p. 72.
28. Goodenough, *Religious Tradition*, p. 86.
29. Goodenough, *Religious Tradition*, p. 94.
30. Goodenough, *Religious Tradition*, pp. 92–93.
31. Goodenough, *Religious Tradition*, p. 93.
32. Goodenough, *Religious Tradition*, p. 93.

33. Goodenough, *Religious Tradition,* p. 94.
34. Goodenough, *Religious Tradition,* pp. 94–95.
35. Letter to Evelyn Wiltshire, 25 September 1939, SL.
36. Goodenough, *Toward a Mature Faith,* p. 32.
37. John W. Flight, review of *Religious Tradition,* by Erwin R. Goodenough, *Journal of Bible and Religion* 5, part 4 (1937): 196.

Chapter 7

1. Letter to Louis Finkelstein, 15 March 1938, YUL.
2. Conversation with the author, to whom she reported Goodenough's remark.
3. Letter of 5 November 1940, SL.
4. Letter to his parents, 28 September 1921.
5. Ibid., 9 May 1922.
6. Letter of 11 April 1940, SL.
7. Goodenough, *Toward a Mature Faith,* p. 52.
8. Interview by the author with Ward Goodenough, 12 July 1988; letter from Jim Goodenough to the author, 20 July 1989.
9. Typed manuscript headed: "The following, copied in Cambridge, was written during my stay at Damascus in the spring of 1962," p. 2, YUL.
10. Goodenough, *Toward a Mature Faith,* p. 34.
11. Goodenough, *Politics,* p. 50.
12. Goodenough, *Symbols,* vol. 4 (New York: Pantheon Books [for the Bollingen Foundation], 1954), p. 57.
13. Letter of Evelyn Wiltshire, 17 June 1940, SL.
14. Ibid., 14 August 1939, SL.
15. Letter of Evelyn Wiltshire to Goodenough, 20 September 1939, SL.
16. Letter of 29 November 1939, SL. This and following letters are from Goodenough to Evelyn unless otherwise designated.
17. Letter of 31 March 1939, SL.
18. Letter of 17 July 1939, SL.
19. Letter of 9 October 1939, SL.
20. Letter of 1 July 1939, SL.
21. Letter of 20 July 1939, SL.
22. Letter of 27 July 1939, SL.
23. Letter of 9 August 1939, SL.
24. Letter of 14 August 1939, SL.
25. Letter of 24 October 1939, SL.
26. Letter of 2 January 1940, SL.

27. Letter of 8 March 1940, SL.
28. Letter of 17 September 1939, SL.
29. Letter of 19 October 1939, SL.
30. Letter of 13 November 1939, SL.
31. Letter of 8 April 1940, SL.
32. Letter of 6 April 1940, SL.
33. Letter of 3 May 1940, SL.
34. Letter of 9 September 1939, SL.
35. Letter of 9 November 1939, SL.
36. Letter of 15 June 1940, SL.
37. Letter of 14 September 1939, SL.
38. Letter of 16 October 1939, SL.
39. Letter of 12 June 1940, SL.
40. Letter of 9 April 1940, SL.
41. Letter of 9 September 1939, SL.
42. Letter of 8 April 1940, SL.
43. Letter of 13 January 1940, SL.
44. Letter of 22 January 1940, SL.
45. Letter of 11 March 1940, SL.
46. Letter of 6 January 1940, SL.
47. Letter of 4 May 1940, SL.
48. Letter of 24 January 1940, SL.
49. Letter of 30 October 1939, SL.
50. Ibid.
51. Letter of 10 May 1940, SL.
52. Ibid.
53. Letter of Evelyn Goodenough Pitcher to the author, 27 May 1992.
54. Letter of Evelyn Wiltshire, 7 March 1940, SL.
55. Letter of 10 September 1939, SL.
56. Quoted in a letter of Evelyn Wiltshire to Goodenough, 6 April 1940, SL.
57. Letter of 7 December 1939, SL.
58. Letter of 24 January 1940, SL.
59. Letter of 20 April 1940, SL.
60. Letter to the author, 26 March 1940.
61. Letter of 9 September 1939, SL.
62. Letter of 6 August 1940, SL.
63. Letter of 3 September 1940, SL.
64. Letter of 13 September 1940, SL.
65. Letter of 19 September 1940, SL.
66. Letter to Andy Morehouse, 1 November 1940, YUL.
67. Letter of 30 November 1940, SL.

68. Letter of 4 February 1941, SL.
69. Letter of 30 November 1940, SL.
70. Letter from Kingsport, TN, Sunday, 4 P.M., 22 December 1940, SL.
71. Letter of Rudolph Willard to Cynthia Goodenough, 18 January 1966, YUL.
72. Recollected by Hally Wood Stephenson, who in 1940 was John Henry Faulk's wife, in a letter of 19 May 1967 to Cynthia Goodenough, responding to Cynthia's request for memories of Erwin. YUL. "Hally" is the spelling on her letterhead, and John Faulk signed "Johnny and Hally" when he wrote to Erwin in 1941. But Erwin always referred to "Johnnie" and "Hallie" in his 1941 letters to Evelyn.
73. Letter of 30 December 1940, SL.

Chapter 8

1. Letter to Evelyn Wiltshire, 29 December 1940, SL.
2. Undated letter; mailed on 4 January 1941, SL.
3. Letter of 1 January 1941, SL.
4. Letter of 7 February 1941, SL.
5. Letter of 6 January 1941, SL.
6. Recounted by Evelyn Wiltshire in interview by the author, 10 June 1990.
7. Letter of 20 January 1941, SL.
8. Letter of 7 February 1941, SL.
9. Letter of 9 January 1941 (misdated 1940), SL.
10. Henry Adams, *Mont-Saint-Michel and Chartres,* Sentry ed. (Boston: Houghton Mifflin: 1963), pp. 89–90.
11. Letter of 13 January 1941, SL.
12. Letter of 30 January 1941, SL.
13. Ibid.
14. Letter of 31 January 1941, SL.
15. Letter of 30 January 1941, SL.
16. Letter of 13 March 1941, SL.
17. Letter of 11 January 1941, SL.
18. Letter of 17 January 1941, SL.
19. Letter of 6 February 1941, SL.
20. Letter of 16 March 1941, SL.
21. Letter of 2 February [1941], SL.
22. Letter of 6 February 1941, SL.
23. Letter of Ward Goodenough to the author, 19 September 1991.
24. Letter of 27 February 1941, SL.

25. Letter of 5 February 1941, SL.
26. Letter of Jim Goodenough to the author, 20 July 1989.
27. Letter of 16 January 1941, SL.
28. Letter of 17 March 1941, SL.
29. Letter of 5 March 1941, SL.
30. Letter to William Gumbart, his attorney, 17 February 1941, SL.
31. Letter of 10 March 1941, SL.
32. Letter of 22 January 1941, SL.
33. Letter of 23 January 1941, SL.
34. Letter to William Gumbart, 17 February 1941, SL.
35. Letter of 1 February 1941, SL.
36. Letter of 11 February 1941, SL.
37. Letter of 18 March 1941, SL.
38. Letter of 27 March 1941, SL.
39. Letter of 11 March 1941, SL.
40. Letter of 9 March 1941, SL.
41. Reprinted by permission of the publishers and the Loeb Classical Library from Philo, "Evil of Bodily Pleasure," in *Philo on the Creation,* transl. F. H. Colson and G. H. Whitaker, vol. 1 (1929; reprint, Cambridge, MA: Harvard University Press, 1981), p. 121.
42. Aldous Huxley, *Point Counter Point* (New York: Avon Books, 1928), p. 124.
43. Letter of 2 March 1941, SL.
44. Letter of 22 January 1941, SL.
45. Letter of 20 March 1941, SL.
46. Ibid.
47. Letter of 29 March 1941, SL.

Chapter 9

1. Letter of 28 April 1941, SL.
2. Letter of 29 April 1941, SL.
3. Letter of Ward Goodenough to the author, 19 September 1991.
4. Letter of 29 April 1941, SL.
5. Letter of 12 May 1941 from Monroe, NY, SL.
6. Letter of 17 May 1941, SL.
7. Letters of 29 May 1941; 5, 9, 10, 18, 19 June 1941; 9, 10 July 1941, SL.
8. Letter of 29 May 1941, SL.
9. Letter of 23 May 1941, SL.

10. Letter of 19 June 1941, SL.
11. Letter of 31 May 1941, SL.
12. Letter of 3 June 1941, SL.
13. Letter of 6 June 1941, SL.
14. Letter of 11 June 1941, SL.
15. Letter of 13 June 1941, SL.
16. Letter of 25 June 1941, SL.
17. Letter of 29 May 1941, SL.
18. Letter of 15 June 1941, SL.
19. Letter of 5 July 1941, SL.
20. Letter of 23 June 1941, SL.
21. Letter of 13 July 1941, SL.
22. Letter of 7 June 1941, SL.
23. Letter of 14 July 1941, SL.
24. Letter of 16 July 1941, SL.
25. Letter dated 1 July 1940; postmarked 2 July 1941, SL.
26. Wilkinsburg, PA, 30 July 1941, SL.
27. Letter to Johnny and Hally Faulk: "August 9, 1941—the day when I got a new wife for myself and a new rear end for the car." SL.
28. Letter of 9 August 1941, SL.

Chapter 10

1. 2 Samuel 23:8.
2. Adolph Behrenberg.
3. Alfred Mattes, the author's husband.
4. Letter of 17 February 1945, YUL.
5. Interview by the author with Evelyn Goodenough Pitcher, 22 May 1990.
6. Letter of 14 November 1945, YUL.
7. Goodenough, *Toward a Mature Faith,* pp. 133–34.
8. Letter of Brand Blanchard to Cynthia Goodenough, 21 August 1966, YUL.
9. Letter of 15 May 1945, SL.
10. Letter of 16 May 1945, SL.
11. Letter of 16 July 1950, SL.
12. Letter of 26 July 1950, SL. Ellen Aitken pointed out the probable emulation.
13. Signed "Conceitedly, Evelyn," n.d., SL.

14. Goodenough, *Toward a Mature Faith,* pp. 127–28.
15. Quoted by Daniel Goodenough in interview by the author, 25 October 1992.
16. Letter of 22 November 1955, YUL.
17. Letter of 5 January 1954, YUL.
18. *Washington University Record,* 2 February 1995, p. 3.
19. Diary of trip, 31 August 1950, SL.
20. Letter of 28 June 1950, SL.
21. Ibid.
22. Letter of 1 July 1950, SL.
23. Letter of 11 July 1950, SL.
24. Letter of 20 August 1950, SL.
25. Letter of 26 July 1950, SL.
26. Undated note to the author.
27. Samuel Sandmel, "An Appreciation," in Neusner, *Religions in Antiquity,* p. 5.
28. Ibid., p. 16.
29. Ibid., p. 16.
30. Goodenough, *Toward a Mature Faith,* p. 127.
31. Sandmel, "Appreciation," p. 6.
32. Goodenough, "The Mystical Value of Scholarship," p. 221.
33. Ibid., p. 225.
34. Erwin R. Goodenough, "John, a Primitive Gospel," in *Goodenough on the Beginnings of Christianity,* ed. A. T. Kraabel (Atlanta, GA: Scholars Press, 1990), p. 59.
35. Robert P. Casey, "Professor Goodenough and the Fourth Gospel," in *Goodenough on the Beginnings of Christianity,* p. 66.
36. Erwin R. Goodenough, "A Reply," in *Goodenough on the Beginnings of Christianity,* p. 70.
37. C. H. Dodd, *Historical Tradition in the Fourth Gospel* (Cambridge: Cambridge University Press, 1963).
38. J. A. T. Robinson, *The Priority of John,* ed. J. F. Coakley (London: SCM, 1985), p. 9.
39. Gerard S. Sloyan, *What Are They Saying about John?* (New York: Paulist Press, 1991), p. 38.
40. Anthony T. Hanson, *The Prophetic Gospel* (Edinburgh: T. & T. Clark, 1991), p. 318.
41. Kraabel, *Goodenough on the Beginnings of Christianity,* p. 27.
42. D. B. Wallace, "John 5:2 and the Date of the Fourth Gospel," *Biblica* 71 (2, 1990): 103.

43. Craig A. Evans, *Word and Glory: On the Exegetical and Theological Background of John's Prologue* (Sheffield, England: JSOT Press, 1993), p. 207.
44. James H. Charlesworth, "Reinterpreting John: How the Dead Sea Scrolls Have Revolutionized Our Understanding of the Gospel of John," *Bible Review* 9, no. 1 (February 1993): 18–25.
45. T. H. Tobin, "The Prologue of John and Hellenistic Jewish Speculation," *Catholic Biblical Quarterly* 52 (2, 1990): 269.
46. Letter of 6 February 1949, YUL.
47. Letter of 9 August 1939, SL.
48. Goodenough, *Symbols,* 1: 29.
49. William McGuire, *Bollingen* (Princeton, NJ: Princeton University Press, 1983), p. 174.
50. Goodenough, *Toward a Mature Faith,* pp. 34–35.
51. Goodenough, *Symbols,* 4:30, 30n15.
52. Fully aware of this dominating emphasis, he wrote the author on 6 November 1942: "I am on Victory and the Crown now, and so far the first has escaped from the phallic. No one will believe me, but it is a *blessed* relief."
53. Letter of Hazel Barnes to the author, 21 February 1990.
54. Interview by the author with Amos Wilder, 12 April 1993.
55. Letter to Evelyn Wiltshire, 7 March 1940, SL.
56. Ibid., 13 March 1940, SL.
57. Letter of 13 May 1940, YUL.
58. Letter of 24 May 1940, YUL.
59. Letter of 14 November 1945, YUL.
60. Letter of 24 September 1946, YUL.
61. Letter of 27 July 1948, YUL.
62. McGuire, *Bollingen,* p. 175.
63. Letter of 18 November 1947, YUL.
64. Letter of 13 April 1948, YUL.
65. Letter of 21 July 1950, SL.
66. Beatrice L. Goff, "The 'Significance' of Symbols," in Neusner, *Religions in Antiquity,* p. 476.
67. Entry of 12 March 1951, Cairo, in Evelyn's two-volume diary of the trip, 1:49. This diary, in the Schlesinger Archives, supplemented by McGuire's *Bollingen,* is the source of all the preceding information about the trip.
68. 17 March 1951, Diary 1:54, SL.
69. 13 February 1951, Diary 1:9. SL.

70. 12 June 1951, Diary 2:110, SL.
71. 12 July 1951, Diary 2:38–39, SL.
72. 30 August 1951, Diary 2:22, SL.
73. Letter of 15 November 1951, YUL..
74. Letter to Ernest Brooks, secretary-treasurer of the Bollingen Foundation, 27 April 1955, YUL.
75. Goodenough, *Psychology*, p. 25.
76. Recounted at dinner table conversation with the author, Yale Faculty Club, New Haven, CT, 6 June 1990.
77. Goodenough, *Symbols*, 1:x.
78. Goodenough, *Symbols*, 12:23.
79. Goodenough, *Symbols*, 1:vii.
80. Goodenough, *Symbols*, 1:viii.
81. Goodenough, *Symbols*, 1:viii.
82. Goodenough, *Symbols*, 1:6.
83. Goodenough, *Symbols*, 1:6.
84. Goodenough, *Symbols*, 1:264
85. Goodenough, *Symbols*, 1:266.
86. Goodenough, *Symbols*, 2:295.
87. Goodenough, *Symbols*, 2:295.
88. Salo W. Baron, review of *Symbols,* by Erwin R. Goodenough, vols. 1–3, *Journal of Biblical Literature* 74(1955): 198–99.
89. Harry Leon, review of *Symbols,* by Erwin R. Goodenough, *Archaeology* 7, no. 4 (December 1954): 262.
90. Ceil Roth, reprinted with permission from *Judaism* 3, no. 2 (Spring 1954):179. Copyright 1954 by American Jewish Congress.
91. Baron, review, p. 199.
92. Leon, review, p. 262.
93. Morton Smith, *Anglican Theological Review* 36 (1954): 218–20.
94. Reported by Evelyn Goodenough Pitcher in a letter to the author, 15 April 1992.

Chapter 11

1. Sandmel, "An Appreciation," in *Religions in Antiquity,* pp. 12–13.
2. Goodenough, *Symbols*, 4:vii.
3. Ibid.
4. Ibid.
5. Ibid.
6. Ibid.
7. Ibid.

8. C. G. Jung, *Modern Man in Search of a Soul* (New York: Harcourt Brace, 1933), p. 117.
9. Goodenough, *Symbols,* 4:30.
10. Ibid.
11. Ibid.
12. William James, *The Varieties of Religious Experience* (1902; reprint, New York: Modern Library, n.d.), p. 497.
13. Goodenough, *Symbols,* 4:54.
14. Goodenough, *Symbols,* 4:55.
15. Goodenough, *Symbols,* 4:62.
16. Goodenough, *Symbols,* 4:87.
17. Goodenough, *Symbols,* 4:211.
18. Goodenough, *Symbols,* 5:99.
19. Goodenough, *Symbols,* 5:111.
20. Goodenough, *Symbols,* 5:112.
21. Goodenough, *Symbols,* 6:46.
22. Letter of 6 January 1941, SL.
23. Goodenough, *Symbols,* 6:47.
24. Goodenough, *Symbols,* 6:53.
25. Goodenough, *Symbols,* 6:219.
26. Goodenough, *Symbols,* 6:221–22.
27. Goodenough, *Symbols,* 7:77.
28. Goodenough, *Symbols,* 8:117.
29. Goodenough, *Symbols,* 8:118.
30. Goodenough, *Symbols,* 8:95.
31. Goodenough, *Symbols,* 8:105
32. Goodenough, *Symbols,* 8:166.
33. Goodenough, *Symbols,* 8:231.
34. Goodenough, *Symbols,* 8:223.
35. Letter of 13 May 1940, YUL.
36. Letter of Nahman Avigad, 29 April 1959, YUL.
37. Letter of Professor Chadwick, 16 November 1959, YUL.
38. Goodenough's comment written on the letter.
39. Samuel Sandmel, review of vols. 4, 5 and 6 of *Symbols,* by Erwin R. Goodenough, *Journal of Biblical Literature* 77 (1958): 383.
40. Ralph Marcus, review of *Symbols,* by Erwin R. Goodenough, *Classical Philology,* 52, no. 3 (July 1957): 264.
41. Neusner focused on Smith's 1967 article "Goodenough's Symbols in Retrospect," in *Journal of Biblical Literature* (1967), whereas I summarize points Smith made in his 1955, 1957, and 1960 reviews of volumes 4, 5, and 6, then of 7 and 8, in *Anglican Theological Review.*

42. Smith, review of *Symbols,* by Erwin R. Goodenough, *Anglican Theological Review* 39 (1957): 264.
43. Smith, review of *Symbols,* by Erwin R. Goodenough, *Anglican Theological Review* 42 (1960): 173.
44. Arthur Darby Nock, *Arthur Darby Nock: Essays on Religion and the Ancient World,* ed. Zeph Stewart, vol. 2 (Oxford: Clarendon Press, 1972), pp. 900–901. By permission of Oxford University Press.
45. Nock, *Essays,* 906.
46. Ibid., 907.
47. Goodenough, preface to *Symbols,* vol.12, vii.

Chapter 12

1. Letter of 2 March 1954, YUL.
2. Letter of 1 November 1940, YUL.
3. Erwin R. Goodenough, "Scientific Living," *The Humanist* (Spring 1942), p. 9.
4. Ibid., p. 10.
5. Letter to Paul S. Minear, 15 August 1941, YUL.
6. Goodenough, *Religious Tradition,* p. 11.
7. Goodenough, "Scientific Living," p. 10.
8. Letter of M. C. Otto, 11 April 1942, YUL.
9. Letter of 1 November 1945, YUL.
10. Described in letters of 13, 14, 15, and 16 May 1945 to Evelyn Goodenough, SL.
11. William F. Buckley Jr., *God and Man at Yale* (Chicago: Henry Regnery, 1951), p. 9.
12. Letter of William Cutter, Hebrew Union College, undated, YUL.
13. Letter of 18 January 1945, YUL.
14. Goodenough, *Toward a Mature Faith,* p. 1.
15. Ibid., pp. 1–2.
16. Ibid., p. 83.
17. Ibid., p. 12.
18. Goodenough, *The Varieties of Religious Experience,* p. 419.
19. Goodenough, *Toward a Mature Faith,* p. 34.
20. Ibid., p. 33.
21. Ibid., p. 41.
22. Chet Raymo, "Science Musings: Big Boost for the Big Bang," *Boston Globe,* 19 March 1990, p. 26.
23. Goodenough, *Toward a Mature Faith,* p. 47.
24. Ibid., p. 50.

25. Halford E. Luccock, *Marching off the Map and Other Sermons* (New York: Copyright 1952 by Harper & Brothers; renewed 1980 by Mary W. Luccock, HarperCollins Publishers), pp. 28–29.
26. Suzanne K. Langer, *Philosophy in a New Key* (New York: New American Library, 1948), p. 19.
27. Langer, *Philosophy,* p. 20.
28. Goodenough, *Toward a Mature Faith,* p. 68
29. Ibid., p. 69.
30. Ibid., p. 174.
31. Ibid., p. 72.
32. Ibid., pp. 106–7, 109.
33. Paul Tillich, *The Courage to Be* (New Haven, CT: Yale University Press, 1952), p. 188.
34. Goodenough, *Toward a Mature Faith,* pp. 140–41.
35. Goodenough, *Toward a Mature Faith,* p. 153.
36. Goodenough, *Toward a Mature Faith,* p. 155.
37. Goodenough, *Toward a Mature Faith,* p. 157.
38. Goodenough, *Toward a Mature Faith,* p. 157.
39. Goodenough, *Toward a Mature Faith,* p. 174.
40. Goodenough, *Toward a Mature Faith,* p. 163.
41. Goodenough, *Toward a Mature Faith,* p. 174.
42. Goodenough, *Toward a Mature Faith,* p. 175.
43. Goodenough, *Toward a Mature Faith,* p. 176.
44. Goodenough, *Toward a Mature Faith,* p. 177.
45. Goodenough, *Religious Tradition,* p. 95.
46. Goodenough, *Toward a Mature Faith,* p. 178.
47. Ibid., p. 179.
48. Ibid., p. 180.
49. Goodenough, *Toward a Mature Faith,* p. 95.
50. Ibid., p. 94.
51. Goodenough's note on the manuscript, YUL.
52. Letter of 30 December 1954, YUL.
53. Letter of 6 November 1958, YUL.
54. Front and back of book jacket of 1955 edition of *Toward a Mature Faith.*
55. Back of book jacket.
56. Front of book jacket.
57. Back of book jacket.
58. Quoted by Evelyn Goodenough Pitcher in an interview by the author, 10 October 1991.
59. Letter of 20 September 1958, YUL.

60. Jacob Neusner, "Introduction to the Brown Classics in Judaica Series Edition," in *Toward a Mature Faith* by Erwin R. Goodenough (Lanham, MD: University Press of America, 1988), p. xii.
61. Erwin R. Goodenough, "Religionswissenschaft," in *Goodenough on the History of Religion and on Judaism,* ed. Ernest S. Frerichs and Jacob Neusner (Atlanta, GA: Scholars Press, 1986), p. 3. The article originally appeared in *ACLS Newsletter* 10, no. 6 (June 1959), without these prefatory remarks.
62. Goodenough, "Religionswissenschaft," p. 4.
63. Ibid., p. 14.
64. Ibid., p. 15.
65. Ibid., p. 16.
66. Willard G. Oxtoby, "Religionswissenschaft Revisited," in *Religions in Antiquity,* p. 608.
67. The author gave Goodenough a copy of a book she wrote, titled *In Memoriam: The Way of a Soul* (New York: Exposition Press, 1951).
68. Erwin R. Goodenough, "Honest Doubt," *Yale Alumni Magazine* (April 1959): 19. Reprinted by permission from that issue of the magazine; copyright by Yale Alumni Publications.
69. Ibid., p. 20.
70. Ibid., p. 21.
71. Ibid., p. 21.
72. Letter to Ruth Nanda Anshen, editor, 16 April 1959. The letter is in a file labeled "Psychology of Religious Experiences," which contains letters regarding the proposed publication of *Religion and Reality* and portions of related manuscripts. Goodenough's widow, Cynthia, gave the file to Douglas Robbe, who was writing a Master of Arts thesis, *"The Development of Agnosticism in the Thought of Erwin R. Goodenough."* After submitting the thesis to the Hartford Seminary Foundation, he had no further use for the material, and when he learned of my projected biography, he gave me the file and other files of letters, articles, lectures, and manuscripts, which I have given to the Yale University Library to add to Cynthia Goodenough's previous gift, with her concurrence.
73. Letter of Melvin Arnold, Harper & Brothers, to Ruth Nanda Anshen, 5 December 1961, YUL.
74. Letter of David Horne, Yale University Press, 24 May 1963, YUL.
75. When Douglas Robbe studied the unpublished materials in the "Psychology of Religious Experiences Unrevised" file, he identified there what he saw as a draft of the unpublished *Agnostic Religion*

and evidence of the inclusion of its main themes in The Psychology of Religious Experiences. (Douglas Robbe, "The Development of Agnosticism in the Thought of Erwin R. Goodenough," a Master of Arts thesis submitted to the Hartford Seminary Foundation, May 1972, pp. 71–73.) I have made no independent study of the subject, but from looking over the file I tentatively share Robbe's conclusions.

Chapter 13

1. Comment in manuscript headed: "The following, copied in Cambridge, was written during my stay in Damascus in the spring of 1962," p. 1, YUL.
2. Letter of 20 June 1957, SL.
3. Letter of 18 July 1957, SL.
4. Letter of 11 July 1957, SL.
5. Letter of 16 July 1957, SL.
6. Letter of 3 July 1957, SL.
7. Letter of 15 July 1957, SL.
8. Ibid.
9. Letter of 23 July 1957, SL.
10. Letter of 9 September 1957, SL.
11. Letter of 21 October 1957, YUL.
12. Letter to Marguerite Block, 26 February 1958, YUL.
13. "The following . . . was written during my stay at Damascus in the spring of 1962," p. 2, YUL.
14. Erwin R. Goodenough, "The Evaluation of Symbols in History" (paper presented at the IXth International Congress for the History of Religions (Tokyo, 27 August to 9 September 1958).
15. Erwin R. Goodenough, "The Evaluation of Symbols in History," in *Proceedings of the IXth International Congress for the History of Religions* (Tokyo: Maruzen, 1960), p. 525.
16. Goodenough, *Symbols,* vol. 11, Publishers' acknowledgments.
17. Goodenough, *Symbols,* 10:206.
18. Goodenough, *Symbols,* 10:199–200.
19. Goodenough, *Symbols,* 10:210.
20. Goodenough, *Symbols,* 10:210.
21. Goodenough, *Symbols,* 9:55.
22. Goodenough, *Symbols,* 10:138.
23. Goodenough, *Symbols,* 9:4.

24. Goodenough, *Symbols,* 9:217.
25. Goodenough, *Symbols,* 10:210.
26. Goodenough, *Symbols,* 10:210.
27. Clark Hopkins, *The Discovery of Dura-Europos,* ed. Bernard Goldman (New Haven, CT: Yale University Press, 1979), p. 212.
28. Elias Bickerman, "Symbolism in the Dura Synagogue," *Harvard Theological Review* 58 (1965): 148. Copyright 1965 by the President and Fellows of Harvard College; reprinted by permission.
29. Sister Charles Murray, *Rebirth and Afterlife* (Oxford: BAR International Series 100, 1981), p. 116. Sister Charles Murray gives examples in 116n.15 and n.17.
30. Jacob Neusner, foreword to Erwin R. Goodenough, *Jewish Symbols in the Greco-Roman Period,* abridged ed. (Princeton, NJ: Princeton University Press, 1988), p. xxix.
31. Letter of 20 February 1958, YUL.
32. Letter of 6 February 1961, YUL.
33. Paul Friedman, "On the Universality of Symbols," in *Religions in Antiquity,* p. 609.
34. Goodenough, preface to *Symbols,* vol. 12, vii.
35. Goodenough, *Symbols,* 12:197.
36. Frederick C. Grant, review of *Symbols,* by Erwin R. Goodenough, *Journal of Biblical Literature* 83 (1964): 418.
37. Ibid.,
38. Friedman, "On the Universality of Symbols," in *Religions in Antiquity,* p. 609.
39. Harry J. Leon, review of *Symbols,* by Erwin R. Goodenough, *Archaeology* 20, no. 1 (January 1967): 77.
40. Morton Smith, review of *Symbols,* by Erwin R. Goodenough, *Journal of Biblical Literature* 86 (1967): 66, quoted in Neusner, foreword, to *Symbols,* abridged ed., p. xxxiv.
41. Morton Smith, review, p. 66.
42. Neusner, foreword, p. xxx.

Chapter 14

1. Letter of Sunday evening, undated, SL.
2. Letter of Monday, undated, SL.
3. Letter of 15 November 1959, SL.
4. Letter of 10 September 1960, SL.
5. Ibid.

6. Letter to Earl Hanson, 18 October 1961, YUL.
7. Interview with Bishop Krister Stendahl by the author, 13 April 1992.
8. Interview with Professor Helmut Koester by the author, 31 March 1992.
9. Letter of 12 September 1960, SL.
10. Letter of 23 May 1961, YUL.
11. Interview with Robert Pitcher by the author, 23 October 1991.
12. Interview with Evelyn Goodenough Pitcher by the author, 3 September 1992.
13. Letter of 13 January 1963, YUL.
14. Letter to "Dear Little Lord Jesus," typed manuscript headed: "The following, copied in Cambridge, was "written during my stay at Damascus in the spring of 1962," p. 2, YUL.
15. Letter to "Dear Little Lord Jesus," pp. 2–3.
16. Letter of 13 January 1963, YUL.
17. Ibid.
18. Interview with Daniel Goodenough by the author, 25 October 1992.
19. Letter to Earl Hanson, 18 October 1961, YUL.
20. Letter of 18 October 1961, YUL.

Chapter 15

1. Letter to Evelyn, 7 September 1962, SL.
2. Letter to Monroe E. Stearns, 10 June 1963, YUL.
3. Letter of 10 April 1956, YUL.
4. "Notation 20 March 1960" on handwritten title page of *Paths to God* manuscript containing handwritten and typed foreword. YUL.
5. Information provided by Cynthia Goodenough in a letter of 8 February 1972 to Douglas M. Robbe, who quoted it in "The Development of Agnosticism in the Thought of Erwin R. Goodenough," p. 73. Used with Robbe's permission.
6. Goodenough, "Religionswissenschaft," *ACLS Newsletter* 10, no. 6 (June 1959): 9.
7. Goodenough, *Psychology*, p. xi.
8. Goodenough, *Psychology*, p. 128.
9. Goodenough, *Psychology*, p. 26.
10. Goodenough, *Psychology*, p. 160.
11. Goodenough, *Psychology*, p. 3.
12. Goodenough, *Psychology*, p. 6.

13. Goodenough, *Psychology,* p. 8.
14. Goodenough, *Psychology,* p. 25.
15. Goodenough, *Psychology,* p. 28.
16. Goodenough, *Psychology,* p. 59.
17. Goodenough, *Psychology,* p. 62.
18. Goodenough, *Psychology,* p. 137.
19. Goodenough, *Psychology,* pp. 138–39.
20. Goodenough, *Psychology,* p. 158.
21. Goodenough, *Psychology,* p. 165.
22. Goodenough, *Psychology,* p. 179.
23. Goodenough, *Psychology,* p. 181.
24. Goodenough, *Psychology,* p. 183.
25. Goodenough, *Introduction,* p. 143.
26. Goodenough, *Religious Tradition,* p. 85.
27. Goodenough, *Toward a Mature Faith,* p. 72.
28. Goodenough, "The Mystical Value of Scholarship," p. 225.
29. "The following, copied in Cambridge, was written during my stay at Damascus in the spring of 1962," pp. 1–2, YUL.
30. Goodenough, *Psychology,* p. 181.
31. A. T. Kraabel, preface to *Goodenough on the Beginnings of Christianity,* (Atlanta, GA: Scholars Press, 1990), p. xx.
32. *Library Journal,* 15 April 1965, p. 1911.
33. Mental Health Association of Westchester County, New York, 13 April 1966.
34. J. Josephine Leamer, *The Iliff Review* (Spring 1966):50.
35. Jacob Neusner, "Book Notes," *Connecticut Jewish Ledger,* 5 August 1965, p. 5.
36. George G. Meyer, "Critical Review," *Journal of Religion,* 46 (January 1966): 85.
37. Arthur A. Vogel, *The Living Church* 151, no. 18 (31 October 1965): 4.
38. Neusner, "Book Notes," p. 5.
39. Goodenough, preface to *Psychology,* p. x.

Chapter 16

1. "Notes made by Erwin Ramsdell Goodenough for an autobiography, begun in Oxford, England, Summer 1964," p. 3, YUL.
2. Telephone interview with Jacob Neusner by the author, 5 December 1994.
3. Goodenough, preface to *Symbols,* vol. 12, vii.

4. Kraabel, preface to *Goodenough on the Beginnings of Christianity,* p. xx.
5. Kirsopp Lake, *The Earlier Epistles of St. Paul* (London: Rivington's, 1911), p. viii.
6. Letter to Walter, 14 November 1964, YUL.
7. Erwin R. Goodenough, "The Inspiration of New Testament Research," *Journal of Biblical Literature* 71 (1952): 4.
8. Letter of 15 August 1941, SL.
9. Goodenough, *Introduction,* p. 29.
10. Letter of 18 November 1946, YUL.
11. Erwin R. Goodenough, "The Bible as Product of the Ancient World," in *Goodenough on the History of Religion and on Judaism,* pp. 38–39.
12. Goodenough, *Symbols,* 12:3.
13. Ibid., 12:188.
14. Gilles Quispel, "Jewish Influences on the 'Heliand,'" *Religions in Antiquity,* p. 244.
15. Letter of A. T. Kraabel to the author, 20 July 1992.
16. 1968 prefatory note of Kraabel to Erwin R. Goodenough, "Paul and the Hellenization of Christianity," in *Goodenough on the Beginnings of Christianity,* p. 124.
17. *Philippians* 3:13. King James version.
18. Goodenough, *Symbols,* 12:3.
19. Goodenough, *Symbols,* 1:3.
20. Letter to WD (letter is typed, but "W.D. Davies" is handwritten vertically on right margin), 20 March 1964, YUL.
21. Goodenough, "Paul," p. 140.
22. Ibid., p. 162.
23. Goodenough describes this interpretation as "the one basic novelty" of his essay, in a letter to Walter, 14 November 1964, YUL.
24. Goodenough, "Paul," p. 151.
25. Ibid., p. 174.
26. Letter to the author, 1 July 1992.
27. Letter of Hester Goodenough Caldwell to the author, 4 July 1989.
28. Letter of 28 February 1965. Goodenough wrote "1964," but the error in the year was corrected by Ward Goodenough on his copy. Quoted with Ward Goodenough's permission.
29. Letter of Evelyn Goodenough Pitcher to the author, 1 July 1992.
30. Letter of Ward Goodenough to the author, 23 June 1991.
31. Ursula Goodenough, unpublished "Memories of My Father," p. 4. Quoted with permission.
32. Letter of 28 February 1965. See note 28.

33. Letter of 28 February 1965. See note 28.
34. W. H. Goodenough, "Last Rites," October 1988, revised August 1993. Quoted with permission.
35. Letter of A. T. Kraabel to the author, 20 July 1992.
36. In an undated typed statement "To my Legatee under Article II of my will," he had requested that the inscription be a quotation from Philo:

When a Scholar has died
Such Scholarship as resides in
    Individual Masters
    Has indeed perished with him.
    But its Prototype remains
And as long as the World lasts
    May even be said to Live.

Philo Judaeus.

In possession of Evelyn Goodenough Pitcher. Quoted with permission.

Postscript

1. Letter of 19 February 1965, YUL.
2. Letter of 28 December 1966, YUL.
3. Allan I. Ludwig, *Graven Images* (Middletown, CT: Wesleyan Press, 1966).
4. Morton Smith, "In Memoriam," in *Religions in Antiquity,* p. 2.
5. Samuel Sandmel, "An Appreciation," in *Religions in Antiquity,* p. 17.
6. Alan Mendelson, "Memoir," in *Religions in Antiquity,* p. 20.
7. Frederick C. Grant, "Psychological Study of the Bible," in *Religions in Antiquity,* p. 112.
8. Paul Friedman, "On the Universality of Symbols," in *Religions in Antiquity,* p. 609.
9. Baruch A. Levine, "On the Presence of God in Biblical Religion," in *Religions in Antiquity,* p. 71.
10. Wayne A. Meeks, "Moses as God and King," in *Religions in Antiquity,* p. 371.
11. William Scott Green, "Introduction to the Brown Classics in Judaica Series Edition," in *The Psychology of Religious Experiences* (Lanham, MD: University Press of America, 1986), p. xx.

12. Jacob Neusner, "Introduction to the Brown Classics in Judaica Series Edition," in *An Introduction to Philo Judaeus*, 2d. ed. (Lanham, MD: University Press of America, 1986), p. xxi.

13. Jacob Neusner, "Introduction to the Brown Classics in Judaica Series Edition," in *Toward a Mature Faith*, p. xvii.

14. A. T. Kraabel, "A Bibliography of the Writings of Erwin Ramsdell Goodenough," in *Religions in Antiquity*, p. 621.

15. Jacob Neusner, Preface to *Goodenough on the History of Religions and on Judaism*, p. x.

16. A. T. Kraabel, Preface to *Goodenough on the Beginnings of Christianity*, p. xx.

17. Pau Figueras, "Jewish Ossuaries and Secondary Burials," *Immanuel*, no. 19 (Winter 1984–1985): 53.

18. Ibid., p. 53.

19. Dieter Georgi, *The Opponents of Paul in Second Corinthians*, (Philadelphia: Fortress Press, 1986), p. 369. Copyright 1986 by Fortress Press. Used by permission of Augsburg Fortress.

20. Ibid., p. 370.

21. Neusner, foreword to Goodenough, *Symbols*, abridged ed., p. xi.

22. Kraabel, *Goodenough on the Beginnings of Christianity*, p. 128.

23. Information provided to the author by Robert Elinor, professor emeritus, New England College, who attended and took notes on the session.

24. Paul Finney, *The Invisible God: The Earliest Christians in Art* (Oxford: Oxford University Press, 1994), pp. 249, 252–54.

25. Goodenough, *Religious Tradition*, p. 93.

26. Joseph Campbell with Bill Moyers, *The Power of Myth* (New York: Doubleday, 1988), p. 5.

27. Rollo May, *The Cry for Myth* (New York: Norton, 1991), p. 15.

28. Goodenough, *Psychology*, p. 138.

29. Morton T. Kelsey and Barbara Kelsey, *Sacrament of Sexuality*.

30. Letter to Evelyn Wiltshire, 2 March 1941, SL.

31. Goodenough, *Symbols*, 12:74.

Index

About the Author

Eleanor Bustin Mattes was born in New York City. She received a B.A. degree at Smith College; an M.A. at Girton College, Cambridge; and a Ph.D. from Yale Graduate School. She also studied at Union Theological Seminary and the Yale Divinity School, where she received a B.D.

She has taught biblical literature and religion at Western Reserve University and Barnard College, English Literature at Connecticut College and English and American literature at Wilson College, from which she retired as professor emerita. She has published *In Memoriam: The Way of a Soul: A Study of Some Influences That Shaped Tennyson's Poem;* articles in *American Notes & Queries Supplement, Women & Literature,* and *Anima;* and reviews in *The Review of Religion* and *Christianity and Society.* She is a member of Phi Beta Kappa and the Modern Language Association.

The author is married to the Reverend Alfred Mattes, has a daughter and two sons, and now lives in Lexington, Massachusetts.

Her friendship with Erwin Goodenough began at Yale and continued for many years.

DATE DUE

HIGHSMITH #45230

Printed
in USA